Elementary Physical Education Teaching & Assessment

A Practical Guide

Second Edition of
Teaching for Outcomes in Elementary Physical Education

Christine J. Hopple, MS

HUMAN KINETICS

Library of Congress Cataloging-in-Publication Data

Hopple, Christine J., 1962-
  Elementary physical education teaching & assessment : a practical guide / Christine J. Hopple.-- 2nd ed.
    p. cm.
  Previous ed. published as: Teaching for outcomes in elementary physical education.
  Includes bibliographical references.
  ISBN 0-7360-4405-1 (soft cover)
  1. Physical education for children--Curricula. 2. Physical education for children--Evaluation. I. Hopple, Christine J., 1962- Teaching for outcomes in elementary physical education. II. Title.
  GV443.H66 2005
  378.1'619--dc22
                            2004027983

ISBN-10: 0-7360-4405-1
ISBN-13: 978-0-7360-4405-9

This book is a revised edition of *Teaching for Outcomes in Elementary Physical Education: A Guide for Curriculum and Assessment,* published in 1995 by Human Kinetics Publishers, Inc.

The Web addresses cited in this text were current as of December 2004, unless otherwise noted.

Acquisitions Editor: Bonnie Pettifor; **Developmental Editor:** Jacqueline Eaton Blakley; **Assistant Editor:** Kathleen D. Bernard; **Copyeditor:** Nancy Wallace Humes; **Proofreader:** Julie Marx Goodreau; **Permission Manager:** Dalene Reeder; **Graphic Designer:** Robert Reuther; **Graphic Artist:** Denise Lowry; **Cover Designer:** Keith Blomberg; **Art Manager:** Kelly Hendren; **Illustrators:** Mary Yemma Long, and Argosy; **Printer:** Total Printing Systems

Printed in the United States of America   10   9   8   7   6   5   4

The paper in this book is certified under a sustainable forestry program.

Human Kinetics
Website: www.HumanKinetics.com

United States: Human Kinetics, P.O. Box 5076, Champaign, IL 61825-5076
800-747-4457
e-mail: humank@hkusa.com

Canada: Human Kinetics, 475 Devonshire Road Unit 100, Windsor, ON N8Y 2L5
800-465-7301 (in Canada only)
e-mail: info@hkcanada.com

Europe: Human Kinetics, 107 Bradford Road, Stanningley, Leeds LS28 6AT, United Kingdom
+44 (0) 113 255 5665
e-mail: hk@hkeurope.com

Australia: Human Kinetics, 57A Price Avenue, Lower Mitcham, South Australia 5062
08 8372 0999
e-mail: info@hkaustralia.com

New Zealand: Human Kinetics, P.O. Box 80, Torrens Park, South Australia 5062
0800 222 062
e-mail: info@hknewzealand.com

                                                                                        E2734

To my mom, Gerry.
(1935-2002)

Contents

Preface

Assessment . . . now *that's* one of our favorite words! What do you think when you hear it? What about your students? Have your thoughts and views on this topic changed since you were a student? As a student in high school physical education, I knew that assessment meant fitness tests—including that darned shuttle run I could never quite do. As a college senior in my tests and measurement class, assessment meant knowing which AAHPERD standardized skills test to use with what unit, and the difference between T-scores and Z-scores. As a beginning teacher, truthfully, I can't recall much of what it all meant!

As I gained experience in teaching, the term *assessment* evolved and took on new meaning in my mind, and in my teaching as well. It meant finding out what my students were learning. It meant being a good observer of their skills. It meant asking my principal to evaluate my program, to give me feedback on what he felt were strengths and weaknesses in what I was doing.

Then, about 12 years ago, my thoughts about assessment changed again. As a new curriculum writer at Human Kinetics Publishers, I was asked to develop teaching materials for physical education teachers and their students. George Graham, whom I studied with when working on my master's degree at Virginia Polytechnic Institute and State University, told me about a committee he was a part of, a committee that was developing something called *outcomes statements* for physical education. "Take a look at those," he suggested. "Think about how you might help teachers assess them. This might become important down the road."

Well, needless to say, that was pretty good advice! Only problem was that assessment at that time—

way back around 1993—was beginning to focus on something new called *alternative assessment*. Little had been published on this topic in general, and nothing at all in the area of physical education. What *were* alternative assessments? What did they look like in physical education? What in the world was a *rubric?* At that time, there were few answers to these questions. Fortunately, I had wonderful guidance from several people, and I read a lot of books and journal articles, trying to make sense of what this term meant. When I authored the first edition of this book, *Teaching for Outcomes in Elementary Physical Education,* I truthfully wasn't sure where it would be even a few years down the road, much less 10. I'm glad to say, it's still around!

We've come quite a way in the past 10 years in terms of standards and assessments. Ten years ago we had 20 outcomes statements from the National Association for Sport and Physical Education (NASPE), and now NASPE has released the second edition of its content standards. Today it's not uncommon to have elementary students completing assessment sheets in physical education class—almost unheard of a decade ago. Journals such as *Teaching Elementary Physical Education (TEPE)* and the *Journal of Physical Education, Recreation & Dance (JOPERD)* devote entire issues to the topic. Teachers can go on the Internet and find examples of alternative assessments that have been tried with students. One particularly good source, the Web site PE Central (www.pecentral.org), didn't even exist 10 years ago. And as professionals, we now know so much more about what works (and what doesn't!) when using assessment with children.

At the same time, this past decade has brought us a number of challenges in applying alternative assessment and standards in our programs. Today, the demand for accountability—and assessment as a means to judge that accountability—is here to stay. For example, on a national level, students in grades 3 to 8 are assessed every year in reading and mathematics. We are asked to assess our students, even in physical education, at most state levels. And even though it is unlikely we will see students assessed nationally in physical education any time soon, it is safe to say that we will be asked to apply assessment in even more ways, some not yet imagined, before the *next* 10 years are over. Also, we've found from conferences, Web sites, and teacher in-services that there is never such a thing as too much practical information to be found on the topic of assessment and standards.

Since the first edition of this book was published, I've discovered firsthand the truth in this statement. I've been blessed—and have thoroughly enjoyed—meeting many of you at conferences and in-services, and I've heard your concerns and questions about using assessment in the trenches. And I've appreciated *all* your comments on the book, especially those on how to make it even better. I've also had the wonderful opportunity to again teach physical education in a public school setting. Because of that, I've experienced assessment on a day-to-day basis—and I wonder why I *ever* wrote some of what was in the first edition!

In this second edition, I've attempted to incorporate what I gained from all of these experiences and make this text as helpful and informative as possible. The book has a similar format as the first, with parts I and II offering a theoretical background on assessment and standards (yet practically written, I hope!). Part III centers on actual assessment tasks and curriculum ideas for the classroom. Each chapter reflects additions and revisions to the first edition as a result of how much more is known about assessment.

We start in chapter 1 with an overview of the alternative assessment of students in elementary physical education. Because the definition of alternative assessment varies from one teacher to the next, this chapter covers more than in the first edition and presents a foundation on this topic. As before, I've included examples, tried-and-true suggestions, and helpful hints for using alternative assessment.

A large portion of chapter 2 is devoted to that topic everyone seems to love to hate—rubrics! You will find more, more, more . . . more background information on rubrics, more examples, and more hints on how to use them as a part of assessment. Information on other methods of scoring alternative assessments and ideas for developing your own are also found in this chapter.

Chapters 3 and 4 present the information that pulls it all together: practical ways to effectively and efficiently manage assessment and assessment data in the physical education environment. I suspect you'll spend much of your time in these two chapters, because they address common questions: How do we best organize our teaching area for assessment? How do we use the results of assessment to communicate to parents? What do we do with all that paper? How can we assess so many children in one day or week? Also included is information on the use of technology to assist with organizing and managing assessment.

Chapter 5 reflects the accepted current educational practice and focus on standards-based education and our professional national standards. This is a major difference from the first edition's emphasis on outcomes. Current terminology and discussion of the national standards are presented and referred to throughout the text.

Chapter 6 explains how to use national standards to design-down your curriculum to best physically educate your students. This chapter will be of particular interest to teachers working on curriculum-writing projects. The examples and forms may be helpful tools in this endeavor.

Throughout parts I and II of this book I offer sidebars called "Tidbits" with supplementary information that give insight to the topic at hand. In addition, sidebars called "Real World" relate my own experiences with assessment as an elementary physical education teacher, as well as some experiences of other teachers and students I've known. I hope you find both types of sidebars interesting and enlightening.

Part III, similar to the first edition, contains curriculum ideas, organized by movement concepts and skill themes, useful when developing lessons and units. These are highlighted by a variety of assessment ideas and performance indicators that correlate with national standards. The biggest change is that you'll find many more of the assessment worksheets you can copy for students—something *everyone* seems to love.

With the first book, I received more feedback than I ever anticipated on the sample grade-specific unit outcomes, renamed *performance indicators* in this book. Many of you told me how handy they were to you in developing your curriculum standards, and you'll once again find them, with minor revisions, in appendix A. They are referenced in the appropriate skill or concept section in part III for your ease while working. You'll continue to find expanded supplementary information, such as a list of NASPE's performance indicators, a glossary, and a bibliography, in the back of the book.

Although this book is written with the elementary physical educator in mind, I have been told that many of those who teach physical education majors at the college level found the first edition to be a helpful supplement to the more traditional assessment courses common in higher education. As you teach your college classes, I hope you find the expanded parts I and II especially useful as you instruct future professionals on the importance

of assessment. In addition, I'd guess that the majority of you have purchased or borrowed other texts on the subject, such as Sue Schiemer's *Assessment Strategies for Elementary Physical Education,* published by Human Kinetics. In keeping with my statement that I believe teachers can never have too many resources on the subject, my hope is that you will find this text to be a complement to Sue Schiemer's book and others.

In conclusion, my overall goal for this edition is the same as for the first one, as written in its preface: that this book achieve that well-worn look, with pages crinkled, notes in the margins, items crossed out, and ideas added. I'll be disappointed if it ends up on the shelf looking as new as the day you bought it! I hope you will let me know what works well (or maybe not so well) in this second edition. I'd love to hear from you; you can e-mail me at chrishpl@lightlink.com. And my best to you as we continue in this ever-expanding journey to improve the teaching and assessment of children's physical education.

Acknowledgments

As I look back at the acknowledgments printed in the first edition of this book, I realize what was written then is just as relevant now. That is, this resource, a long time in coming, wouldn't be in this form today without the time, energy, support, and dedication of many individuals. Therefore, I'd like to recognize the following professionals:

First thanks to Scott Wikgren, director of Human Kinetics' HPERD division, and Bonnie Pettifor, acquisitions editor, for your patience, understanding, and unending commitment to this project. Thanks to developmental editor Jackie Blakley for your hard work on a task that was full of, well, drama, shall we say. The professional and personal support each of you has shown has been unequalled, and I truly couldn't ask to work with anyone better. Thank you.

I would also like to thank those fellow professionals whose experiences and expertise greatly enhanced this second edition, especially Marina Bonella, Nathan Brubaker, Mark Manross, Larry Satchwell, and Mark Searles. Thanks, too, to the many teachers I've had the pleasure to work with through various workshops and in-services; you've helped me crystallize my thinking and gain a deeper understanding of the topic of assessment. The same must be said for the children at my former school, Crystal Spring Elementary School in Roanoke, Virginia. You've taught me as much as (if not more than) I taught you, I'm sure.

Last, I must recognize three special people. Thanks, R, for your love and support, as well as the great setting that was so inspiring as I wrote. And also Aunt Barb and Uncle Bill, I couldn't have done this without *your* love, support, motivation, and feedback (not to mention, the computer!). I have truly been blessed to have each of you in my life.

PART I

Assessment in Elementary Physical Education

I'm sure you will agree that the job of an elementary physical education teacher certainly is not an easy one. We teach hundreds of students weekly—students whose developmental skills range from those of preschoolers to preteens. We teach in outdoor settings that challenge us in myriad ways, and if we have an indoor teaching space, we're considered fortunate. The amount and type of equipment available to us influences the type of curriculum we offer, and our budgets do not necessarily meet the financial assistance we need. We interact on a daily basis with parents, classroom teachers, and school administrators—some of whom may not always understand or support what we do. And this only scratches the surface. We have issues related to developing our curriculum, staying current with our national profession, and dealing with assessment and grading. It is no wonder we are exhausted by the end of the week.

Given all of this, we do not always have the time to analyze our curriculum and develop assessments to track student progress. Yet because these topics are so integral to our job (not to mention their priority at district, state, and national levels), it is important that they be addressed.

To maintain the emphasis of this book on the use of alternative assessments in elementary physical education, part I examines the topic of alternative (performance-based) assessment in our content area. In chapter I we explore the pervasive issue of assessment and look at the "new" topic of alternative assessment and how it relates to seamless assessment. In chapter 2 we examine ways to score assessment tasks (for example, through the use of rubrics) and tips for developing these tasks. Chapters 3 and 4 include practical, down-to-earth strategies to find time for assessment in your classes, as well as ways to use the results to your benefit.

Depending on the educational climate and events in your state or district, and on your level of expertise, you may find one chapter more useful than another. For example, you might even start with chapters 3 and 4 and work backward. Because the chapters generally do not build on each other, you will find that you can begin in one chapter and skip around. With all of this in mind, I hope you discover some ideas and tactics in part I that you can apply to your teaching. And because your time is valuable, let's begin. Happy reading.

Introducing
Alternative Assessment

Uh-oh, there's that word again. You know, the one that makes us cringe when our principals mention it in faculty meetings or the school board brings it up as a goal for the coming year. Even before hearing the particulars, we immediately know that assessment means more testing for the students and more work for us (read: paperwork, paperwork, paperwork). Does this sound familiar?

You're not alone. Teachers and students across the United States have felt the effects of the focus on assessment over the past few years, and its repercussions have not always cast assessment in a favorable light. Why is it that this aspect of the educational process, with such potential for positively influencing curriculum, instruction, and learning, is looked upon so negatively?

One reason assessment has received such a bad rap is that the term has taken on a new meaning in the politically charged educational environment of the past 20 years. Rather than considered a helpful educational tool, assessment has become synonymous with the high-stakes, one-shot testing situations many students confront at various times in their school years. Consider that at the time of this writing, every U.S. state has at least one mandatory student competency test or assessment program—a tenfold increase in the past 40 years—with each student taking an estimated three to five standardized tests annually (Madaus and Raczek, 1996).

This testing culture affects more than students. In an increasing number of districts a principal's annual raise is determined by student performance on the state tests (scores are published in the local newspaper and on the Internet). A teacher's effectiveness is judged by the percentage of students who pass the state tests. Classroom curricula are affected by the amount of time needed to administer the numerous tests, with a common complaint being that teachers have to teach to the tests instead of actually being able to *teach*. Add to all of this the federal emphasis on testing students as a way to determine school accountability, which, in turn, is tied to federal funding (or lack of it for failing schools), and it is easy to see why many teachers and administrators hold a negative view of assessment. In fact, we might even call assessment the Rodney Dangerfield of education because it seems to get no respect.

If assessment is so maligned, then why use it? Because at its best, the process of assessment is a powerful and even necessary tool for students to learn and apply important skills they'll need for future success. It holds promise to motivate them to take charge of their learning. Assessment can also assist teachers in a variety of ways as we strive to become more effective. As Smith, Smith, and DeLisi state, "Assessment . . . is not an add-on, a necessary evil, or a nuisance that we wish we could avoid, it is part and parcel of teaching. Assessment *is* part of instruction" (2001, p. 13). Unfortunately, we have (often, with good reason) come to look at the worst aspects of assessment: the planning, paperwork, and time it demands—time most teachers feel is better spent on instruction.

It's time to erase our traditional viewpoints about assessment and realize that the assessment of today—with its emphasis on the alternative assessment of students—is not the assessment of yesterday. So in our quest to relearn assessment, we first need to be clear about what it is—and what it is not.

Defining Alternative Assessment

Think back to your years of schooling; if they were anything like mine, the majority of your assessments were probably tests consisting of, for example, true or false, essay, and multiple choice questions. As figure 1.1 suggests, these traditional assessments required us to either select an answer from the list provided or develop (construct) a very short answer in response to a prompt or question (e.g., What is one cue to help you dribble a ball better?). The main purpose of these traditional assessments, I'm sure teachers would agree, was to determine what we knew about specific subject matter (mathematics, grammar, history, science, and so on). The tests did not require much more from us than putting forth our knowledge in a very specific, narrow manner, with little to no creativity required.

Yet if we search our memories, we might recall times we were asked to demonstrate knowledge

> *tidbit* Although certainly related, a number of terms such as *grading*, *evaluation*, and *testing* often take the place (erroneously) of *assessment*. For exact definitions of each term, check out the glossary at the end of the book.

in ways other than these traditional methods of assessment. For example, in middle school I had to make a diorama of an ecosystem after a particular unit in science class. I loved making cutouts of trees, animals, and physical surroundings that I pasted in three-dimensional view inside that cardboard shoebox. Talk about fun! And what about home economics in high school? I don't recall ever taking a paper-and-pencil test, but I did have to sew a top (I did not receive an A, for the record) and demonstrate how to measure ingredients when baking. Then there were physical fitness tests in physical education, and showing my ability at these tasks was fun, as you'll probably agree.

As you reflect on your school memories, you may remember some of these same assessments—tasks that demonstrated your knowledge or skill in a nontraditional manner. Creativity and ingenuity were (typically) important here. When I made a diorama, I did not just answer questions on paper about different ecosystems—I took information about geography, and plant and animal life of a particular environment, and illustrated it in a unique way. In home economics I did not take a written test on how to sew—I actually sewed.

Today, we call these kinds of practical assessments *alternative* or *performance assessments*. Alternative assessment tasks require students to do something, such as construct a tangible item, perform an artistic event, or demonstrate a physical skill. Students are expected to do more than recite information or memorize discrete facts; they're asked to apply knowledge in ways that are relevant in a changing landscape. Baron and Boschee perhaps summarize this best:

> The rapidly changing conditions characterizing our increasingly global society demand that we explore alternative strategies for preparing students to face life after school. Traditional instructional and assessment techniques fail to provide adequate measures of a student's chances for success in a world being transformed by changing social, political, economic, and cultural conditions. [Authentic] assessment, on the other hand, challenges students to demonstrate proficiency on tasks designed to develop the academic skills essential for successful citizenship in tomorrow's world. (1995, p. xii)

Traditional Assessments

Selected response	Constructed response
Multiple choice	Short answer
True or false	Concept mapping
Match the picture to the word	Fill in the blank
Circle the correct word or picture	Essay question

Figure 1.1   Types of traditional assessments.

Advances in communication and technology have changed how we live (imagine life today without computers), and some have argued that these changes have even altered how our brains think and learn. It has been posited that during the previous century, building a base of knowledge by memorizing discrete facts and information was important because of less access to books and attendance in higher education, and fewer modes of communication. But because students today can easily retrieve information unavailable to earlier generations, the challenge is not so much to memorize information, but to know how to access it, analyze it, use it, and apply it. When viewed this way, it becomes apparent that alternative assessment is in many (but, admittedly, not all) cases the most appropriate means for determining whether students have indeed mastered these complex skills. Fortunately for us in (elementary) physical education, using performance assessment is a perfect fit with what we do and how we teach. Let's take a closer look at the types of alternative or performance assessments and their characteristics.

The Four Ps of Alternative Assessments

There are four basic types of alternative assessment tasks, known as the four Ps (McTighe and Ferrara, 1998; Puckett and Black, 1994):

- **Products** are tangible, concrete items that students create through either the written, visual, or auditory media. For example, in elementary physical education a product assessment task could include students' drawings of themselves performing a physical activity, student-created brochures advertising the benefits of physical activity for parents and friends, or collages of pictures and photos showing healthy habits.

- **Process-focused tasks** show the thinking processes and learning strategies students use as they work. For example, a group of students might solve a physical task (such as getting all the students to the other side of the gym without their feet touching the floor), or students might write down (and maybe even explain, especially if they are young) how or why they designed a game or movement sequence.

- A **portfolio** is a collection of student work and additional information gathered over a period of time that demonstrates learning progress. Portfolios may include results from traditional (selected- and constructed-response) assessments, product tasks, process-oriented tasks, and other information.

- **Performances** are observable affective or psychomotor behaviors put into action. For example, students might demonstrate their abilities to throw by stepping off with the opposite foot and their cooperation with others during an activity.

In elementary physical education, the most common type of assessment task is the performance task. Figure 1.2 shows several examples of the four Ps and how they can be used in K–12 physical education. Keep in mind that sometimes, one alternative assessment task may involve the

My friend Larry Satchwell, a former NASPE (National Association for Sport and Physical Education) Elementary Teacher of the Year and elementary specialist in Gwinnett County, Georgia, once shared an experience that illustrated the power of alternative assessment. After instructing first and second graders in the proper way to throw underhand by stepping off with the foot opposite the throwing arm, Satchwell administered an assessment that shows two students throwing: a chubby youngster stepping with the correct (opposite) foot, and a slender child stepping with the incorrect foot. After evaluating the sheets, to his surprise, Satchwell found that many of his students (despite what he thought was good instruction) circled the youngster stepping with the incorrect foot. Curious, he took students aside and asked them how they made their choices. Their answers? "Fat kids can't throw." Satchwell discovered (and needed to address) much more about his students than their knowledge of the underhand throw—something a formal assessment would never have uncovered.

real world

Alternative Assessments			
Products	**Process-focused tasks**	**Portfolios**	**Performances**
Web site Bulletin board Collage Banner Public service announcement (PSA) Sculpture Photograph Drawing picture Videotaping sequence or game Designing a brochure or book	Problem solving an adventure-type task (group or individual) Creating a game Creating educational gymnastics/dance/creative movement sequence Creating an obstacle course Analyzing partner's performance Self-reflections Journal entries Research reports	A product itself made up in part of individual assessment sheets (portfolio tasks) that may be traditional or alternative in nature. They may also include information based on performance assessment tasks, health data, and more.	Skills/cue checks during tasks or game play Role playing Officiating a game Teaching the class a skill Affective (cooperative) behaviors toward others during participation Physically solving an adventure-type task Debates Fitness tests Performing educational gymnastics/dance/creative movement sequences

Figure 1.2   Types of alternative assessments used in physical education.

use of two or more Ps (see the information on *complex* assessment tasks in this chapter, page 10). At times, it may also be difficult to know under which P a given assessment task falls; there is not always one right answer. However you decide to classify it, what's most important to remember is that we are asking students to interact in unique and relevant ways with the content they are learning.

In short, alternative or performance assessment tasks determine students' knowledge, skills, and attitudes in ways that are enriching, motivating, and more instructional than a written test. Alternative assessment tasks tell us much about students:

where their talents or strengths lie (for example, how they complete a product reveals their level of creativity), how they best think, or what they think about a specific topic. Alternative assessments go far beyond the data and numbers we get from standardized tests. And they are a lot more fun both to take and evaluate.

This is not to say that the more traditional assessments have no place or use in modern education. It is simply that alternative assessments hold richer instructional potential and are better suited for the goals of contemporary learning. But simply performing an alternative assessment once in a while with students is not going to help us accomplish

tidbit

In part III of this book you will find performance tasks for every grade level, beginning with kindergarten, for the skills and concepts found in the elementary physical education curriculum. In addition, a variety of portfolio tasks allow students to demonstrate their knowledge of the same concepts and skills. Some of these portfolio tasks will be either product- or process-oriented tasks, while others may be assessment sheets that are more traditional in nature (i.e., incorporate selected or constructed responses). These more traditional forms of assessment tasks are included because younger students are generally not developmentally ready to complete many of the higher-order thinking processes required by some of the alternative forms of assessment. These assessment sheets can be completed easily by younger students as part of a physical education lesson. Other examples of assessment tasks can be found in NASPE's *Moving Into the Future: National Standards for Physical Education*, Second Edition (2004) and on the PE Central Web site (www.pecentral.org).

these goals. Rather, using alternative assessments challenges us to rethink how we work with the three educational processes of planning, instruction, and assessment to achieve what is known as *seamless assessment*.

Seamless Assessment

Traditionally, teachers have been trained to think of the link between planning curriculum, delivering it to students (instruction), and assessing it in a linear fashion. Simply put, we plan and instruct, and then assess at the end of the instructional period (e.g., unit), one right after the other. After assessment takes place, we begin another instructional unit.

In the modern model, however, it helps to think of the planning, instruction, and assessment processes as a braided rope (see figure 1.3) (Puckett and Black, 1994). Each part of the educational process is intertwined with the others, with each

Figure 1.3 The seamless assessment process represents teaching, learning, and assessing as interwoven.

AUTHENTIC ASSESSMENT OF THE YOUNG CHILD by Puckett/Black, © 1994. Reprinted by permission of Pearson Education, Inc., Upper Saddle River, NJ.

affecting the others and in turn being affected by them. When this happens, what Chappuis and Stiggins (2002, p. 40) call *assessment for learning* occurs: "Assessment becomes an instructional tool that promotes learning rather than being an event just to get grades." It involves and motivates students in the learning process. Asp tells us, "Approached in this way, assessment becomes integrated with curriculum and instruction, frequently serving as an instructional activity and guiding the development of curriculum and teaching strategies" (1998, p. 20).

In other words, assessment for learning occurs during, not just after, the teaching and learning process. This is quite different from our traditional view of assessment, to be sure. This new approach to assessment is *seamless*; it is difficult to tell when instruction ends and assessment begins. In fact, when we begin to look at assessment as a part of the instructional process, not apart from it, it "looks like instruction . . . because it *is* instruction" (Smith et al., 2001, p. 23).

In elementary physical education, I have a favorite example from my teaching to illustrate the idea of seamless assessment. I loved teaching educational gymnastics, with its skill themes of rolling, balancing, and transferring weight. In grades 1 and 2, I would introduce various skills, such as rolling different ways, balancing on different body parts, and transferring weight with only our feet. At the end of these lessons, I would have students develop a three-part sequence to showcase their skills, and I would then videotape their sequence. I would set one whole lesson aside for them to develop the sequence, and I would take them through each part. They'd decide first on a roll they could do well, a balance second, and a transfer of weight third. They would write this sequence down and

When the first edition of this book came out in 1995, the concept of assessment actually being a part of instruction was not as easily communicated and posited as it is today. This is partly because we educators were in the middle of figuring out how assessment fit in—and, it was so different from how we had typically thought about it. And even though I had written a book on the topic, I could not clearly define this concept. But that changed when I was giving a workshop with teachers and trying to explain what an assessment task was, and a teacher said out loud, "Oh, you mean, it's an *instructional* task?" This teacher got it much better, in some ways, than anyone else in the room, including me. I'll always be grateful to her (I would give her credit if I knew her name) for so simply but effectively and eloquently saying what is at the heart of this "new" assessment idea.

real world

then practice it. On the next physical education day, they would practice as I took one student at a time to be videotaped.

It always amazed me how motivated the students were to work on and improve their sequences. They knew I would be watching how well they did each part, and, in fact, I came to find out that second graders could easily evaluate their own performances according to a simple rubric—and many times they were tougher on themselves than I had been. (More on all of this rubric stuff later.) At any rate, this assessment task did take up quite a bit of instructional time, but to me, it was also learning time. I did not mind taking two whole lessons out of instruction, because students actually developed skills relating to analyzing and critiquing their own work, not to mention their physical skills, as they worked on the assessment task. As I went around to the students and gave them ideas and feedback on what they had developed, I found out much more about how each child worked and learned. It was an instructional, assessment, and educational experience for us all, and one I (and the students, it seemed) always looked forward to.

Just when this new notion of alternative, seamless assessment begins to sound pretty good, there is a flashing warning light to be heeded. Keep in mind that *any* assessment poorly developed, planned, or implemented—whether alternative or traditional in nature and tied perfectly into instruction—is still nothing more than a poor assessment. For an assessment to give quality results and be of maximum benefit to students and teachers, it must first have quality as an alternative assessment, woven together with planning and instruction. So what exactly does this mean? Let's next explore this idea of quality assessment.

Characteristics of Quality Assessment

Just as appropriate (and inappropriate) practices have been delineated for quality instruction

tidbit

Children Moving by George Graham, Shirley Holt/Hale, and Melissa Parker, and *Teaching Children Gymnastics: Becoming a Master Teacher, Second Edition,* by Peter Werner, are two great resources (and two of my favorites) on the planning, teaching, and assessing of educational gymnastics.

and instructional programs, so can appropriate practices and characteristics relative to quality assessment (whether it is traditional or alternative). Many scholars in education in general have already contributed to this body of knowledge. Rather than reinvent the wheel, I have gleaned the most common characteristics of quality assessment from these and other experts and compiled a list. I've also added thoughts of my own. Let's take a closer look at each of these characteristics that help define quality assessment.

- **Quality assessment is valid.** Good assessment measures what it is supposed to measure. In physical education, a written assessment administered in kindergarten or first grade, for example, may be less a reflection of the students' actual knowledge than of their (limited) vocabulary or ability to print words on paper. Nor would this written assessment tell you how well they could actually, for example, dribble or kick a ball. Care must be taken to ensure that an assessment truly measures what it has set out to measure.

- **Quality assessment is reliable.** The results from an assessment should be consistent. The results of an assessment today should be similar to the students' results on that same assessment tomorrow (assuming, of course, that additional learning has not taken place). Students getting answers on an assessment correct by guessing, for example, would not lend to that assessment being reliable. An assessment being both reliable and valid are the "cornerstones" of quality assessment.

- **Quality assessment is fair.** It allows all students, regardless of socioeconomic status, race, or gender, to have an equal chance to perform well. The assessment should be free from cultural, racial, and economic bias, and treat all students in an ethical manner. For example, asking students to perform an assessment outside of class requiring skills with golf clubs or hockey sticks may not be fair, because not every student has access to this equipment at home. Also, in some locales, students may be unfamiliar with certain skills, words, or equipment that an assessment might address.

• **Quality assessment uses many methods.** One method is not enough to determine the scope of students' knowledge and abilities. Judgments should never be based on just one assessment or one P type, no matter how fair or valid it may be. Multiple, varied measures of assessment should be used over time to yield the most accurate picture of students' capabilities.

• **Quality assessment uses repeated observations of performance.** Using data gathered during a number of observations is a more dependable way to determine what a child has learned. In other words, assessment should never be a one-shot deal. Unfortunately, too many times we require students to complete an assessment (such as a fitness test) on demand that results in an inaccurate representation of their skills. The best assessment situation gives students repeated opportunities not only to learn but also to demonstrate what they have learned.

• **Quality assessment is efficient and practical.** If teachers perceive assessment as impractical and inefficient, it likely will not be considered important. In addition, an impractical and inefficient assessment may be administered incorrectly, generating unfair results.

• **Quality assessment both enhances and develops out of instruction.** In other words, as we've already discussed, it is seamless in nature. It is derived from not only what you teach but also what is important to teach. In turn, good assessment then adds to (not detracts from) the instructional process and time for instruction. Seamless assessment makes a lot more educational sense.

• **Quality assessment reflects clear targets for accomplishment.** It sets out specific and appropriate expectations for students. They are told how the assessment will be scored and exactly what knowledge or skills will be required. It is then their responsibility to perform at an acceptable level—or not. There is also a clear link between the content taught to students and the assessment of that content. A prime example of the contrary is the class in which you studied your notes, did the readings—and the test (assessment) included none of that. When it comes to assessment, there should not be any surprises.

• **Quality assessment serves instructionally relevant purposes.** Because assessment has loomed so large in recent years, there is a danger of overdoing it just for the sake of gathering interesting information about student performance. Quality assessment practices, rather, have clear intentions for who receives the results and how they will be used.

• **Quality assessment appropriately incorporates technology.** It does not rely on technology merely to try out the newest gadget. Instead, there is a specific, appropriate reason for using that equipment. Care is also taken to give teachers adequate training. (Imagine trying to use a handheld computer to record fitness scores—without any previous instruction or practice.) In addition, if students are expected to use the technology to complete the assessment, they also need previous, repeated exposure to it.

• **Quality assessment communicates results quickly.** Students should receive timely feedback on their performance and the opportunity to see what they did correctly (or not). This information can help them further their learning. Involving students in the assessment process encourages them to take charge of their own learning, instead of making it a process that is out of their control (and therefore, not valued).

When reflecting on some of the characteristics of quality assessment, I cannot help but think of a particular college experience. In one of my classes we used a timed run to assess our cardiorespiratory endurance. Running has never been easy for me, and my results indicated I lacked cardiorespiratory endurance. I remember thinking that had to be an inaccurate measure of my endurance, because I could easily swim a mile in less than 30 minutes. I did not quite understand it at the time, but this is the value of multiple, valid measures. Had we been given a swimming assessment (or maybe even a different type of test such as a step test), I'm confident my results would have been different. I've since wondered how often I, or we, give an assessment and make a judgment about particular students based only on that one—when in fact, it might not be a true representation of their abilities.

real world

Attributes of Assessment Tasks

Any assessment task, whether traditional or alternative, of quality or not, can be further described or defined by a series of attributes. These attributes, typically found along a continuum, do not make one assessment task right and another one wrong, or one of quality and the other not. Understanding these attributes and their advantages and disadvantages can help us choose the most appropriate assessment task for its purpose. When these characteristics are combined, they make high-quality assessment tasks that add to instruction, not take away from it. Details of these attributes follow.

Informal Versus Formal

Effective elementary physical education teachers are good observers, and you'll find that they hold a wealth of information about their students. They are masters of *informal assessment*—relying on visual observation and scanning, for example—as a means of determining large amounts of information about their students. In other words, these teachers excel as "on-their-feet assessors." Through the course of their day-to-day teaching, they can tell that Johnny did not get enough sleep the night before, how much Susie improved her throwing skills during the year, and what activities this particular third grade class needs to work on. While not always written down or used for specific purposes, informal assessment data helps us to really know our students.

In addition to observing, teachers incorporate other informal assessment techniques into their lessons. For example, "checking for understanding" (Graham, 2001) is a quick, verbal indicator, such as "thumbs up if you think the answer is number 1, thumbs down if you think the answer is number 2." The results tell teachers if students get an idea or concept or direction. Informal assessments can also take the form of anecdotal records we write in our planners after a lesson (detailing information we observed), data we enter into our PDAs or on a cue checklist we complete about students' abilities, or information we gather from an assessment sheet. Informal assessments can provide us with hard-and-fast data we need to objectively grade students, report to parents about their child's progress, or tell our principal or school board about the effectiveness of our program.

By contrast, *formal assessment* can be thought of as the standardized tests prevalent in today's public schooling system. They are formal because typically they are administered under structured, prescribed conditions (e.g., "Put your pencils down") that involve when and how to give the test, and its duration. Examples of nationwide formal assessments can include the fitness tests, the SAT or ACT, the Iowa Test of Basic Skills, and the Peabody test battery that is administered in many elementary schools. They can also include teacher-made tests (e.g., a multiple-choice exam given at the end of a unit). Typically, the scores from standardized tests are used to compare one particular student's scores with others of the same grade and age. Many times, data from formal assessments are used to place students in a specific achievement group or used collectively to determine the efficacy of a school or school district's curriculum.

The most effective teaching and assessment practices call for us to rely less on data from formal assessments in our programs and more on observation of students during informal assessment tasks throughout the school year. Informal assessments seem less threatening or stressful (for both teachers and students) and are more similar to instructional tasks than are their formal counterparts.

Simple Versus Complex

To distinguish the simple from the complex assessment, think of it this way. You ask second graders, after one or two lessons on dribbling, to trace their hands on a piece of paper and color the part of the hand that touches a dribbled ball. This assessment task can easily be completed as part of one lesson; it also entails the use of only one P. Therefore, it is defined as a *simple* assessment.

In contrast, think of an assessment task that includes more than one type of alternative assessment (or P) or includes information covered over a series of lessons, not just one. This type of task is a *complex* assessment.

As an example of a complex assessment, say your fifth-grade students have been working on their gymnastics skills. As a culminating task for the unit, you break them into groups to develop, refine, and perform an educational gymnastics sequence. Each group's sequence has to consist of one type

As I became a more experienced teacher I decided to try to give students one alternative assessment per unit. Sometimes it was simple (performance only) and formative in nature; other times, complex and summative. The task could be an assessment sheet for the portfolio administered by teachers in the classroom or done as homework. It was not always possible to give one informal assessment per unit, but it was a good goal that definitely took time to get close to happening. (Chapter 3 explores ways to make it easier to assess throughout the year.)

of roll, one group balance, and one transfer of weight, and the sequence must be done in unison (a performance task). You may ask students to write down the sequence for their portfolios (a product), and you may then videotape the performance to show students and parents at a later date (also a product). This assessment task involves many Ps; it also is a result of knowledge and skills learned over the course of many lessons (i.e., an unit). It is complex in nature.

Generally, because students in lower grades have less advanced psychomotor, cognitive, and affective skills, they should receive simple assessments; they have not developed the tools necessary to combine or attend to many facets of a more complex assessment. Conversely, simple assessment tasks in the upper elementary grades would fail to gauge the higher-order cognitive and more complex physical skills that older children at these levels should exhibit. Therefore, it is best to adjust the complexity of assessment tasks as children develop during their elementary school years.

Formative Versus Summative

Formative assessments can be defined as those ongoing throughout a unit, with the purpose of determining whether students are on track to developing and meeting the desired skills and concepts. Formative assessment can be done after one lesson. *Summative assessment,* on the other hand, typically is thought of as assessment that takes place at the end of a unit—that is, it sums up a number of facts or skills students should have learned over a longer period of time. Think of this in terms of college courses—a quiz each week would be formative in nature, but the midterm and final would be summative.

Again, it would be inappropriate to use only formative or only summative assessments with students during their elementary years. Effective

teachers and assessors use a variety of assessment types.

Authentic Versus Contrived

The term *authentic assessment* is widely used by educators, many times synonymously with the term *alternative assessment*. But because these two terms define different characteristics, they are not interchangeable.

An assessment task defined as authentic is one performed in a real-life context that approximates, as much as possible, the use of that skill or concept in the real world. In opposition is a skill or concept performed in a setting that is artificial or contrived and has little carry-over to everyday life. As an example, consider the mile-run (1.6 km) fitness test. It is certainly performance-oriented and alternative in nature. But think of the setting in which it typically takes place. On a day determined by the teacher, students are required to run a mile on a course around the school grounds or play area. Off they go (for a while, anyway). For most elementary students, this situation is not authentic at all. Think about it. How many young children (or adults, for that matter) typically run a mile over a particular track in their everyday lives? There are some, but it is not the norm. In addition, sit-ups and other standardized fitness tests are certainly performance or alternative in nature, but they are not authentic to how we use these skills (in these cases, the components of fitness) in everyday life.

Typically, the more authentic the context or situation, the more meaningful and motivational the assessment is for the students. For example, it would be fun and interesting for students to learn in the classroom how to bowl and score their games, but playing at a bowling alley is more fun. Another example might be older students expressing what fitness means to them. It is one thing to write this on paper; it is another thing to write a

My favorite "authentic" story is about Amanda, a 9-year-old who knew she was not athletic. My community's DARE program sponsored a 5K run on a Saturday morning through the streets of downtown Roanoke, Virginia, and for the first time it offered a 1-mile (1.6 km) run for children. Because I was required to give the mile-run fitness test to my students, I told them that if they participated in the DARE event, I would count their time as official, and they would not have to do the mile test at school. (Even better, I would run with them—and I am *not* a runner.) Early that morning, students picked up their entry numbers and T-shirts and submitted their stubs for door prizes. Amanda, who would have been one of the last students to complete the run at school, had the time of her life jogging with me through the streets. I will never forget her excitement as she partook in a real event, knowing it was not important who came in first. Plus, she won a door prize. She had fun doing it, and she **could** do it. I'm hoping it made an impression on her she will not quickly forget.

public service announcement (PSA) that could air on the local radio station during National Physical Education and Sports Week. You can understand how fifth or sixth graders may react to the possibility of their PSA being read on the radio.

Although an authentic assessment is always alternative in nature, an alternative assessment is not always authentic. It is not feasible or possible (or even desirable) to make every assessment authentic, but it is good to keep in mind when designing assessment tasks. As adults, too, it is important to remember that what is authentic to us is not necessarily authentic to a child's life. To determine where different alternative assessments fall on the authenticity continuum, see figure 1.4.

So Why Assess?

To sum it up, quality alternative assessment offers a number of benefits to those involved in the educational process.

- It improves instruction.
- It guides the process of writing effective curriculum (units, time spent on each, and so on).

- It shows the overall effectiveness of a program.
- It gives information about each student's progress.
- It helps teachers make placement decisions.
- It helps us communicate the effectiveness of our program to others.

Sometimes we assess ourselves as teachers (Are my students learning what I'm expecting them to? Should I go on to my next unit of instruction?), while at other times we assess to give others, such as parents or administrators, information on the success of a program (Is the physical education program helping students become physically fit?). As you can imagine, our assessment audience determines our purposes for assessment (and vice versa) as well as the type of assessment task we use.

Though all of these purposes are important, one of the best arguments is that, given the limited instruction time in elementary physical education (with some elementary physical education teachers seeing students as few as 16 hours a school year), assessment can be a primary means of determining whether we are spending our teaching time wisely.

Fitness tests	Collages	Skills check during game play
Traditional assessments	Debates	Physical events in community
Standardized tests	Teaching the class a skill	PSAs
		Web sites

Less authentic ←———————————————————————→ More authentic

Figure 1.4   Authenticity continuum.

It is interesting to note the reactions of students when they hear the term *assessment* rather than *test* in class. Although kindergartners have a good sense of what a test means (and first graders on up definitely do), my experience is that students do not have the same (negative) reaction to the term *assessment*, likely because they are not used to hearing it as often as the word *test*. When teaching, I would say, "Okay, let's do a quick assessment to see what you know," and it always amazed (and amused) me that students did not equate this with a test, even though the process often was similar (e.g., writing an answer on paper). At times, they would even write down, "I don't know yet" in response to a question, something I'm sure they would never do on a test.

real world

Assessment allows us to answer the one question that any contemporary, quality physical education teacher should be asking: "Are my students becoming physically educated through their involvement in my (elementary) physical education class?"

There is no doubt that many issues make assessing students difficult. You may face some of them on a daily basis.

- Large numbers of students per week
- Double classes per teaching period
- Travel time to different schools to teach
- Limited time with students per week and year
- Full schedule of 8 to 10 classes per day
- Short class periods
- Lack of technology and other resources
- Inadequate facilities
- Lack of time to deal with assessment results
- Lack of personnel to assist with the assessment process

Difficulties such as these are, unfortunately, realities for many teachers. But these challenges should not dissuade us from the basic premise that quality planning and quality instruction by themselves are not enough to constitute a quality physical education program. Quality assessment must also be present for the program to be truly of quality. Fortunately, there are small things that can assist us in conducting quality assessment tasks as part of the planning and instructional process. You can read about these in the next few chapters.

Summary

Quality assessment tends to be more alternative, authentic, and appropriate for students than most traditional assessments. There is no doubt that moving toward this method of assessment is not easy, but given time, experience, and support from fellow teachers, I bet you will find you actually enjoy rather than dread the process of assessment. In fact, our next few chapters will focus on strategies and other information that can help the assessment process. Who knows? When we're done, maybe assessment will finally get more respect.

Scoring and Creating Alternative Assessment Tasks

If the answer to physical education lay in a true or false question, our jobs as teachers might be simple. But what we do is much more involved than the choice of a T or F on a piece of paper, and so it should also be for the assessment of students in our classroom. The action-oriented aspect of our profession dictates that our assessments measure the performance part of learning that takes place in our elementary school classroom. To this end we also need ways to accurately and objectively score these alternative methods of assessment. In this chapter we'll take a look at three different scoring methods, examples of them from elementary physical education, and suggestions for using them.

Three generally accepted methods for scoring an alternative assessment task are checklists, rating scales, and that weird word that reminds us of a toy—rubrics. Each has its own specific uses and attributes, which we'll explore in more detail.

tidbit

The word *rubric* comes from the centuries-old Latin term *rubrica terra,* which described the red earth used to mark or signify something of importance. In layman's terms today, it refers to an established or authoritative rule, something that we've built off of in education today. I only wonder *who* in education thought of using that word?

Checklists

Checklists are one of the easiest methods for scoring performance-based assessments. The criteria in the checklist (i.e., the specific skills, cues, or tasks) are considered separately, according to whether they have been accomplished. This may take the form of a simple yes or no (i.e., criteria present or not present), point given or not given, or item checked off or not checked off for each criterion in the checklist. A narrow scale such as "never, rarely, and frequently" or "can do almost all the time, sometimes, and rarely" are also sometimes used when scoring a checklist. Figure 2.1 shows an example of a checklist used to assess elementary physical education students' ability to dribble in hockey.

Checklists are valuable tools in the classroom for a number of reasons. First, because they have a simple format, they are easy to understand—enough so that even young students can use them to evaluate themselves or peers. Second,

Name	**Class** **Date**

✔ +	I can dribble a puck with a hockey stick in a straight pathway, keeping the puck close to the stick.
✔	I can dribble a puck with a hockey stick in a curved pathway, keeping the puck close to the stick.
✔	I can dribble a puck with a hockey stick in a zigzag pathway, keeping the puck close to the stick.
✔ −	I can dribble a puck around two cones in a figure eight, keeping the puck close to the stick.
✔ +	I can dribble a puck while running, keeping the puck close to the stick.
✔	I can pass a puck between two cones (one hockey stick apart) from 20 feet (6.1 m) a total of 3 out of 5 times.

✔ + A skill you can do very well

✔ A skill you can do sometimes but still needs work

✔ − A skill you cannot do most of the time

Figure 2.1   Example of a simple checklist used by students to personally assess ability.

Used with permission of Larry Satchwell.

they are very simple for teachers to use. Even in an action-packed gym, checklists are time-savers when recording data. Third, they help increase the degree of objectivity used as tasks are scored. For example, a checklist forces you to look at and judge only one criterion at a time, and it reduces the chance that you will score the total assessment higher because of the influence of one or two individual parts. Last, because they are organized in a step-by-step fashion, they can aid students in cognitively organizing and recalling information inherent in a particular checklist (for example, the order in which a skill is to be performed).

Another positive aspect of using checklists is that they are neither difficult nor time-intensive to develop (especially compared with other, more complex alternative assessments). Any of the checklist examples in this book can easily be revised to reflect a variety of skills and are well within the scope of

most teachers. For additional examples, check the PE Central Web site (www.pecentral.org.), which includes forms you can download and reproduce. You can also find information in resources such as Sue Schiemer's *Assessment Strategies for Elementary Physical Education* (2000), *Classroom Assessment: Enhancing the Quality of Teacher Decision Making* (Anderson, 2003), and *The Logic and Methodology of Checklists* (Scriven, 2000) to help you develop checklists for yourself or students.

Rating Scales

While checklists typically have a "check yes or no" or "give a point or not" format to determine if a specific criterion is met, rating scales judge the degree to which the criterion is present. They answer questions such as how much, how good, and how often. As might be expected, this type of measure is more subjective than a checklist. Yet, because rating scales are still fairly simple in format, elementary school students can generally handle them.

One common use of rating scales in physical education allows teachers to receive input and opinions from students by asking questions such as, "On a scale of 1 to 4, with 4 being the best and 1 being the worst, rate how well you think you cooperated with others today, and why." Rating scales can also be combined with a checklist. For example, students can check whether a specific criterion is present (or not), and then rate the degree to which it is present. Figure 2.2 gives one example of a rating scale that can be used by older students to evaluate the creative dance performance of their peers. A rating scale such as this can help students form a basis for making constructive comments to another group about the quality of a performance.

In figure 2.2, there are only three points in the rating scale because of the informal nature of the assessment. More complex evaluations would likely consist of a four-, five-, or six-point scale, although keep in mind that younger students will have more difficulty distinguishing the finer points of scales with too many options. Before students use a rating scale (especially a more complex one), it would be helpful to discuss what distinguishes each point in the scale. In this case, it would help to accompany the rating scale with anchors, or samples of student work that illustrate each point in the scale. Anchors help students clearly see what constitutes a score of 1 versus a 2, 3, or 4 performance. This information is clearly conveyed

> **tidbit**
>
> Rating scales (like their checklist counterparts) are not difficult to develop by even inexperienced teachers, so this resource will not focus in detail on their development. Rather, the majority of scoring time will be spent on rubrics. Based on my experience, that's probably a good thing, because this scoring option can befuddle even the most veteran teacher.

Name _____   **Class** _____

Group you are evaluating _____

Rate the group you watch on a scale of 1 to 3, with 1 being the lowest and 3 being the highest. In the space provided, write a reason why you gave the number you did.

	Low 1	2	High 3
How well did their movements match each other's? **Reason:**			
How well did their sequence flow without mistakes? **Reason:**			
Did their choice of music match the type of sequence they developed? **Reason:**			
Were they creative in developing their sequence? Did they think of unusual or unique ways to move? **Reason:**			

Figure 2.2   Sample rating scale.

by pointing out aspects of students' performances and giving specific verbal instructions. If necessary, previous videotaped performances can be shown so students witness the level of work expected. Providing these anchors and expectations can help raters become less subjective in their evaluations and result in greater scoring reliability. In addition, when evaluating students with a rating scale, it is helpful to include comments to explain a specific score.

Checklists and rating scales, while helpful, cannot adequately measure each type of alternative assessment. They are limited by the very simplicity that makes them easy to use, and they are not appropriate to use with more complex, detailed alternative assessments. In these cases, rubrics are required.

Rubrics

A rubric is a list of statements explaining in detail the possible levels of performance for each criterion involved in an alternative assessment task. As opposed to a checklist, where one or more criteria are evaluated by a simple "yes" or "no" judgment, a rubric may describe each criterion according to three, four, five, or even more levels of judgment. Depending on the nature and complexity of the task, rubrics can be holistic or analytical as well as task-specific or generic in nature.

Holistic Rubrics

Holistic rubrics generally are applied to evaluate the *overall* quality of a student's work. In this type of rubric, multiple criteria are grouped together into one statement for each specific level of performance (e.g., descriptor scale) in the rubric, typically totaling four to six in number. As the number of descriptor scales in a holistic rubric increases, the detail and specificity found in each of the descriptor statements also increases. Many times, holistic rubrics are used to score writing and related tasks in which a summative big picture of each student's work is desired. They are also appropriate for use when it is difficult to separate the individual criteria because they overlap.

In elementary physical education, a holistic rubric might be used to evaluate a student's affective behaviors during class. Figure 2.3 shows a rubric developed using Hellison's (2003) levels of self-responsibility as a guide. His levels are the descriptor scale, and each level is further detailed by the exact behaviors that typify that specific level.

When developing a holistic rubric, care must be taken to include all criteria in each descriptor statement across the scale. In other words, each level should include information about each criterion and address the same amounts and type of information. For example, you would not want creativity and smoothness to be addressed in two levels of the rubric but not in the other two. In addition, one shortcoming of a holistic rubric is that students may perform well on one criterion or a few criteria in a particular descriptor statement, but poorly on one criterion or two criteria in that same descriptor statement. This indicates that the particular descriptor statement may not be the best representation of the student's work. In these cases, it is better to use an analytic rubric.

Level 4	Level 3	Level 2	Level 1	Level 0
• Helping others without being asked • Being partners with more than just my friends • Doing kind deeds for others • Always safe	• Always doing my work • Trying my hardest • Taking care of equipment • Working nicely with others • Including everyone	• Trying my best only some of the time • Doing my work only sometimes • Needing reminders about my behavior and care of equipment	• Not doing my work • Not taking care of equipment • Not following directions • Saying "I can't" • Talking while others are talking	• Bothering others • Hurting others' feelings • Acting disrespectful • Choosing not to participate • Not safe to self, others, or equipment

Figure 2.3   Sample holistic rubric.

I have always been intrigued by Hellison's model of affective development in physical education, and I was convinced to use it in my gym after attending a workshop seminar given by fellow Virginia elementary physical educator Fran Zavacky. Her idea of hanging neon-colored signs and smiley and frowny faces on the gym walls became a great visual reminder for my students and, perhaps more important, their parents to see as they came through the gym.

Analytic Rubrics

In contrast to holistic rubrics, *analytic rubrics* allow for the separation of specific criteria important to the evaluation of an assessment task. Each criterion is judged against a specific number of levels of performance (that is, the descriptor scales), which are further defined by a descriptor statement. The number of points can then be totaled to indicate the overall effectiveness of the assessment task. An analytic rubric for a gymnastics performance for grades 1 and 2 is shown in figure 2.4. This type of rubric is especially well suited to alternative

---

Name _____   **Class** _____

_____ How well did you perform the skills in your sequence? (Did you remember the hints to help you do your skills well?)

3 pts: You were able to perform *each* skill in your sequence correctly; you stretched your body parts to make them look good!

2 pts: You were able to perform *most* of the skills in your sequence correctly.

1 pt: You were able to perform *some* of the skills in your sequence correctly.

0 pts: You weren't able to perform any of the skills in your sequence correctly.

_____ Did your sequence flow smoothly? Did you correctly remember the sequence you made up?

3 pts: Your sequence was very smoothly performed, and you correctly remembered it.

2 pts: Your sequence was pretty smooth—you may have had a few small stops. You correctly remembered your sequence.

1 pt: Your sequence was somewhat smooth, but you had some stops. You may have forgotten some of your sequence.

0 pts: Your sequence was not smooth at all—you had lots of stops. You forgot the sequence you wrote down.

_____ Did you remember all the parts of your sequence?

	Yes (3 pts)	No (0 pts)
Includes at least one roll	_____	_____
Includes at least one balance	_____	_____
Includes at least one weight transfer	_____	_____
Has an ending shape	_____	_____

_____ Total points

18: Congratulations! You practiced well—you are an "Olympic Gymnast!"

16–17: Great job! You worked hard during class, and it shows—you are a "Terrific Tumbler!"

7–15: You did okay, but you need to improve a little more. You can do it—keep practicing! You are a "Junior Gymnast."

0–6: You need to work a little harder; you can improve if you try! Practice at home or in the yard—you are on the "Practice Team."

Figure 2.4   Sample analytic rubric.

assessment tasks that have a number of dissimilar criteria or parts, and those that require feedback on each specific criterion.

When developing descriptor statements for an analytic rubric, vague words such as "adequate," "some," "well done," and the like would leave the assessor to interpret what each of these words means. Take care to describe each level on the descriptor scale adequately and accurately to reduce subjectivity by the assessor.

Task-Specific Rubrics

A *task-specific rubric* is one that has been developed especially for one particular assessment task. In this type of rubric (which can be either holistic or analytic), the descriptor statements are specific to the objectives of the assessment and worded in a way that reflects the requirements of the task. The analytic rubric in figure 2.4 is also an example of a task-specific rubric because the wording in each descriptor reflects the unique nature of the gymnastics sequence it measures.

Generic Rubrics

Many times, task-specific rubrics have been developed out of or from a *generic rubric*. As the name suggests, generic rubrics (sometimes called *global rubrics*) are general enough in wording that they can apply to the evaluation of a variety of assess-

ment tasks. In elementary physical education, a generic rubric might detail how well fifth-grade students apply offensive and defensive strategies in a variety of games, not one particular game (see figure 2.5). Another example might involve students designing and performing a creative dance and gymnastics sequence; similar criteria inherent in both tasks may allow the same rubric for either task. Evaluating students on how well they demonstrate affective behaviors is another instance; a generic rubric can apply to most any activity. Obviously, the advantage to using generic rubrics is that of time—once developed and perfected, the rubric can be used repeatedly.

No matter the rubrics you use, there is no doubt that they take time, practice, and patience to perfect. The suggestions outlined in the next section may streamline the process.

Developing Your Own Rubrics

The key to successfully scoring a performance assessment depends on the quality of its rubric. The following hints, listed in sequential order, may help as you develop any type of rubric.

Step 1: Define the Crucial Elements for Student Learning   To determine the criteria you will use to evaluate students' work, ask yourself this question: What about this task is so important that students must demonstrate that they have mas-

Competent	Achieving	Needs practice
• Student is able to consistently create space by moving to open spaces to successfully pass object; pass is not broken up by defender; student does not need to be reminded by teacher or teammates to move. • Student consistently creates space by moving to open space to receive object; needs no reminders to move to open space. • Student is able to consistently move body in between object and goal; is consistently in close position to make a play on the object or break up the play.	• Student is able to sometimes, but not always, move to open spaces to pass an object; many times, pass is blocked by defending guard. • Student is able to sometimes, but not always, move to open space to receive object; at times, stands in location where first moved, no matter where teammates or defense have moved; may need prompting by teammates or teacher to move to open area. • Student is able to sometimes, but not always, move body in between object and goal; at times, is not in correct position to make a play on the object or break up the play.	• Student does not grasp the concept of moving to open spaces to pass an object; makes no attempt to move away from guarding defender. • Student does not grasp concept of moving to open space to receive object; makes no attempt to move away from defender in order to receive object from teammate. • Student is rarely able to move body in between object and goal; consistently gets "beat" out of position by offense.

Figure 2.5   Sample generic rubric.

tered it? For example, in the gymnastics rubric discussed earlier (see figure 2.4), the criteria students were expected to demonstrate included

- performing a successful roll, balance, and transfer of weight (successful was defined both in instruction and the rubric);
- practicing the sequence enough so they could remember and perform it without having to stop; and
- forming an ending shape.

These criteria were determined before the unit of instruction was taught and could be modified, as needed, depending on what happened during instruction.

As you consider the qualities you want to measure, it should become clear which type of rubric, holistic or analytic and task-specific or generic, is best suited to your task. In figure 2.4, the unique criteria measured and their importance in the unit dictated that a task-specific analytic rubric was appropriate.

tidbit

Because every teacher, their expectations, and their students are different, rubrics were not developed for the performance tasks in part III of this resource. Instead, you will find Rubric Clues that prompt you to the specific criteria you can use when developing a rubric for that task, one that will work for your students and your instruction.

Step 2: Define the Descriptor Statements for the Rubric

Now that you have identified your criteria, you must next define them. Begin by considering the top (proficient) performance level. What does it look like? For each criterion, determine what qualities mark a proficient performance. Be sure to use descriptive rather than judgmental statements. For example, saying that the sequence demonstrated excellent flow is too abstract. What does excellent look like? It is more helpful to say that the sequence flowed smoothly with no stops or hesitations, an evaluation that clearly defines what excellent looks like.

After defining your top level, define your lowest level of performance. What does an unsatisfactory performance look like? Again, use descriptive language to address each criterion. Once both of these are done, write your middle performance expectations. One strategy that may help you at this step is to have a class actually perform the task. Once this is done, categorize their results in order,

according to the descriptor scales in your rubric. In other words, determine which students' work is at the highest level, the lowest, and each level in between. With your criteria and results in hand, analyze both to decide how best to explain what you are looking for in your top level and so on, and then write your descriptor statements.

Step 3: Decide How Many Levels Make Up Your Rubric

Generally, a rubric should define four to six levels of performance. The advantage of generating four levels instead of three is that with three levels teachers tend to put a few students in the bottom level, a few in the top level, and everyone else in the middle. This results in very little discrimination among the students in the middle level, although realistically there would have to be differences between a student who performs near the bottom level and one who performs close to the top level. Four or more levels, then, requires more discernment. A teacher cannot sit on the fence—in other words, you must more precisely evaluate the performances of the majority of the students.

There are times, however, when it may be desirable to have three levels in a rubric. For instance, when observing students' throwing skills, having only three levels allows you to quickly and easily judge their performances (i.e., "most of the time, some of the time, little to none of the time"). This provides information so you can tailor instruction or give a progress report to parents (this data should not be the sole determinant for a child's grade). In addition, when children evaluate themselves or peers, it is easier for them to select among three levels rather than four or more.

When does your rubric have enough levels? When you can no longer make distinctions among the levels—if you cannot articulate the difference between a 4 performance and a 5—then you probably have too many. "It is better to have a few meaningful score categories than to have many score categories that are difficult or impossible to distinguish" (Moskal, 2002, p. 92).

Step 4: Give Each Descriptor Scale a Label What you decide to call each level in your rubric will depend on a couple of factors. First, does your school or district use certain terms that are reflected on report cards or in your grading scheme? This may be a good place to begin, as these terms may already be familiar to parents and others. One example would be to use "E" (excellent), "S" (satisfactory), "N" (not satisfactory), and "U" (unsatisfactory)—the same labels that may be found on a report card—for your descriptor scale labels.

Second, which level do you expect students to achieve to pass the task? For example, in a four-point rubric, if you consider the third-highest level to be a passing grade (which is common), then you might label that particular level as acceptable, satisfactory, 3, or You've Got It. After you determine your passing level, you can decide the performance appropriate for the levels above and below it. As a caution, stay away from negative or derogatory terms to describe levels; you want students to know that their performance—not them personally—is being judged.

Once you have completed the previous steps, your rubric should be completed. But, before you use this rubric with students for a grade, there are a few things to keep in mind.

Hints for Working With and Using Rubrics

You thought developing the rubric was the hardest part? Now all you need to do is use it? As anyone familiar with rubrics will tell you, it is not always this easy. Remember, developing rubrics takes

> I have found my most successful rubrics, for both elementary and college students, tend to include either three or four descriptor scales. For most (but not all) of my tasks, five or six levels in the rubric became unwieldy, and it is rarely necessary or useful to have that many levels.

time—and patience—so do not get frustrated. There are a few more strategies you can use to ensure that your rubric is as good as it can be.

Use It in a Test Run Before using your rubric in the classroom—especially if it will determine a grade—first try it out with a specific class or group of students. It seems that most teachers, when they first develop a rubric for a new assessment task, end up revising one or more parts of the rubric or assessment task once they determine what works and what does not. There is nothing like the real thing to confirm if you were specific enough with your criteria. It also may be constructive to ask a colleague with a similar curriculum and teaching style to try your rubric in his or her classroom. Working together is more helpful than working alone.

Include Anchors Once your descriptor scales and statements are set and you've used the task and rubric with students, include at least one or more *anchors* (examples) of student work with the rubric for your benefit; these will be helpful as you compare results of this task with future ones. Expect to revise your rubric at a future date and share your rubric and how you developed it with other teachers. If colleagues will be using the rubric, these anchors are absolutely necessary to maintain the reliability of the rubric across users.

Recycle You may find you can use the basic criteria of a rubric for more than one assessment task, especially if the rubric is generic. Examine your other

> As I developed the grades 1 and 2 gymnastics performance rubric discussed earlier (figure 2.4), I went through four versions before I was satisfied with how it worked. Because I taught many first- and second-grade classes (I worked at two different schools), I could test my rubric on a few classes before I used it for real. I recall developing other rubrics and giving them test runs during particular units, then revising and using them the next year once the units came back around. It is all a part of the process, and when it came time to actually use the revised rubric, I knew each descriptor scale inside and out.

I had to laugh when, in one of my college classes, I discussed the merits of sharing rubrics with students before they are evaluated. A student in the class asked, "Well, wouldn't some students just say, 'Hey, I'm only going to do what I have to do to get a fair grade'? How is this motivating to them?" In one of those rare moments when I knew *exactly* what to say to make my point, I replied, "Well, isn't that what sometimes you all do when I give an assignment? You look at everything you have to do, or things outside of school you want to do, and you say, 'Hey, I could go for the highest level, but right now, given everything, I'm fine with getting a fair grade?'" It was their turn to chuckle; indeed, some of them did just that.

rubrics—see what worked, what did not, and how you wrote criteria—to help you develop or revise a rubric. Borrow rubrics from other sources, such as classroom teachers (especially helpful for portfolio-type tasks) or workshops (just be mindful of copyright laws). You may find wording of descriptor labels or statements you like and can use in the development of your own rubrics, even if they are not from your subject area.

Share It With Students   Have you ever had a teacher tell you to expect a test, but not tell what it will cover? Remember how frustrating that was? One of the great benefits of rubrics is that they can (and should) be shared with students before they are assessed, preferably as you begin instruction in new units. A rubric gives students a clear idea of what is expected of them. Sometimes termed instructional rubrics (Andrade, 2000), they help form a cognitive scaffold for your instruction (i.e., understanding how the parts fit together to make the whole). When rubrics are discussed in class, they motivate students to perform at their highest level and provide a basis for your feedback during the instructional process. When it comes time for evaluation, there should be no surprises.

Summary

Our job is not simple. It is much more like an essay question than one answered true or false. The responsibility of developing our own assessment tasks and rubrics adds to the complexity of what we do, to be sure. Fortunately, many resources are available to help with this process, both in physical education and education in general. It is also helpful to know that, as the saying goes, "perfect practice makes perfect." In other words, the more you use your tasks and rubrics and see what does and does not work, the easier the process will become. Before long, you'll be a pro at it—and developing tasks and rubrics will become second nature. In fact, you may end up asking yourself how you ever survived without them.

Managing the Assessment Process

By now you may be thinking, Finally, we're getting to the nitty-gritty. There is no doubt that talking about alternative assessments is one thing, but finding the time to incorporate them into your already jam-packed elementary physical education program can be quite another. I mean, why should teaching nine classes a day and 500 students a week, hauling around equipment, gulping down lunch, and having barely enough time to visit the restroom affect what you do?

Seriously (and realistically) though, *doing* assessment is nearly impossible without the use of organizational strategies to help you best manage the process. That's why in this chapter we'll look at strategies that can help make the assessment process a little easier. They center on the topics of finding time for assessment, using organizational protocols (especially those that enhance the use of portfolio tasks), and recording data efficiently (including the use of technology).

Finding Time to Assess

Too many times we plan for instruction but fail to factor in assessment. Or we do not want to relinquish our instructional time to assessment. The result? Assessment becomes an afterthought, the first thing to go if we run out of time in a unit or lesson. Fortunately, however, this does not have

to happen. With seamless assessment, smart planning, and a few other strategies, we can make the most of our instructional and assessment time.

Plan Ahead

This may be an obvious strategy, but planning ahead is often overlooked (especially if we are just beginning to incorporate assessment tasks into our instruction). Before each unit, take the time to realistically determine how many lessons (or minutes in a lesson) you need for students to complete an assessment task, and then work this amount of time into your unit calendar (see "Step Four: Revise Your Unit Overview" in chapter 6). By looking at instruction and assessment together in your planning, it can help to make your assessment seamless.

As an example, it would be downright impossible for a group of fourth-grade students, in just one 30-minute lesson, to design, refine, and perform a movement sequence combining locomotor and nonlocomotor movements, with the use of equipment, that focuses on concepts such as matching, mirroring, and unison (see locomotor skills theme in chapter 9, grades 3 and 4, for the related task). Before they can meet this objective, planning needs to encompass the skills students need to complete the task, the movement concept experiences that will assist them, and the time it will take to allow them to demonstrate their finished product (in this case, their performance). Adding at least one lesson to your unit to allow time for students to demonstrate their routines ensures that you have adequately adjusted your schedule for both instruction and assessment of this unit. Without leaving enough time (especially if it happens over a number of units), your lesson plans have to be rethought.

Of course, how much time to set aside for assessment in each unit or lesson will depend on a variety of factors: the type of task you are asking students to complete, its complexity, whether students have had experience with the task, and the effectiveness of their instruction. For complex performance tasks that are movement-sequence related, provide students enough time to demonstrate their routine to others or be videotaped for viewing later. (Asking students to design a sequence and then not giving them a chance to perform it is frustrating to them.) This may take up a half to a whole lesson, but it is time well spent, especially if you held high standards for the development and refining of the sequence. For more game-oriented performance tasks, it is likely that a keen observer could quickly and easily assess for a skill or strategy during time allotted for the lesson.

If you will be administering a portfolio task, plan on roughly five minutes or so for a group of experienced first or second graders to complete the task. It will take more than this the first few times you give them the portfolio tasks, but once students are familiar with assessment protocols (and as they become more independent), this time can be reduced. For older students more experienced with the routine of the portfolio tasks, allow even less time.

Enlist the Aid of Classroom Teachers

Another way to build in time for assessment is to solicit help from your classroom teachers. (No doubt, this will work better with some teachers than others.) For example, three first-grade teachers I worked with made a strong team, and they were more than happy to include my portfolio assessments in their classroom learning centers. The students loved doing the tasks (they weren't seen as classroom work, and therefore became favorites), and it was a great way for me to buy assessment time. And the fifth-grade teachers had students write journal entries about a particular question related to physical education (e.g., "Why do you think teamwork is important when playing games or sports? When else is teamwork important?"), and then evaluated their responses when the journals were turned in on a daily or weekly basis.

Assign Homework

You can give an assessment task as homework to save classroom time. With our goal of promoting student activity outside of school, some tasks are a natural fit. Again, my experience is that many students see physical education work as fun work, compared with other homework assignments. There is the added benefit of involving parents in the homework. Be careful, though, in using homework assessments as part of a child's grade as it is unlikely that every student will return the homework.

Use Rainy Days

Rainy days do not have to be filled with games of Seven Up and Eraser Tag. Use days when students are confined to the classroom for assessment tasks, especially portfolio tasks. This works especially well if you can have a task ready and waiting for a rainy day. For example, a task that focuses on students' likes and dislikes about physical activity works well and is not specific to a particular unit. Fitness-related lessons, such as students interpret-

tidbit

Ever hear of a multitasking task? This is one that can serve more than one teacher, each evaluating a different aspect of the task. For example, in the previous journal-writing example, you as the physical education teacher will be looking at the content of the writing. The classroom teacher, not as concerned with what is being said as how, can look at the grammar. Assessment tasks that involve artwork, computer skills, and research skills also can be multitasked by a number of teachers.

I want to share story from my friend Larry Satchwell, a teacher in Gwinnett County, Georgia. We were discussing how he is expected to teach one class of mathematics and writing to fifth graders on a *daily* basis (other "specials" also had similar classroom duty). In discussing it, we realized it might make a good multitasking assessment opportunity, as he could have students write about their physical education experiences. I guess that's what they mean by making lemonade out of lemons.

ing their fitness scores, are also very well suited to the classroom.

Assess at a Station

You can save class time by setting up a station solely for assessment. For example, toward the end of a unit on dribbling, post different stations around the gym that test aspects of this skill; the station near you is the one used to observe and record student performance data. The advantage is that you are looking at a few (five or less, likely) students at a time instead of scanning the whole group. This setup works well both inside and outside, and it could include videotaping (by a volunteer) the students at the designated station if you couldn't devote your time strictly to the observing portion.

Organizing and Setting Up Protocols for Assessment

Getting your gym or learning area set up for easy and quick assessing (especially portfolio tasks) is tantamount to success. There's just no other way around it. Once you do this, assessment will be much smoother. The trick is to find a system that works for you, your students, and the particulars of your teaching situation.

It is important to get students used to your system through the use of *protocols,* or predetermined routines that are practiced until they become second nature (Graham, 2001). For maximum effectiveness, introduce students to these protocols at the start of the year. That way, students have plenty of time to get used to the routine, and you can determine what works and what does not and make the necessary adjustments before the end of the year. I will share my experience with incorporating assessment into my program, as well

as the organizational strategies and protocols that I instituted to help make it easier. Not all of this will pertain to your situation and students, but you may find insight from the processes, strategies, and difficulties I encountered.

Setting Up and Using a Bin System

Using Sue Schiemer's assessment stations (Schiemer, 2000) as a guide, I decided to take the organizational plunge one year and set up what I called a *bin system* in my gym (although this can be done just as easily in an outside area). By doing this, I was hoping to make portfolio tasks much more efficient and easy. I set up the system with the following supplies:

- Five colorful signs depicting sports activities, purchased as part of a premade bulletin board set from a teacher's supply store
- Five stackable, 8.5- by 14-inch (21.6 by 35.6 cm) plastic bins with handles (big enough to hold legal-size folders)
- Twenty-five to thirty legal-size (8.5- by 14-inch) tabbed manila folders in various colors (one per grade level per bin) to hold student portfolio assignments
- Five colored legal-size manila folders (one per bin) to hold returned papers
- One class-set of clipboards
- Five plastic cups to hold pencils
- One class-set of pencils (obtained by picking up dropped ones found around the school)

First, I labeled each sign with a number (1 to 5) and then laminated them. I spaced them at intervals around the gym like stations and taped them to the wall (these signs stayed up the entire year). I then taped a laminated number from 1 to 5 on the front of each bin and taped a cup for pencils into a corner of each bin. Next, I placed five or so clipboards sideways into the back of each bin, one colored manila folder for each grade level (i.e., five total, starting with first grade) labeled Grade [5] Look for Papers Here, and one colored manila folder in the very front for returned assignments (labeled Return Completed Papers Here). I then put each numbered bin under the corresponding sign (against the wall or on the outside of the playing area) and assigned students to the sport that the picture depicted; this would serve as their bin and sport for the entire year.

When it came time to do a portfolio assessment, I would ask students to go to their bins, look in the colored manila folder with their grade level written on it, take an assessment task sheet from the folder, and grab a pencil and clipboard. They would take their materials to either a self-space or a group, write their first name and first letter of their last name, and their teacher's name on the paper, and they were ready to go. Only five students were at a bin at the same time. This was much more manageable and time-saving than before the bin system, when they were all after the same pile of papers and cup of pencils. As students finished, they returned their completed papers to the manila folder in the front of the bin that read Return Completed Papers Here, placed the pencils and clipboards into the assigned box, and we were done. At the end of the school day, I would take the boxes and place them in my office (this is where the stacking came in handy), remove the folder, and take it home to read the completed papers.

tidbit

Remember the part on planning for assessment? If you are setting up assessment protocols, such as using bins or stations, plan on taking a part of one lesson at the beginning of each year to introduce students to this system.

Once students designed their portfolios (see the following section, "Making and Storing the Portfolio"), I added the portfolio folders to their designated bins, behind the colored folder belonging to their specific grade level. In all, there would be approximately five student folders per class multiplied by the number of classrooms in that grade level (for example, with three first-grade classes, there would be 15 student portfolios behind the first-grade colored folder). I did not worry about an exact order for these folders—there were not that many, so students had no trouble finding their own. Students generally put their folders back in the appropriate places if they took them out to look at their papers or any other information I placed into them.

Dealing With Portfolios and Portfolio Tasks

Once I introduced students to the bin system, it worked out great. After a few practices, completing a task during class took a minimal amount of time. But then I had to figure out what to do with all those papers I had collected. Here are ideas I found useful in my teaching situation.

Making and Storing the Portfolio Each year, I had the first-grade students design portfolio folders that would hold all their work papers from physical education class. (If you return portfolios to students at the end of each year, you'll repeat this process at the beginning of the next school year. Plan to purchase the appropriate number of folders.) This typically was done on the first "lost day" of the year when I had to have students in

real world

Younger kids love carrying clipboards, especially when they use them to assess a partner. Perhaps it is because the students get to play the role of teacher. If you do not have the funds to buy enough clipboards for the class, chances are your principal or parent organization has some instructional funds for such a need. I've known teachers who said their clipboards ended up damaged or ruined by students. I was concerned about this, so as part of my lesson on working with the assessment bins I showed a new clipboard and a marred one, and we discussed how to care for equipment. Although this might not work in every teaching situation, I simply asked students not to write on the clipboards—and to my amazement, it worked. I also found out that a pencil just does not stay attached to a clipboard (and believe me, I tried everything short of duct tape).

the classroom (for me, it usually fell during the week when book fair took over the gym). At the end of the previous year, I ordered enough 8.5- by 14-inch tabbed manila folders for twice the number of the enrolled first-grade students. (Buy the type that have tabs spaced at various places on the folder, otherwise the tabs align and obscure the students' names.) On our portfolio-designing day, I took the students step by step through the process of writing their names—last name first—on the folder tabs (those of you who teach first grade can relate). Students then decorated their folders, drawing their favorite physical activities. Later, I stapled each folder to a plain one along both sides and the bottom, creating three pockets to hold papers.

Grading and Storing Papers   After students completed a physical education portfolio task, I would grade or give feedback on the portfolio sheets (stamps, stickers, and check marks work well) and put them into the first pocket of their folders. When we next used the bin or had a spare moment (for example, as they sat in the gym before class in the morning), students got their folders, looked over the marked papers inside, and then moved the graded papers to the back pocket of their folders. This signaled me that they had seen the most recent papers.

Filing Papers   I enlisted a parent volunteer at my school to help file papers in the students' folders, although at times I did the filing. Besides parents, high school students or retired senior citizens may be willing to help. Once I was familiar with what folders were in each bin (I would make a note of this in my grade book), the filing process went quite quickly.

Using the Portfolio   During parent-teacher conferences, back-to-school night, and other appropriate times during the year, the bins and folders were available to students and parents. At the end of the year, I would take the year's worth of papers from each, staple or clip them together, and send them

home with the student. Fifth graders could take their folders home with them.

It truly surprised me just how much the older students loved seeing the collection of work they had done in earlier grades. But I also realized that sending papers home more often allowed parents to track their child's progress, and that is why I began giving them back on a yearly basis. Although, with all the other papers students take home at the end of school, I sometimes wondered if parents ever saw them.

Chalkboards

Another organizational tool to make assessment easier was the chalkboard I placed near the gym entrance. I would write instructions on the chalkboard before class, indicating what the students needed for that day's activity. Students would follow my written notes and simply go to their bins, get the materials, and come together in a group or go to their self-space, whichever they had been directed to do. Having students read the instructions and follow them, without my verbal prompting, not only saved time but also allowed me to talk with an individual student, collect lunch money to hold for a child, take attendance, and so on without making the group wait.

> **real world**
>
> I admit that I tried a few different ways to deal with papers accumulated in a portfolio over a school year. At the beginning of the bin system, I did not send the papers home at the end of the year, but instead saved them year to year and gave them to the fifth-grade students—each year's papers clipped together—when they moved up to middle school.

Recording Performance Data

If organizing the physical teaching area is half the battle in assessment, then efficiently recording assessment data for hundreds of students just might be the other half (or pretty darn close to it). Because I did not have my own desk during class time and was in constant motion, recording grades was a challenge. I discovered a few different methods—ranging from checklists to rubrics to forms of technology—that made this easier. As each is presented, take into account your personal preferences and comfort level, the method of evaluation you are using, and your physical teaching area, just to name a few.

Recording Data From Checklists

Because checklists typically involve a choice between two options (criteria present or not present), they are quick and easy ways to record data as you evaluate students, which makes them perfect for use in elementary physical education classes. While a checklist typically addresses one particular skill or concept, data from multiple checklists can be recorded on a single form, such as PE Central's cue checklist sheet on their Web site (www.pecentral.org).

Or you could easily set up a class roll and data form similar to the one I used with my classes (see figure 3.1). I printed students' names on the original form at the beginning of the year and made copies as needed, adding new students at the bottom of the list or crossing out names of those who had withdrawn. Or, use a word processing software program to make this even easier.

This class roll and data form served multiple purposes for me. First, I could keep track of students' performances by date and quickly compare results for improvement. Second, it allowed me to record individual data about the students, such as whether they turned in a permission slip, their attendance, and level of self-responsibility or behavior for the day. As students left the gym, they either told me or held up their fingers to indicate the behavior level (see the bottom of the rubric in figure 3.1) they were working on that day (this helped determine the report card behavior grade). If no level was marked, I knew the child was absent and marked "ab." By taking attendance at the end of class during what is always noninstructional time, I had more time to instruct and assess. Third, it was helpful to put data for multiple tasks on one sheet, giving me a complete record of all scores for performance, product, and portfolio tasks.

You'll note that on this form, I also recorded information relative to the students' abilities on a performance task—stepping off on the opposite foot during underhand throwing. For this particular task (on Thursday, October 17), I used a check mark if they consistently stepped correctly while throw-

ing and an X if they did not. This system made observing and writing down a score very simple. On the next class roll and data form, I could have easily recorded data about the students' abilities to skip or hop, for example, and their levels of self-responsibility. For older students, results of fitness tests, for example, can quickly be written on this type of form. In this way, it is apparent that you can use the class roll and data forms to record multiple types of data on a single form.

Recording Data From Rubrics

Methods for recording data scored by a rubric include the type of form in figure 3.2 (page 30), which is already completed as an example. This definitely low-tech form is particularly helpful if your rubric has only three levels, because it will be fairly simple to assign students to a level. This allows you to record data as the performance takes place. In this case, it may be easier to include the names of the students in the top and bottom levels; the "at standard" level, where most students should fall, will be filled in later with the remaining students' names. You will find a blank copy of this form in figure 3.3 (page 31), if you decide to use this form when assessing students in your class.

You could also use the class roll and data sheet shown in figure 3.1 to record performance based on a rubric. The two best times to record these data are either right after the live performance, or, in the case of videotaping, after you watch the tape. If you choose to judge the performance on the spot, you will need a copy of your rubric for reference. (This is when all the time it took to develop your rubric comes in handy—you will likely know it by heart.) For example, I have found that I can watch a group's performance of a movement sequence, score it immediately on an analytic rubric, and record the score on my class roll and data sheet.

If desired, you can give a copy of your rubric to each student; then you actually write the score and any comments on the rubric and put this paper into the student's portfolio. Or, you could keep track of each student's performance progress with a form like the one in figure 3.4 (which is filled in as an example, page 33). This form is filed in the student's portfolio, and data are added

Student	W 9/25	Th 9/26	W 10/2	Th 10/3	W 10/9	Th 10/10	W 10/16	Th 10/17	UH throw*
	Teacher Erin Kaufmann					**Grade** 1			
Austin W.	4	4	4	4	2	4	4	4	✓
Brittany B.	4	4	4	4	3	3	2	4	✓
Carter T.	4	4	4	4	4	4	4	3	✓
Cate S.	4	4	4	4	4	4	4	4	X
Donyelle W.	4	4	4	4	4	4	4	3	✓
Heather C.	4	4	3	4	3	2	3	3	✓
Jessica K.	4	4	ab	4	4	4	4	4	X
John B.	4	4	ab	4	4	4	4	4	✓
Joshua R.	4	4	4	4	4	4	4	3	✓
Kelly H.	4	4	4	4	4	4	4	3	✓
Kendall K.	4	4	4	4	4	4	4	4	✓
Kyra S.	4	4	4	4	4	4	4	4	✓
Lauren C.	4	4	4	4	4	4	4	4	✓
Mikah N.	4	4	4	4	3	4	4	4	X
Tim T.	4	4	4	4	4	4	4	3	✓

* UH throw: Did student step with opposite foot? Check for yes, X for no

4: Follows all class expectations; receives no reminders from the teacher; 3: Follows most class expectations; receives only one reminder from the teacher; 2: Follows some class expectations; receives some reminders from the teacher; 1: Follows few class expectations; receives many reminders from the teacher.

Figure 3.1 Sample class roll and data form.

Unit _Kicking—inside of foot_		Grade _2_	Date _10/3_
Rubric level	**Class:** _Peebles_	**Class:** _Ketcham_	**Class:** _Samuel_
Above standard	Larry Sue Rosie Dianna Mark Scott George Vicky Manny Harriet	Trinesha Adjahnae Barry	
At standard	_(Fill in all other names of students in class at a later time, if desired.)_		
Below standard	Trent Lisa	Johnny B.	
Absent	None	Marcus John W.	

Figure 3.2   Sample form for recording data from rubrics.

Rubric level	Class:	Class:	Class:
Above standard			
At standard			
Below standard			
Absent			

Unit _____ Grade _____ Date _____

Figure 3.3 Form for recording data from rubrics.

From *Elementary Physical Education Teaching & Assessment: A Practical Guide,* by Christine J. Hopple, 2005, Champaign, IL: Human Kinetics.

as the year goes by. The advantage of this is that you can see multiple levels of information on one student. The downside is the time it takes to write this information on each student's sheet. Instead, use a master copy listing the tasks or units, and then make a photocopy for each child's portfolio. Perhaps a volunteer can help with this (see "Filing Papers," earlier). You will find a blank example of this form in figure 3.5 (page 34), if you want to use it in your situation.

Another option for scoring performance tasks is a ready-made system, such as Karyn Shellhase's "Grades K–6 Assessment System" (1998), available for purchase through PE Central's Web site (www.pecentral.org). Shellhase developed ready-made forms (now on CD-ROM) based partly on the grade-specific unit outcomes (appendix A) from the first edition of this book (now called "Performance Indicators" in this edition) that you can use to keep track of students' progress, by class, on a variety of performance tasks (see figure 3.6, pages 35–36, as an example of one of the forms from her system). Each form is organized by the different skill themes found in part III of this book (e.g., throwing and catching, dribbling, and the like); a form for each skill can be found for every grade-level range (kindergarten, 1 to 2, 3 to 4, 5 to 6). The performance indicators and tasks are at the headings of the columns; once you write or type in the students' names from each class in the first column, the form can be duplicated and used as you observe students. Her rubric is set up according to the tasks NY (Not Yet Achieved), DEV (Developing), and ACH (Achieved). The beauty of her system is that the forms can travel with you, they are easy to use, and they have spaces for the date each task was achieved. (Shellhase also developed assessment reports for parents; the reports are based upon these outcomes. See chapter 4 for more information.)

Using Technology in Assessment

A number of products are available that can simplify your assessment practices (particularly recording and analyzing data). Unfortunately, it can sometimes take a year or more to enter all the curriculum information into the systems so you can use them, depending on the technology and your expertise with it. The good news is that once this is done, it saves time on recording, compiling, and inputting data into report and progress forms.

While a comprehensive review of current technology is beyond the scope of this book, there are a few products that can serve elementary physical educators.

Video Cameras

Technology today is certainly far beyond the use of the low-tech camcorder; now we have choices from DVD recorders to digital cameras. But, for simplicity and ease (not to mention lower cost and accessibility), the old-fashioned video camera is still a best bet for most of us when it comes to filming student performances.

When using this or any camera, you must consider where to locate it for the best filming, how to make the situation safe for moving students, and who will be videotaping. Personally, I found the best place to set up the camera is on a tripod in a corner (or as close to it as possible), with the lens on wide-angle to capture as much of the learning space as possible. For example, if students are working on dribbling, the wide-angle view usually catches everyone. Students are not permitted to move behind the camera, so it is usually not a hazard. Be careful if you use power cords to run to the camera. (This is assuming that you are not

---

When I first used a rubric to score students' educational gymnastics sequences, I took the videotaped sequences home, watched each performance, and rated them. Partly because my rubric was not specific enough, it took me quite some time to score each student (not to mention there were more than 60 sequences). It did not take long for me to figure out that this was too time-consuming. But once I refined my rubric, I could watch each student, rate the performance according to the different criteria, and give a total score on the spot. This would take about 30 seconds a student, more or less—a much better procedure.

Date	Performance task/unit	Rubric level			Comments
		AS	**AT**	**BS**	
9/10	Body awareness	✓			
10/18	Space awareness	✓			Moves well to open spaces.
11/20	Kicking		✓		Sometimes uses toe to dribble.
1/8	Throwing			✓	Doesn't keep side to target.

Student *Mark Manrove*   **Class** *Sanders*   **Grade** *2*   **Year** *2002*

AS = Above standard; AT = AT standard; BS = Below standard

Figure 3.4   Sample performance assessment record.

Student		Class			Grade	Year

Date	Performance task/unit	Rubric level			Comments
		AS	**AT**	**BS**	

AS = Above standard; AT = AT standard; BS = Below standard

Figure 3.5 Performance assessment record.

From *Elementary Physical Education Teaching & Assessment: A Practical Guide,* by Christine J. Hopple, 2005, Champaign, IL: Human Kinetics.

Third Grade: Weight Transfer and Balance

Student Names:	Outcome 1 Transfer weight from one body part to another (hands, knees, feet) in a variety of ways.	Outcome 2 Use a variety of body actions to move into and out of a number of weight transfers from feet to hands with large extensions.	Outcome 3 Step into weight transfers from feet to hands over low equipment or apparatus (box, crate, beam, bench).	Outcome 4 Use balances to move smoothly into and out of different weight transfers.	Outcome 5 Design and perform gymnastics sequences that focus on changes in directions, levels, pathways, and extensions (using 1 or a combination of 2).	Comments
Date of Assessment:						
	NY DEV ACH	NY DEV ACH	NY DEV ACH	NY DEV ACH	NY DEV ACH	
	NY DEV ACH	NY DEV ACH	NY DEV ACH	NY DEV ACH	NY DEV ACH	
	NY DEV ACH	NY DEV ACH	NY DEV ACH	NY DEV ACH	NY DEV ACH	
	NY DEV ACH	NY DEV ACH	NY DEV ACH	NY DEV ACH	NY DEV ACH	
	NY DEV ACH	NY DEV ACH	NY DEV ACH	NY DEV ACH	NY DEV ACH	
	NY DEV ACH	NY DEV ACH	NY DEV ACH	NY DEV ACH	NY DEV ACH	
	NY DEV ACH	NY DEV ACH	NY DEV ACH	NY DEV ACH	NY DEV ACH	
	NY DEV ACH	NY DEV ACH	NY DEV ACH	NY DEV ACH	NY DEV ACH	
	NY DEV ACH	NY DEV ACH	NY DEV ACH	NY DEV ACH	NY DEV ACH	
	NY DEV ACH	NY DEV ACH	NY DEV ACH	NY DEV ACH	NY DEV ACH	
	NY DEV ACH	NY DEV ACH	NY DEV ACH	NY DEV ACH	NY DEV ACH	
	NY DEV ACH	NY DEV ACH	NY DEV ACH	NY DEV ACH	NY DEV ACH	
	NY DEV ACH	NY DEV ACH	NY DEV ACH	NY DEV ACH	NY DEV ACH	
	NY DEV ACH	NY DEV ACH	NY DEV ACH	NY DEV ACH	NY DEV ACH	
	NY DEV ACH	NY DEV ACH	NY DEV ACH	NY DEV ACH	NY DEV ACH	
	NY DEV ACH	NY DEV ACH	NY DEV ACH	NY DEV ACH	NY DEV ACH	

Figure 3.6 Example of a performance task recording form.

Used by permission of PE Central (www.pecentral.org), the premier Web site for physical educators.

(continued)

Third Grade: Weight Transfer and Balance (continued)

Student Names: Date of Assessment:	Outcome 1 Transfer weight from one body part to another (hands, knees, feet) in a variety of ways.	Outcome 2 Use a variety of body actions to move into and out of weight transfers from feet to hands with large extensions.	Outcome 3 Step into weight transfers from feet to hands over low equipment or apparatus (box, crate, beam, bench).	Outcome 4 Use balances to move smoothly into and out of different weight transfers.	Outcome 5 Design and perform gymnastics sequences that focus on changes in directions, levels, pathways, and extensions (using 1 or a combination of 2).	Comments
	NY DEV ACH	NY DEV ACH	NY DEV ACH	NY DEV ACH	NY DEV ACH	
	NY DEV ACH	NY DEV ACH	NY DEV ACH	NY DEV ACH	NY DEV ACH	
	NY DEV ACH	NY DEV ACH	NY DEV ACH	NY DEV ACH	NY DEV ACH	
	NY DEV ACH	NY DEV ACH	NY DEV ACH	NY DEV ACH	NY DEV ACH	
	NY DEV ACH	NY DEV ACH	NY DEV ACH	NY DEV ACH	NY DEV ACH	
	NY DEV ACH	NY DEV ACH	NY DEV ACH	NY DEV ACH	NY DEV ACH	
	NY DEV ACH	NY DEV ACH	NY DEV ACH	NY DEV ACH	NY DEV ACH	
	NY DEV ACH	NY DEV ACH	NY DEV ACH	NY DEV ACH	NY DEV ACH	
	NY DEV ACH	NY DEV ACH	NY DEV ACH	NY DEV ACH	NY DEV ACH	
	CUES Soft landings Behind up Strong arms/tight muscles Arms take weight first	**CUES** Feet to hands—behind up, tight muscles, arms take weight first	**CUES** Head up when moving onto equipment Tight muscles Soft landings	**CUES** Keep center of gravity over bases of support Tight muscles Inverted—kick feet up high; hips, shoulders, and hands in line; control balance with fingertips	**CUES** Directions—forward, backward, sideways, up and down Levels—low, medium, high Pathways—curved, straight, zigzag Extensions—near, far	

Figure 3.6 (continued)

36

using the camera battery pack.) Be sure to secure cords with duct tape to prevent tripping.

If you are trying to record your (or a student's) voice, a cordless microphone may be your best bet. The camera's built-in microphone likely will not pick up voices from across the gym (especially if there is background noise). Electronics stores typically carry an inexpensive microphone that clips onto your waistband. The mouthpiece clips onto your collar, and the accompanying receiver attaches to your camera. The external microphone picks up the voice of whomever is speaking into it and can be heard loud and clear on the videotape.

If you cannot (or do not want to) do the taping, ask your media specialist or a parent volunteer (or even a fifth-grade student) to move the camera back and forth on its tripod to get everyone in the picture. Also, keep in mind that today's handheld cameras make it easy to film around the gym, but a camera of this type on a tripod keeps the picture from jumping.

When assessing students' movement sequences, I typically handled it in the following way. Most often I set up a mat in front of the camera; other mats would be set up around the gym, as usual. The mat by the camera was the assessment mat, and as I filmed one student, other students practiced at their mats. I would call on a student to perform or ask for a volunteer, but usually students are happy (albeit a little shy) to be videotaped. In a few instances, I might ask a group to perform for the rest of the class (for example, a rhythmic sequence that peers evaluate) and tape the performance. It is imperative to label your videotape right away with the class, date, and topic to keep track of what is on the tape.

Personal Digital Assistants

Computers come in desktop and laptop forms, and now the recent handheld versions called personal digital assistants (PDAs). They are basically small computers with installed software programs, such as Microsoft Excel and Word, and also a calendar and address book. PDAs come in a variety of versions, each with its own operating system and software, just as desktop models come in either PC or Mac versions. Two types especially seem to be used largely by educators: the Pocket PC and the Palm. A Pocket PC is a Windows-based PDA such as Dell's Axim model. An advantage of the Pocket PC is that the software and operating system are completely compatible with the corresponding PC desktop and laptop systems and software. The Palm has its own operating system; special conversion software (which comes with the Palm) converts data on a Palm to a computer with either a Windows- or Mac-based operating system.

The requirements of each system dictate the software programs installed when you purchase the device, which ones can be installed later, and the capabilities of each version; see your school district's technology staff for assistance to figure out the best model for you.

The beauty of working with a PDA is that it allows you to create your own Excel spreadsheet file for each class (you can do this on your desktop system and easily upload it onto your PDA). You can then add columns for each performance task and quickly and easily input data into the file when you are observing students in your classroom. In other words, you can create your own class roll and data form and continue to add data (columns) to it without adding more pages. Later, this updated file can be downloaded (or "synched") into your desktop system (the ease of this process depends on the model you have). At this point, you can set up progress and grade reports that pull data directly from the cells in your spreadsheet file.

For those unfamiliar with PDAs, the small screen can take some getting used to, as does working with the stylus to input information. Too, getting used to the system and setting up the technology can take time, patience, and a huge learning curve. But its portability makes this handheld device worth the drawbacks for elementary physical education teachers. It conveniently can go inside or out, and it saves time on inputting information, because you only have to do this once, when the performance takes place. For example, you do not have to write information on paper and key it into your computer later. There also are software programs that come ready-made for you to add your students' names and your tasks or indicators (see the following section). Because the system is already developed, you just add the data.

Software Programs

A variety of software programs can be used to efficiently deal with recording and using assessment results. Certainly one of the most common is Microsoft Excel, the spreadsheet software that allows you to design your own class roll and data form, keep assessment data on each child in different columns, and easily modify the files (i.e., add or delete student information) as needed. Data from the spreadsheet can be pulled from the file to a report template (which you develop in Microsoft Word) that summarizes assessment information for each child. The advantage of Excel is that it is accessible and you can quickly set up simple forms such as the class roll and data form. The disadvantage is that you have to set up (make) the forms yourself, and setting up and using the more advanced document features (such as the merging of data into a report) can be more time-intensive.

tidbit

The computer is used in so many aspects of today's school environment that it is possible that your school secretary can download class rolls onto a disk for you or even send them to you as an e-mail attachment. With access to that information, you can copy and paste the students' names into your files.

Other software has been developed for use by educators. Classroom teachers or the media specialist at your school can be one of your best resources on this subject. For those looking for a more advanced and versatile program beyond Excel, the Learner Profile software may be of assistance. Specifically geared toward organizing and working with assessment results, the software (found at www.learnerprofile.com) allows you to input your class rolls and then add assessment data according to specific performance indicators. The beauty of software such as this is that the template is already set up; it takes you through the steps involved in setting up the system. Another positive feature of this software is that it is compatible with Palm and Palm-OS PDAs.

You can also find software to help you keep track of and print out reports for fitness test scores. Specific software for the FITNESSGRAM health-related fitness test (found at www.HumanKinetics.com) is available for both the PC and Mac computer. Another program, HealthStar Manager (www.microfit.com), allows you to track fitness test, health, and skill (performance) data, as well as attendance and other managerial-related information. (It has Palm-compatible software as well.) PE Manager software (www.polarusa.com) is another tracking program that may be of assistance to you

as you look to technology to make recording and reporting data from physical education easier. You may also find information about software specific to other individual fitness test batteries at the respective test's Web sites.

You may also find the software at www.rubrics.com of assistance in developing your rubrics as well as aligning your curriculum and assessment tasks to your standards and benchmarks. Although their software has been developed with the classroom (versus physical education) teacher in mind, many times there is enough flexibility that you can easily modify the information to fit your program.

Certainly the topic of technology and the number of products available to help you deal with assessment goes far beyond this short overview. For additional information on using technology in your teaching and assessment, refer to a variety of books and recent journal articles on the use of technology in physical education as well as technology information in classroom teachers' catalogs (see the references at the end of this book for some of these sources). Too, your district technology staff, sessions at professional conferences, and expertise from teachers on professional list-servs are other good sources of the nuts and bolts of using technology in physical education.

For many of us, myself included, going beyond the basic computer can be a daunting experience. But talking with teachers who use PDAs, for example, to record assessment data has convinced me that it can be worth any problems that may be encountered. The fact that the technology gets easier to use, the kinks work out as time goes by, and experienced teachers can help in these areas make it more comfortable for those of us who are less technologically inclined to use these systems in our classrooms.

Summary

As you can see, there are a variety of strategies you can use to make your assessment life easier. Finding and developing these strategies takes time and effort, to be sure. What is most important is not to expect it to all be there when you start out—it just will not happen. If you'll allow me, I'd like to end this chapter with one more personal experience. When I first went back into teaching after my years of curriculum writing work at Human Kinetics, I felt like a beginning teacher all over again. I was now teaching kindergarten through fifth grade at two schools in Virginia rather than the kindergarten through second-grade students at one school in Florida. And I had two programs to set up from scratch, versus entering one that was already established. Believe you me, it was a very rough few years.

I'll never forget my sister-in-law, Vicky (also an elementary physical educator, in Florida), asking me that first year, "Well, Christine, have you used any of your assessments yet?" I remember saying something to the effect of, "Getting to assessment? You have to be kidding. I'm just working on the curriculum part!" Indeed, it took me a few years before I got a system down and really began to work with assessment in the way I wanted to (which, I can tell you, was quite frustrating at times). The moral of the story? Be patient, and do not expect it all to happen at once. Pick one class or one grade level. Start small—and before you know it, you'll be there!

Chapter 4

Using Your Assessment Data

It's great to be able to say, "Hey, I'm using alternative performance tasks to assess students—and they work." But not using the results from these assessments is like being all dressed up with no place to go—they look good, but essentially it has been wasted effort. So how do you successfully use the results from your assessments? The answer lies in what you do before you begin assessing students. Knowing beforehand why you are giving an assessment and how you intend to use the results can help ensure that you will know what to do with them and that they gathered the right information for your purpose.

If you recall, we discussed those purposes of results as part of our introduction to assessment in chapter 1. In this chapter, we elaborate on these topics, focusing specifically on five different uses for assessment.

- Improving curriculum
- Placement
- Grading and reporting
- Communicating assessment results to parents
- Communicating assessment and program results to administrators

Improving Curriculum

My guess is that the most common purpose of teachers' assessments is to adjust curriculum.

Through assessment tasks, we can ascertain whether students are learning what we set out to teach. If results do not meet our expectations, the following questions should be asked.

- Was my instruction adequate on the material? Did the students perform to potential? Was it something else?
- Was my instruction too advanced or too fast for the students' developmental levels? Did I expect too much of them?
- Do I continue with this unit (and thereby take time away from another unit)?
- Do I plan more time for this unit next year?
- Did something about the assessment task affect their performance?

If students performed well on the assessment, we can be assured that they learned what we intended; but we should still consider a few questions, such as these two:

- Should I spend less time on this unit next year?
- Should I change my instruction to challenge this group more?

How you answer the previous questions depends on you, your students, and your situation. It is also important to reflect on the answers to make future decisions. To this end, save space on each page of your teacher planning book to write comments about the lessons you'll teach that week. Based on your informal observations as well as formal assessments, jot down what worked and what did not, and ideas for changing the lesson in the future. Although it takes practice to develop the habit of recording your ideas, once you begin to incorporate them the following year (or in upcoming lessons), you'll realize the value of this strategy.

Placement

Assessment results can determine student placement into a specific group; for example, whether a student requires special (adapted) physical education services. Although many packaged test batteries are available for diagnostic purposes, your results from formal and informal alternative assessments are the most important pieces in student evaluation of special needs.

Beyond alternative assessment data, anecdotal (written) observations can offer a more complete picture about the students' strengths and weaknesses. If you notice a student is having difficulties, either note this on an index card for review later or write it down in your daily planner, as mentioned earlier.

During special services committee meetings my input about how particular students learned and performed was valuable in determining their needs. The completed work in their portfolios and the information on their motor skills many times confirmed the difficulties they had in the classroom. (Sometimes my observations gave a picture of the student the classroom teacher never saw.)

The use of levels of behavior in my classroom also provided insight; this daily record gave a snapshot of the student's social interactions with other students and me.

The hard part about all this was not compiling the information—it was getting the information to the committee. Asking the special services committee to inform you and other special area teachers when a child is up for a review is a first step. Even if you cannot be present, you can duplicate the information and pass it to the committee. When it comes to helping students, the more information the better, to make a judgment.

Grading and Reporting

Talk about an attention-grabbing topic. As teachers, we each have our own little grading system. In fact, I would bet that if I asked 10 elementary teachers how they determine a grade and what it signifies on a report card, I would likely get 10 answers (not to mention some heated discussion). One thing the majority of these teachers may agree on is that determining a grade, whether for an assignment or a marking period, is one of the least important reasons to give assessment tasks in elementary physical education. They are also likely to agree that grading has the least amount of time devoted to it. (If you're like me, grades are figured out in a few minutes, a day or so before they are due.) Yet because grading is, for better or worse, a critical part of the educational process, it is an area that deserves more attention than we generally give it. The following gives a closer look at characteristics of grades, the dos and don'ts of effective grading,

Another way, albeit uncommon, to use assessment results in physical education is to identify students for "gifted" programs. I hadn't heard of this until a colleague, Carolyn Nelson from Olentangy Elementary School in Columbus, Ohio, recently asked fellow teachers if they had any experience in this arena. As a special yearly focus for her school, her principal charged each teacher (including "special area" teachers) with identifying students who perform at an exemplary level and who might benefit from "enrichment" activities. Carolyn's question of any (formal) assessments used to identify these students in physical education class was an interesting one, and one with which I hadn't had any previous experience. I wonder how many other teachers have dealt with this question in the past, or will so in the near future?

and some personal experiences and ideas I have to improve the process.

Characteristics of Grades

As we know, grades signify many facets of instruction in the classroom. So let us start by defining the term as the "process by which descriptive assessment information is translated into marks or letters that indicate the quality of a student's classroom behavior, effort, or achievement" (Anderson, 2003, p. 149). Educational researcher Lorin Anderson goes on to describe characteristics of grades—whether specific to one assignment or an entire school quarter—for any school level.

1. [As] they should represent the quality of a student's behavior or effort or achievement, separate grades should be given for each of these attributes.
2. There should be a clear connection between the assessment information available for each student and the grade assigned.
3. Students should *earn* grades; teachers should not be in the business of *giving* grades. (p. 150)

Unfortunately, all too often in physical education we are constrained in meeting some or all of these criteria because of

- the restriction of one physical education grade on the report card;
- a lack of available valid and reliable assessment data on which to base a grade;
- a lack of understanding by students that their grade reflects their achievement in physical education;
- a lack of time to effectively grade;
- a lack of respect from the educational community toward grading in physical education; and
- the large number of students we teach each year.

Some of these issues are addressed more easily than others. Even if we cannot change some issues, we can critically look at our grading practices and procedures and make them as sound as possible

under our given constraints. The following dos and don'ts can help this endeavor.

Dos and Don'ts for Effective Grading

McMillan (1997) offers succinct guidelines for grading and the reporting of grades (see figure 4.1). By following these guidelines, we can establish a more sound, defensible approach to our grading and giving of report card grades. We know, for example, that it is inappropriate to base a grade on only one or two assessments—especially if these are scores from fitness tests. We do not want these tests to become, as Wendy Mustain says, "grist for the grading mill" (1994, p. 1), with the grade based on little or no other data. We also want parents to know at the start of school how we will determine their child's grade (something we cannot always detail in advance). Also, grades should be based on what we believe is essential for students to learn and to do (i.e., the important standards we set for our students), not extraneous factors that have no bearing on achievement. When we focus on these points, we may ponder whether grading our students on perceived effort or dressing out is the essential basis of grades, especially those on report cards.

Communicate Your Grading Policies Though at times it seems that parents do not care about physical education grades, it is wrong to assume this is true. The recent emphasis on physical activity is making parents more concerned about their children's performance in your class. With this in mind, parents need to know how students achieve a grade in physical education. This can be accomplished several ways, such as through a parent letter at the start of the year or in a grade-level newsletter sent home quarterly by teachers in a specific classroom or grade level. Spelling out your grading policies helps you when parents question a grade.

Give Specific Feedback When Possible Let's face it: Adults love to get feedback on their undertakings. Children are no different. Even in physical education class, both parents and students welcome written comments explaining how to improve or praising a good performance (whether

Do	Don't
• Grade fairly	• Allow personal bias, labels, or previous teachers' comments to affect students' grades
• Grade students based on their achievement of realistic, important objectives and standards that the majority of students should be able to achieve.	• Lower grades for misbehavior, lack of effort, or not dressing out or wearing shoes. • Increase grades because of good effort on student's part, even if he or she has not mastered the desired objective. • Assign a grade relative to other students' performances.
• Inform students, parents, and administrators in writing of grading procedures at the beginning of the year.	• Keep grading procedures secret.
• Use multiple assessments in order to determine a grade.	• Rely on only one or two assessments for a grading period. • Rely on the same type ("P") of assessment in order to determine a grade.

Figure 4.1   The do's and don'ts of effective grading.

Reprinted, by permission, from L. Anderson, 2003, *Classroom assessment: Enhancing the quality of teacher decision making* (Mahwah, NJ: Lawrence Erlbaum Associates, Inc.).

on paper or a physical task). In that same way, the more specific the feedback on portfolio and performance tasks, the more the students and parents will benefit from that feedback. Certainly there are times when a check mark, stamp, or smiley face will do. For example, when noting that students completed a survey of their favorite physical activities, when there is no right or wrong answer, a sticker will do. But, for most assessment tasks, there is a big difference between OK and Very Good, and our feedback should reflect this. In these situations, even a short comment beyond the check mark can be helpful. Or why not institute a student-friendly three-level rubric system (e.g., check plus, check, or check minus; or two smileys, one smiley, check minus) to quickly evaluate portfolio tasks? (I think students, especially younger ones, understand the smiley system better than numbers.) For your grading purposes, each level in the rubric could be designated by

a number (e.g., 1, 2, 3). This number, along with rubric scores from performance tasks, would be entered into your record-keeping system and converted into letter form at the end of the grading period (more on how to do this later). While this takes more time than giving a check mark, it also gives more feedback to students and bases their grade on more concrete data.

Using Rubric Scores to Determine Letter Grades

Once you type your rubric scores on each student into your record-keeping system, how do they turn into a grade? My sense is that this is when most elementary physical education teachers eyeball scores and decide on an overarching grade for a student. But, if we want to be as objective and consistent as possible in this process, we'd best be a little more exacting. (Warning! If you really are

It is demoralizing to work in a profession that appears to get so little respect from parents. Yet sometimes I think our attitude toward this does us an injustice. That is, do we sometimes assume parents do not care about their child's progress in physical education? And do we follow this by not adequately communicating information (including grades) to them? Conversely, if we set out to inform parents as much as possible, could it eventually result in a groundswell of interest?

tidbit

Should we grade on effort? How do we quantify effort? What about students who don't wear the correct shoes for physical education? Should a student be penalized because of delayed development of motor skills? Raise these questions at a meeting of physical education teachers, and the talk can get pretty intense. No doubt, the extent that a student's overall physical education grade is based on behavior, effort, and skill is guided by our own values and personal beliefs. I will not address this issue here—that is grist for another book. What I will emphasize is that since the majority of us are required to give grades in elementary physical education, let's work to make this practice as appropriate and sound as possible.

not interested in going this far with figuring your student's grades, it is fine to stop here and skip ahead. The next section gets pretty detailed, and you may feel it does not fit your situation. Believe me, that is okay.)

There are a number of ways to convert rubric scores to a letter grade for a report card (Carr, 2000), some more acceptable than others for a true measurement. The challenge for us is to make this process as simple as possible, knowing that we are not statisticians, that we do not have a lot of time to devote to grading, and that we typically are not interested in being so strict with letter grades for young children. Yet we want to base our grades on defensible, accurate data and records, and the methods we use should be professionally, if not mathematically, sound. With this in mind, here are some thoughts regarding this process.

One important guideline is to average scores of rubrics with a like number of levels. For example, if all of your portfolio and performance tasks were evaluated on the same three-level or four-level rubric, you could easily average these scores into one overall rubric score, which could then be converted into a letter grade. (Figure 4.2

shows one example of how this might be done; check if your school district has standards for letter grades on report cards, based on rubric scores.) Do not take scores from a three-level rubric and scores from a four-level rubric and average these together, since a score of 3 on a three-point scale is quite different from a 3 on a four-point scale. For example, if you have portfolio task scores based on a three-level rubric scale and performance tasks based on a four-level rubric scale, average the scores from each rubric level separately, and then combine these two scores to derive a letter grade. However, this process can become slightly more complicated.

Using the previous example, let's say a student's score from all the tasks based on the same three-level rubric is a 2.25, and the score based on tasks using a four-level rubric is 3.45. Using a chart like the one in figure 4.3, you determine that this student would receive a grade of S+—showing slightly higher than solid, proficient grade-level achievement. Of course, the chart in figure 4.3 is only an example; you may set up your own score ranges and letters differently, and you may choose not to use a + and −.

A parent volunteer or a high school student who wants on-the-job experience can provide the help you need to transfer rubric results into your record-keeping system (emphasize the need for confidentiality). Volunteers can type class rolls, input data, and possibly even keep track of your spreadsheets or computer data files (high school students are great with technology). If volunteers are scarce, the next best thing is a spreadsheet program or other technology aid (see the information on PDAs in chapter 3). At the end of the nine weeks, all you have to do is type a formula into your software program, and just like that it automatically figures the total or average for each student. The time up front is the most intensive, but at the end, it sure makes life easier. Most school districts have a technology expert who will help you set up a spreadsheet. Or perhaps this is your next horizon to tackle.

Average rubric score (four levels)	Letter grade on report card	Letter grade represents
3.01–4.00	E	Achievement beyond what is expect-ed for student at this grade level
1.75–3.00	S	Solid, proficient grade-level achievement
1.00–1.74	N	Achievement reflecting some but not all concepts and skills

Figure 4.2   Sample conversion of rubric scores to letter grades.
Reprinted, by permission, from Susanne Canavan.

What happens if a student does very well on one set of assessments, but not on another? For example, if he or she averages to an S, does this grade represent the child's overall performance? Or what if the majority of performance assessments are on four-level rubrics instead of three-level rubrics? In this case, you may decide to give more weight to one set of scores.

As you can tell, there is no right or wrong way to handle these questions. The main thing is to figure all the students' scores in the same way. Fortunately, once you set up a chart like the one in figure 4.2 or 4.3, it could be used throughout the course of the year. In fact, you may find it helpful to use these charts as guides for your grading. Simply adjust the information according to your school district's grading policy.

> **tidbit**
> Remember, when working with rubrics you always want to decide the satisfactory level on the rubric beforehand. For example, on a four-level rubric, what score do you consider indicative of solid, proficient, grade-level work? This rubric level should relate to your average letter grade (e.g., C or S).

Communicating Assessment Results to Parents

Communicating student assessment results to parents can (and should) take a number of forms. A report card is just one method. Interim reports, end-of-semester reports, and parent-teacher conferences also are opportunities to share information with parents. Some of these strategies are impractical for elementary physical education teachers strictly because of the large number of students we teach, often at more than one school. Nevertheless there are ways to connect with parents.

Part of the challenge of communicating is to find a way to write or express to

Average of scores from four-level rubric	Average of scores from three-level rubric		
	4.00–3.01	3.00–1.75	1.74–1.00
3.01–4.00	E	S+	S
2.01–3.00	S+	S	S–
1.01–2.00	S	S–	N
0.00–1.00	S	S–	N

Figure 4.3   Sample form for combining scores of rubrics with different levels into letter grades.
Reprinted, by permission, from Susanne Canavan.

parents an aspect of their child that is not so positive. For example, how do you inform parents that their child is not very coordinated or is overweight or too physically inactive? Even coming up with meaningful positive comments to write on report cards can sometimes be difficult. To help, first consider the manner in which we convey information to parents—verbally or through the use of written comments. These topics are more fully explained in the next section.

The Three Fs of Communication

Whether verbal or written, communication with parents follows three basic principles, what Anderson (2003) terms the three Fs: focus, friendliness, and forthrightness. Let's look at each in more detail before we look at specific methods of communication.

Focus   Be succinct. In other words, know what topic you want to discuss (you have a point), and then cover it without adding superfluous information. Do not talk around the subject; otherwise it will be lost or unclear. Especially with today's busy parents, getting straight to the point is important. But temper this; being too blunt alienates parents. It is now that friendliness comes into play.

Friendliness   Set a respectful tone with parents, but also speak in a manner that relates to them. Think of it as user-friendly: Do the parents understand the terminology and language you are using? This is especially important in physical education. For example, the phrase spatial awareness may not be familiar to parents of first graders. And how many parents know what the concept of weight transfer using a variety of body parts is all about?

In my master's program at Virginia Polytechnic Institute, professor George Graham stressed that we should "write for the mail carrier"; that is, we needed to use language that a mail carrier, unfamiliar with physical education terms, could follow. Since then, I always try to envision the mail carrier in the back of my mind when I write, as a reminder to tone down the technical talk.

Forthrightness   Forthrightness suggests that our delivery of information be honest and direct. Our credibility is questioned when we do not seem up front with parents. Are we straightforward and frank, even if it means saying something they do not want to hear? Can we explain and justify the report card grade we gave? Do we beat around the bush or talk in vague terms?

Again, just as with the aspect of focus, forthrightness does not mean being harsh or hurtful, but it does entail being sincere, honest, and understanding. A good standard is to deliver information the way you would want to hear it about your own child. Use this as a guide in your communication with parents. Sometimes it is hard to raise the difficult stuff, but laying it out clearly, honestly, and professionally can go a long way in opening a positive communication channel.

Words to Use—and Not Use

Keeping the three Fs in mind, some words or phrases are more appropriate than others when making comments to parents, either verbal or written. For example, Shafer (1997) reminds us not to use terms such as *always* and *never* (see figure 4.4 for negative terms), because they suggest that a student's behavior cannot change. Instead, use alternative words or

Words and phrases that promote positive view of the student	Words and phrases to convey that student needs help	Words and phrases to avoid or use with extreme caution
• Gets along well with people • Has a good grasp of . . . • Has improved tremendously • Is a real joy to have in class • Is well respected by other classmates • Works very hard	• Could benefit from . . . • Finds it difficult at times to . . . • Has trouble with . . . • Requires help with . . . • Needs reinforcement in . . .	• Always • Never • Can't (or "is unable to . . .") • Won't

Figure 4.4   Alternative words or phrases to use when talking about student assessments.

I never sent interim reports home before report cards came out, that is, not until a mother came back to me questioning her child's grade (which was not a good one). In discussing the matter, the parent asked why she had not been contacted about her child's poor performance (a behavior problem). She said she would have addressed it if she'd known. Suffice to say, she was not happy with me. What could I say? She was correct; parents should be told if their child is not doing well. After that, I always sent interim report to parents of children having difficulties.

phrases, also found in figure 4.4, that convey ways to help a student. Tend toward words and phrases that promote a positive view. By using constructive terms and avoiding negative ones, teachers seem more forthright and our opinions more valid.

Methods of Communicating With Parents

There are a number of ways to make parents aware of student assessment results. Reports sent home during the middle of a grading period (e.g., interim reports and fitness forums) and those sent home at the end of a grading period (e.g., end-of-term and quarter reports) keep parents up to date at long range. Face-to-face meetings (e.g., parent-teacher conferences and portfolio reviews) are more immediate. Each can be used to our benefit in physical education, at different times and for different reasons.

Interim Reports   Most schools require teachers to send interim reports home midway through a quarterly marking (grading) period, indicating difficulties a child may have. They serve as an advance warning of report card grades at the end of the marking period. In physical education, a simple checklist can serve as an interim report (see figure 4.5), which conveys the student's progress quickly and easily. Classroom teachers generally will agree to send your forms home with their information.

End-of-Term or Quarter Reports   Because parents cannot tell much about their children's accomplishments in physical education from a report card grade, a more detailed end-of-term or quarter report can give a bigger picture (see figure 4.6 for an example from Brubaker, based on his standards in figures 5.8 and 5.9). The

---

Physical Education Interim Report
Washington Elementary School

Name _____ Class _____

Dear Parent or Guardian:

During the first part of this grading period, your child has shown difficulty with the following (checked) skills or behaviors:

- ☐ Not bringing shoes to class
- ☐ Not completing homework assignments or not turning them in
- ☐ Being disrespectful to others in class
- ☐ Not participating in class activities
- ☐ Not completing class assignments

Continued difficulty may result in your child receiving a less than satisfactory grade in physical education on his or her report card for the nine weeks. Please contact me at school (123-4567) to set up a time we can meet in person or talk on the phone so that we may best help your child to be successful in physical education.

Thank you,
Christine Hopple
Physical education teacher

Figure 4.5   Sample interim report.

Name _____	**Class** _____	
Teacher _____	**Date 1** _____ **Date 2** _____	
3: Achieved the standard	2: Nearing the standard	1: Below the standard

Date 1	Date 2	Grade 4 Expectations

_____ _____ _____	_____ _____ _____	Performs a lead pass to a moving partner in a game of keep away
		  Turns to the open space ahead of the moving receiver
		  Steps toward the open space with the opposite foot
		  Tosses gently to the open space ahead of the moving receiver

_____ _____ _____	_____ _____ _____	Develops, refines, and performs a gymnastics floor routine with another person
		  Includes two balances and rolls, a change of level, and an action of choice
		  Moves smoothly from movement to movement
		  Clearly matches another person's movements

_____ _____ _____	_____ _____ _____	Strikes a ball with a paddle using mature forehand form
		  Faces side to target
		  Holds paddle back with arm/hand/paddle straight
		  Swings across body in the direction of the target
		  Places the ball consistently over the net, inside the tennis court

_____ _____ _____	_____ _____ _____	Accurately identifies the following critical elements of forehand striking
		  Side to the target
		  Paddle way back
		  Swing across the body toward the target

_____ _____ _____	_____ _____ _____	Develops, refines, and performs a repeatable dance sequence to 4/4 music
		  Includes all the required movements
		  Moves rhythmically and smoothly to the music
		  Demonstrates clear use of different movement concepts

_____ _____ _____	_____ _____ _____	Expresses positive feelings about exercise and physical activity
		  Running for a long time without stopping, exercising to get in good shape
		  Playing catch, kicking a ball with others, and playing on a sports team
		  Moving to music, dancing with others, and doing a gymnastics routine

_____ _____ _____ _____	_____ _____ _____ _____	Exhibits health-enhancing levels of physical fitness as defined by FITNESSGRAM
		  Cardiovascular endurance: Runs or walks one mile (1.6 km) in less than 9 minutes, 15 seconds
		  Muscular strength: Completes 25 or more curl-ups in 1 minute
		  Muscular endurance: Hangs from bar with flexed arms longer than 10 seconds
		  Muscular flexibility: Sits and reaches toward toes with a score of 8 inches (20.3 cm) or more

_____	_____	Demonstrates an understanding of basic fitness concepts
		  Having good endurance helps you go for a long time without stopping
		  Being active helps you get in good shape, feel good, and stay healthy

Figure 4.6 Sample semester report.

I'll always remember the first time I sent semester reports home to parents of my kindergartners. One mother made an appointment to discuss her son. I had mentioned in his report that he had problems with gross motor movements such as running, jumping, and the like. From my perspective, he was lagging behind his classmates, even given developmental differences. I felt he could benefit from extra attention to his motor skills. She was very receptive to my thoughts and had been concerned about her son's motor skills for some time, especially because her older son had always seemed uncoordinated, compared with children his age. She felt that her youngest son exhibited many of the same difficulties, but when she asked the boys' pediatrician, he said there were no problems. I had confirmed her gut feeling, much to her relief. From this point on, this mother and I forged a rapport we both enjoyed, and this taught me to never underestimate parents' interest in their children's physical education progress.

low-tech version involves developing the form on the computer, making copies of it, and then filling it out by hand for each student. To be a bit higher-tech, design a template of the form on the computer, and then merge the data from your Excel spreadsheet or other program directly into the form. Many of the software programs for assessment have a reporting form template set up; you simply input your classroom data and merge the information. Whatever form you use, make it short and simple.

There's no way around the time it takes to complete these forms, whether by hand or by computer. To ease this crunch, alternate when you give reports. For example, instead of waiting until the final weeks of school, send home reports for some grades (e.g., grades 3 to 5) at the end of the third marking period and the others (e.g., kindergarten to grade 2) at the end of the year.

Fitness Forums Improving physical fitness scores is a priority of many school districts and states. Fitness forums are one means parents have to decipher their child's scores. Once fitness scores go home (on forms such as the one from the FITNESSGRAM tests), you can use the forums—opened-ended meetings held in early eve-

ning or after school—as a time to meet with parents, answer questions about the tests, and maybe have a child demonstrate the test items.

Portfolio Reviews A child's portfolio holds all the work sheets up to that point in the year. Sending the portfolio folder home for review provides parents with a progress report as they thumb through their child's accumulated papers. The portfolio has a cover letter stapled on the outside (figure 4.7) that explains what was taught during the semester and what is in the portfolio, and it contains comments from the teacher. Parents have a large space to write their comments and a place to sign the portfolio after review. Be sure to follow up parents' questions with a conference, phone call, or note. While you likely will not want to do this with every grade or more than once a year, it can be a positive method of communicating assessment information to parents.

Parent-Teacher Conferences Many teachers, including me, find the prospect of speaking with parents in a face-to-face meeting quite stressful, as it typically happens only when there is a problem. To make conferences go more smoothly, the three Fs and positive words or phrases discussed

Who says the fitness tests required in your district have to be given during class time? What if interested students and their parents came to school one evening a month for assessment with an item from a health-related fitness test such as FITNESSGRAM? Both parents and children could review a computer printout of the results. Students might begin to realize the importance of fitness, particularly since their parents are participating. Perhaps parents will become more involved in health-enhancing activities with their children. And teachers might end up with more instruction time during the day.

Date

Dear parent or guardian,

Enclosed in your child's **Physical Education Portfolio** you will find information related to just some of the concepts and skills your child has been working on in physical education during the past nine weeks. These include the following:

• A sequence your child designed and practiced that combined the gymnastics-related skills of rolling, balancing, and transferring weight from feet to hands. The child performed the routine during class for one part of his or her physical education grade.

• Your child's physical fitness scores from some of the fitness tests taken earlier in the fall (see enclosed FITNESSGRAM and information/cover sheet).

• Some daily assessments your child was asked to complete during or after a particular day's activities. If none of these are present in the portfolio, your child was either absent that day or did not fill in his or her name on the assessment (causing the child to receive a grade of "0" for that day's assessment).

Should there be any specific information for you regarding your child's physical skills, knowledge of concepts, or behavior in physical education during this past nine weeks, I have noted it here:

_____

_____

Should you have any questions or comments regarding any of the materials in this portfolio or your child's physical education class, feel free to write it in the space provided next. I will be glad to respond as soon as possible.

_____

_____

Please sign below to indicate that you have reviewed your child's portfolio, and then have your child return this form and the portfolio to the physical education class by [insert due date]. Thank you!

Sincerely,

Your physical education teacher

Parent/guardian signature: _____

Figure 4.7   Sample portfolio review cover form.
Used by permission of PE Central (www.pecentral.org), the premier Web site for physical educators.

previously can come in handy. Other techniques for a constructive, positive conference include listing important points (to keep the focus) and rehearsing diplomatic ways to make these points (to be forthright). Having hands-on data helps back up your statements; it's hard to argue with written documentation. Being prepared is many times the best offense when meeting with parents. Come to think of it, it is also the most successful approach when communicating assessment results to administrators, the topic we'll look at next.

Communicating Results to Administrators

If the major use of assessment results is to improve curriculum, my hunch is they are least used to communicate to administrators (principals, school board members, and superintendents). When this does happen, it is usually because teachers are on the defensive, trying to keep physical education funds or jobs from budget cuts. An opposing school of thought might say that if we communicated with administrators more often, we might not find ourselves needing to justify our actions. But certainly, our jobs are demanding enough without having to collect and present data to the school board. What, then, is realistic for us to expect and accomplish when discussing assessment data with the decision-makers?

For one thing, communicate results to the right people. My feeling is that principals are the primary administrators when it concerns student progress in your gym. Yes, principals are busy people, and yes, many times it may seem that they do not care about the physical education program. Even if this is the case, it cannot hurt to tell them what is going on with your students. Who knows, perhaps they'll become more interested. And few principals, if they are truly good at their jobs, will find what students do to be uninteresting. My experience is that principals care about student progress, especially if this learning cuts across the curriculum.

You can keep your principals informed in a number of ways. Begin by picking out the most interesting results from portfolio assessments and periodically give them to your principal to peruse. Pass on a copy of any parent reporting form you designed, and ask for feedback before sending it home. Also, choose a few completed ones for inspection; perhaps there is a problem student the principal is interested in or for whom there was a red flag you should discuss.

When you know you'll be showing videotaped performance tasks such as gymnastics or rhythmic sequences (for example, on a rainy day), invite your principal to come in and watch with the students. Few can resist taking in at least a few moments.

My principals always wanted to know fitness assessment results because of the emphasis put on them by our school board. I always shared a copy of the FITNESSGRAM report card and condensed data into a report detailing the statistics on test results. Periodically, I'd meet with them to discuss ways to improve student performance. I would also invite them to any fitness forums or other events pertaining to the physical education program.

Today's technology is making it easier than ever to collect and condense data into the numeric form that school boards and other administrators seem to love. It may be helpful when you give a performance assessment, for example, to keep track of the percentage of students in that grade who pass (or who do not pass) the assessment task. If desired, these data may be organized by standard to show the progress students are making toward the larger course standards, whether instituted at the state or district level or developed by you. If desired, this information could be presented on a yearly basis to the school board, along with examples of students' work; a little offense might prove to be the best defense. Talk with your physical education supervisor about ideas like this.

As an example of this idea, take the results from my task on students' abilities in grades 1 and 2 to step off with the opposite foot when throwing (taken from the checklist found in figure 3.1). I can easily report these data as "X percent of first and second graders are able to step off with the opposite foot when throwing," under the course outcome of "demonstrates mature motor patterns for a variety of basic manipulative and nonmanipulative skills." Using data gained from my educational gymnastics results—based on my rubric—I can also explain, for this course standard, the percentage of students who met or exceeded minimum expectations for the task. What is nice about this is that a calculator is all that is needed, although computer software programs that focus on assessment can generate reports without you having to do it by hand.

Because there is always strength in numbers, data is more effective or more positively received when it comes from a number of sources. If there is no formal accounting system in your district,

If you find yourself or a group going to the school board to report on student learning in physical education, start by showing a videotaped sequence of students performing, and use this as a springboard for the rest of your number data. (Get permission from the parents of the students first.) The human interest angle is always more compelling, and because they were expecting to hear dry data, board members and the audience will undoubtedly be much more responsive after viewing a performance instead!

tidbit

perhaps an interested group of teachers can work together to present their data to the school board. If this is too daunting a task, simply sending the board, superintendent, and director of curriculum a yearly written report can help. The important thing is to get your information out so others know what you are doing. Being proactive can keep you from having to be reactive.

Summary

By this point, I hope your head is not swimming with all the things you wish you could be doing regarding the planning, instructing, and assessment of your elementary physical education program. If so, take a step back and take a deep breath. Remember, Rome was not built in a day. Do not put pressure on yourself to have it all done now—it is not only unrealistic, given our hectic jobs, but it will drive you crazy. Rather, be realistic about what you can accomplish in one year, and develop one or a few worthy goals or steps to get you to your desired point. Once you get comfortable, you can address a different aspect of the teaching process. Over the course of a few years, you'll have made progress in each area, only to find yourself ready to start again on the same topics in a continuous cycle of reflection and improvement. But then again, isn't that what quality teaching (and assessment) is all about?

PART II

Standards and Curriculum in Elementary Physical Education

Do you know what SOL, TEKS, SSS, and QCCS have in common? No, they're not names of the latest video games, computer models, or extreme-sports moves. They are, however, acronyms for those requirements that drive curriculum at the state level (and many times, drive teachers and principals crazy). If your answer was "unique names thought up by an administrator for a particular state's educational standards program," yes, you would win the prize. Whether they're the Standards of Learning from Virginia, the Texas Essential Knowledge and Skills, Florida's Sunshine State Standards, or Georgia's Quality Core Curriculum Standards, they all have one thing in common—an emphasis on standards (in other words, what students should learn and do before they graduate from public school).

In the next two chapters, we'll visit the standards-based movement that has begun to influence education in our country and examine how this educational reform movement has resulted in national initiatives in our profession of physical education. In chapter 5 we'll review the multitude of terms relative to the standards-based movement in education and take a look at the important process of designing-down—a key difference in how curriculum is designed in a standards-based versus a traditional model. In chapter 6 we take a closer look at each step in the designing-down process, which will enable you (or a committee you may be on) to more fully align your curriculum with the standards. Although it might not be an exciting process to most, it is an important step in ensuring that your curriculum and assessment practices are in line with the national standards. And as you move through the chapter, you'll find a variety of forms and examples to assist you in this process. The end result? Students who are physically educated.

Chapter 5

Standards and Curriculum

Today, just as with assessment, teachers in almost every state and school in the United States are required to work with standards in some form or fashion. Along with this, we seem to be inundated with terms such as *content standards, performance indicators,* and *benchmarks,* to name just a few. If you are brave enough, bring up the word *standards* in a teachers' lounge and then look out—chances are that some heated conversation will follow. The fact is, love them or hate them, we just cannot seem to escape standards in today's school environment. And if recent history is any indication, this focus on standards and the assessment of them will intensify.

So, how do we deal with this push on standards? Perhaps most important, how do we use them to improve our curriculum, and then assess them in ways that are positive and beneficial to our students (and us)? To answer these and other questions, examine the following overview of the standards-based movement, definitions of different types of

standards, and summation of how our profession of physical education has responded to this initiative.

A Brief History of the Move Toward Standards

The push toward the use of standards in education can be traced back to the National Education Goals Panel (NEGP), commissioned by President George H. Bush in the late 1980s. The panel was instituted in response to the 1983 document *A Nation at Risk,* which questioned whether American students had the necessary knowledge and skills for our society to remain dominant in the global marketplace. The panel developed six national standards that were adopted by President Bush and the nation's governors at the historic education summit of 1990 in Charlottesville, Virginia (see figure 5.1). And so was born the standards-based reform movement in American education.

The current focus on accountability has spurred an increased use of the more traditional, high-stakes statewide assessments. These can be easily and quickly administered and then validated over a wide population of students. It also appears that the emphasis on standards may be resulting in less *authentic* means of assessing students in physical education (for similar reasons). Paradoxically, this is in contrast to the older outcomes movement, which relied on the *alternative* assessment of students. In this rapidly changing arena, stay tuned to see what develops next.

tidbit

1. All children in America will start school ready to learn.

2. The high school graduation rate will increase to at least 90 percent.

3. Testing at four grade levels will demonstrate that students have competence in challenging subject matter, and schools will ensure that all students learn to use their minds well in preparation for responsible citizenship.

4. U.S. students will be the first in the world in science and mathematics achievement.

5. Every adult American will be literate and will possess the knowledge and skills necessary to compete in a global economy and to exercise the rights and responsibilities of citizenship.

6. Every school in America will be free of drugs and violence and will offer a disciplined environment conducive to learning.

Added as part of the Goals 2000 Act (1994):

7. Increase parent involvement.

8. Improve teaching education and professional development.

Figure 5.1   Six national education standards.

Reprinted, by permission, from J. Ardovino, J. Hollingsworth, and S. Ybarra, 2000, *Multiple measures: Accurate ways to assess student achievement* (Thousand Oaks, CA: Corwin Press).

A few years later in 1994, President Bill Clinton signed the Goals 2000: Educate America Act, which added two standards to the earlier six. More important, the act

• established a framework for the development of national goals in various subject areas, which provided a strong direction for what should be taught in those subject areas;

• granted funds for states to develop their

individual goals and train teachers how to improve curriculum and instruction; and

• established entities within the federal government to help states develop goals and the assessment systems to measure their effectiveness.

As a result of Goals 2000, experts in various subject areas began to develop national standards. By 1996, most subject areas, including health and physical education, had developed some form of content prerequisites. In addition, every state (except Iowa, which sets district standards) has developed, or is in the process of developing, statewide standards, many times using the national versions as a guide. Although the quality of these standards, as well as their effectiveness in influencing teaching and curriculum at the district and school levels, are questioned at times, there is no doubt that the use and assessment of educational standards today is a force to be reckoned with. If there were any doubt of this, the No Child Left Behind (NCLB) Act of 2001 (P.L. 107–110) signed by President George W. Bush, with its call for elevated standards for students and schools (as well as monetary and other consequences for schools that do not comply), is a reminder of this fact.

Definitions and Types of Standards

The emergence of education standards has brought with it a plethora of associated (and, at times, conflicting) terms. It is nearly impossible for teachers to keep up with the ever-changing vocabulary and definitions. To help make sense of the terminology, the following section defines the most common types of standards and explains how they relate to physical education.

When the first edition of this book was published in 1995, its title, *Teaching for Outcomes in Elementary Physical Education*, reflected the national emphasis in the late 1980s and early 1990s on the development of outcomes—the first phase, you could say, of the standards-based education initiative. The concept of teaching toward outcomes was revolutionary to education, and the term became politically charged because of its effort to define the values that children should hold by the time they graduated from high school. As national guidelines were determined and accepted by teachers in the mid- to late-1990s, the term outcomes began to metamorphose into "standards." With some differences from its forerunner, the term standards has gained political and educational acceptance, while sidestepping many of the issues that outcomes encountered. Today you will hear it being used in arenas from the teachers' lounge to school board meetings to state congressional hearings.

Content Standards

Content standards "describe information or skills essential to the practice or application of a particular discipline or content domain" (Marzano et al., 1993, p.14). They are what sets each content area apart and delineates what students should know and be able to do in that discipline. These standards may be defined by knowledge inherent in an entire subject area (e.g., mathematics), or in the content of a particular unit in that subject area (e.g., calculus). Today, most state departments of education have set standards for each content area, many times using the respective national content standards as a guide.

In the early 1990s, a team of experts was commissioned by the National Association for Sport and Physical Education (NASPE) to develop content standards for the profession. In 1992, the committee published a landmark document, *Definition and Outcomes of the Physically Educated Person*. These 20 outcome statements in the document served as a foundation for developing physical education curriculum throughout the United States. Later, these outcomes served as a springboard for the development of seven content standards for physical education (published in 1994 by NASPE in the resource *Moving Into the Future: National Standards for Physical Education*). A decade later, these seven standards were condensed into the current six standards, found in the second edition of the same resource (see figure 5.2). Developed through a long process of review and input from teachers, the standards have been almost universally accepted by professionals in the discipline. Many states have used the NASPE content standards as a basis for their state physical education content standards, often approving them verbatim (why reinvent the wheel?) or using them with slight modifications.

Performance Standards

If content standards define what students should be able to know and do, *performance standards* measure how well they know and are able to do it. They are a "translation of the content standard that additionally provides an expectation level and answers the question, how good is good enough?" (Solomon, 2002, p. 58). Performance standards may be related to a cognitive concept (the knowing) or a physical performance (the doing), but either way, a good performance standard should answer two questions.

1. "To what depth has each student learned the content standard?
2. What degree of quality is considered acceptable [to have met the standard]? (Ardovino et al., 2000, p. 78)."

For an example of a performance standard in one particular content area of physical education, refer to figure 5.3. When you consider the NASPE content standard of "Demonstrates competency in motor skills and movement patterns needed to perform a variety of physical activities," you might ask yourself these questions: How do I know if my students are competent in motor skills and movement patterns? What does this mean? What does this look like, if I had to measure it? One answer could be the performance standard of "Jumps a self-turned rope using at least three different types of footwork skills, each for a minimum of five consecutive jumps, with no stops or errors in each set of jumps." This statement outlines what the student should do to demonstrate the skill standard and the quality with which it should be performed (i.e., the *degree* of proficiency). It clearly indicates the intent of the standard and tells teachers how to measure student progress by providing an easy assessment tool.

A physically educated person . . .

1. demonstrates competency in motor skills and movement patterns needed to perform a variety of physical activities.
2. demonstrates understanding of movement concepts, principles, strategies, and tactics as they apply to the learning and performance of physical activities.
3. participates regularly in physical activity.
4. achieves and maintains a health-enhancing level of physical fitness.
5. exhibits responsible personal and social behavior that respects self and others in physical activity settings.
6. values physical activity for health, enjoyment, challenge, self-expression, or social interaction.

Figure 5.2   NASPE content standards.

Reprinted from *Moving into the Future: National Standards for Physical Education* (2004), with permission from the National Association for Sport and Physical Education (NASPE), 1900 Association Drive, Reston, VA 20191, USA.

Content standard	Demonstrates competency in motor skills and movement patterns needed to perform a variety of physical activities. (NASPE Standard #1, 2004)
Performance standard	• Jumps a self-turned rope using at least three different types of footwork skills, each for a minimum of five consecutive jumps, with no stops or errors in each set of jumps. • Demonstrates the ability to consistently (over a number of trials) bend knees and swing arms forward and land on balls of feet when jumping for distance.
Performance indicator	• Jumps a self-turned short rope at least three different ways. • Jumps in and out of a turning long jump rope. • Jumps for distance and for height.
Benchmark	By the end of grade 4, can correctly perform the five different jumping patterns (hop, jump, leap, one foot to two feet, two feet to one foot).

Figure 5.3   Examples of different types of standards based on one specific content standard.

If content standards are to be applied and of value to teachers, they must be accompanied by well-written performance standards. Content standards that lack these qualities do not help teachers who try to use them as guides for their curriculum.

Performance Indicators

Performance indicators define content standards by determining what students should be able to *do* with the content—not what they know about the content or even their degree of proficiency. Another way to look at them is to think of performance indicators as the part of performance standards that relates only to students *doing*. For examples that reflect the content standard given earlier, refer again to figure 5.3. Note how each indicator further describes and gives direction to the content standards, but they do not address how well students should be able to perform the skill.

It is important to remember that in subject areas that are concept-oriented, such as mathematics, performance indicators could potentially focus on problem-solving or analyzing skills—processes student *do* with the content they know. In physical education, we might expect students to apply concepts of fitness, for example, to develop a personal fitness plan—not just describe or define concepts of fitness.

To assist you in planning and developing your physical education curriculum, you will find teacher-reviewed and approved performance indicators listed by skill theme and concept in appendix A of this book and cross-referenced in the respective concept or skill section in part III.

They appeared in the first edition of this book, and I've been told they were extremely helpful to teachers wishing to incorporate the standards in their curriculum.

Benchmarks

Benchmarks are statements that further define the K–12 standards at various points in the educational process (see figure 5.3). Benchmarks can specify what is expected to be met by a particular grade level (e.g., grade 4), or by a grade range (e.g., grades 6 to 8). Through the years, there have been numerous interpretations of the term *benchmarks*. While this term is still used at times (in its varying forms), it appears that more emphasis in recent years is on the exact delineation of performance standards and indicators, and not on benchmarks at various grade levels. Either way, the intent of the term helps us understand that content standards must be specified in more detail at various points along the way—in whatever form that may take—if they are to be of most use.

Opportunity-to-Learn Standards

The Goals 2000 Act signed by President Clinton spawned the *Opportunity-to-Learn (OTL) Standards,* "the conditions and resources necessary to give all students an equal chance" to meet the content and performance standards (Ardovino et al., 2000, p. 80). These resources included instructional materials, personnel, professional development of the personnel, and quality of the learning environment for students to meet the proposed standards. The

OTL standards were designed to establish a fair and equitable base for all students and schools in meeting the content standards. For example, in physical education an OTL standard may stipulate at the state level the required number of minutes per week students have physical education, or who is qualified to teach physical education. Generally, district and school administrators, not the classroom teachers, work with OTL measures. Because of this, the OTL will not be discussed in detail in this book.

> *tidbit*
>
> Are you confused yet? You are not alone. Because these terms are used in different ways in different states and districts, even educational leaders disagree over their meanings. Perhaps the best thing is not to get hung up on the term, but instead focus on its intent.

Principles of Standards-Based Education

Now that we've taken a look at the different types of standards, let's examine the underlying premise that defines the standards initiative in American education, and how these standards are used in the educational setting.

1. **Achievement of high standards** is expected of all students—not just the college-bound, for example, or students of a particular race or socioeconomic status. These high standards anticipate the qualities needed to make the United States the leader in a rapidly changing, technologically advanced world; in other words, we are not setting arbitrary goals, but goals with specific outcome intents. This focus on high expectations, not just minimal expectations is unique to the standards-based movement and is one distinction between it and its outcomes-based predecessor.

2. The standards movement requires a **clear definition of what is to be taught and what students should learn.** Well-written standards, in theory, convey to teachers, parents, students, and the community the purpose and role of schools. All curricular, instructional, and assessment activities direct students toward these desired standards. As we are seeing with the NCLB act, this clear intent brings—for better or worse—the obligation of monitoring how well schools are achieving the stated aims.

3. The standards movement advocates **consensus and sharing of information.** While the earlier outcomes movement and its requirements were contested by parties in both the educational and political arenas, the concept of standards has been fairly well received by administrators, content specialists, teachers, and parents. There has been an accompanying drive for districts and states to share the impact of standards among these same groups. Under the NCLB legislation, the public is notified if schools fail the requirements.

4. **Expanded opportunity** is valued in the standards movement. All students should have the opportunities and resources to obtain and practice the knowledge and skills needed to achieve the standards. Care is taken to assure that students meet the prerequisites before they move to higher levels; students receive additional instruction to master the content. This is in direct response to President Clinton's OTL legislation.

> *real world*
>
> It is interesting to note how much the Internet has changed information-sharing in regard to standards. States that I have taught in, including Virginia and New York, publish schools' state performance rates on their Web sites. This information is very accessible and often used by citizens considering relocating to a particular school district. You can imagine the pressure put on and by stakeholders (e.g., school boards, superintendents, principals) for schools to perform better than others in their locale. In fact, the annual monetary raise that the principal at my former school in Virginia receives is related, in part, to the performance of the students on the state test relative to the state standards. In some districts throughout the United States, I've heard that teachers' merit pay is based on the same measure. Is sharing this information a good thing? No doubt there are proponents on both sides. One thing is for sure, I know I'm not the only one slightly concerned about these trends.

5. The last principle of the standards initiative is **designing-down** (also called *backward mapping;* for ease, I use *designing-down* throughout the text). This process was first proposed by educational leaders Grant Wiggins and Jay McTighe (1998) in their resource *Understanding by Design* and quickly became a hallmark of the outcomes and standards movements. At its core is the belief that teachers begin with the main goals for students—what they should achieve by high school graduation—and then design curriculum backward from that point, eventually down to what is expected in kindergarten (see figure 5.4). In other words, curriculum is "purposefully planned" for optimal learning. Instruction is then "delivered up" so that what is taught at each grade level is cumulative, allowing students to build toward the desired goals.

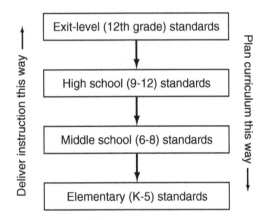

Figure 5.4   Designing-down sequence.

To draw an analogy for the designing-down process, think of a car trip. You begin with the destination and plan accordingly: How much time will you need to reach the destination? Can it be done in one day or must it be split over two days? Do you need hotel reservations? Where are the rest areas along the way? What landmarks will you pass? Contrast this to just heading off in a general direction without a map or directions. There may be gorgeous scenery and great experiences along the way, to be sure, but there are also numerous pitfalls for the unprepared traveler—who ultimately may not make the desired destination.

The designing-down approach contrasts with the traditional manner in which curriculum has been developed. Often a goal is developed at different grade levels without thought to whether it is redundant to previous content or in line with what will come (or if students are ready for it at that particular time). As a result, students may be taught similar content over multiple grade levels or may miss key lessons that build on what they have been expected to master. In an effective designing-down model, a school district brings teachers of similar subject areas in the elementary, middle, and high school levels together to ensure that content is purposefully planned and taught at each grade level. To this end, we take a closer look at how standards can be used to design-down curriculum (see also chapter 6).

Levels of Standards in the Designing-Down Process

Earlier in this chapter you were introduced to different types of standards that national and state professional organizations and state departments of education have drawn up (e.g., content standards, performance indicators, benchmarks). All of these relate to the planning of your physical education program as a whole—or the big picture. In contrast, the designing-down process leads us through varying levels of standards—each more specific than the preceding one—that help us move from the broad

In discussing the designing-down of standards, I recall that during district-wide meetings for physical educators, the middle school teachers would turn to the elementary teachers and say, "What do you do all day? Don't you teach students [this]?" Likewise, high school teachers would say, "I can't believe you middle school teachers didn't teach them [this]." What a perfect example of how curriculum is traditionally developed—each school level (and many times, each school) does its own thing . . . with mixed results. Some students gained some skills; others did not. By designing-down and agreeing on what should be done at each school level, a district curriculum can become much tighter and more effective in helping all students reach designated outcomes. Learning, then, is not left to chance.

standards down to the very specific unit and lesson standards that affect our curriculum daily.

Is there any overlap, then, between the various big-picture standards and the standards at the different levels in the designing-down process? Yes, in the sense that they all begin from the same ending (or is it the beginning?) point—the national content standards. I do my best to illustrate in the remaining part of this chapter where this overlap takes place, as well as to introduce you to the elements unique to each level in the designing-down process.

Exit Standards

In designing-down curriculum, increasingly specific levels of standards are developed, starting with those that students must meet to graduate from, or *exit,* high school (see figure 5.5). These broad statements of achievement set the tone for learning required at subsequent grade levels. We can think of the kindergarten through 12th-grade content standards developed by NASPE (see figure 5.2) as the exit-level standards for our profession of physical education.

Program Standards

Program standards are designed from these national exit-level standards. These standards typically delineate the overall kindergarten through 12th-grade goals for a specific subject area (i.e., a program of study, such as physical education or mathematics) for students in a particular state or district. Program standards are usually developed by a state department of education committee or a team of teachers working in a school district, and they take a variety of forms.

In physical education, states or districts generally use the NASPE standards for physical education or edit them to fit their needs. They may have grouped the program standards together according to different *strands,* or similar content areas (e.g., fitness, health, manipulative skills). In some states, physical education program standards might be combined with those of another content area. For example, New York's standards addressing physical education are also combined with those for health and family and consumer science. In rare cases, a content area, such as physical education, may not have program standards specific to it, but, rather, professionals in that content area address the state's program standards that most apply (e.g., the standards addressing areas of responsible behaviors, decision-making, healthy choices, and the like).

Frequently, program standards are clear enough that they can easily be used to communicate an overall picture of the physical education curriculum to parents and administrators. Figure 5.6 gives an example of program standards designed by Florida's State Department of Education.

Course Standards

The next set of standards below the program level is the *course* standards. Individual teachers (or a state- or district-wide committee of teachers) develop course standards, using program standards as a guide. Course standards outline more specifically

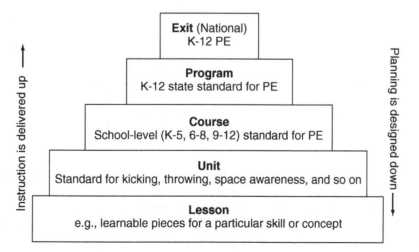

Figure 5.5　Designing-down curriculum model.

Physical education literacy	Responsible physical activity behaviors	Advocate and promote physically active lifestyles
1. The student develops competency in many movement forms and proficiency in a few forms of physical activity. 2. The student applies concepts and principles of human movement to the development of motor skills and the learning of new skills. 3. The student analyzes the benefits of regular participation in physical activity.	4. The student achieves and maintains a health-enhancing level of physical fitness. 5. The student demonstrates responsible personal and social behavior in physical activity.	6. The student understands how participating in physical activity promotes inclusion and an understanding of the abilities and cultural diversity of people. 7. The student understands that physical activity provides the opportunity for enjoyment, challenge, self-expression, and communication.

Figure 5.6   Example of program standards designed by Florida's State Department of Education.

Reprinted, by permission, from Florida Department of Education, 1996. [Online] Available: http://www.firn.edu/doe/curric/prek12/frame2.htm.

what students at a specific school level (e.g., elementary, middle, or high) or, in the case of high school, in a specific course of study (e.g., Personal Fitness I or Weightlifting I) should achieve within that particular school level. Because the elementary school years include as many as six grades, they often are clustered into developmental groups (e.g., kindergarten to second grade, third to fifth) to facilitate planning and allow for students' developmental differences. Typically, the highest grade in a cluster becomes the benchmark, meaning the year by which students should have achieved the given course standards.

Course standards are basically a bridge between what you teach daily or weekly and the bigger picture of eventual student goals. These goals give curriculum a direction and allow us to plan units and lessons that are more rational than random. Course standards are written broadly enough to encompass various units; instruction from a number of different units might help students achieve one particular course standard.

Figure 5.7 provides examples of elementary, middle, and high school course standards developed from one program standard at the state level,

in this case Florida. (I've chosen course standards for each grade range the state recognizes—in this case, prekindergarten to second, third to fifth, sixth to eighth, and ninth to twelfth—to more fully illustrate the designing-down process beginning with the program standard.) Figure 5.8 shows elementary course standards that Nathan Brubaker, a former elementary physical education teacher in Vermont, designed for his Underhill Elementary School curriculum in 1999 (personal communication, August 24, 2001). You'll see that he set his benchmark years at kindergarten, second, and fourth grades in a program he designed down from NASPE (exit) content standards.

If you work on a district or statewide standards team, it helps to periodically present the new course standards to physical education teachers in other school levels. This ensures that there is continuity of goals at the different school levels. You will also find that course standards help illustrate the goals of your elementary physical education program to parents, administrators, and classroom teachers, and they aid in presenting information to parents on report cards and progress reports.

tidbit

Most states provide physical education teachers with a set of program standards, and many times these are accompanied by course standards. At the elementary level, these course standards are typically provided for either the highest grade in a cluster of grades, or the grade(s) at which students are tested statewide (i.e., benchmarks). Even if your state lacks course standards, ask your district which grades are considered benchmarks. Aligning your standards with these specific years can be helpful, especially if your state establishes course standards later.

Strand: Physical Education Literacy			
Standard 1: The student demonstrates competency in many movement forms and proficiency in a few forms of physical activity.			
Pre-K–2 course standards (PE.A.1.1)	**3–5 course standards (PE.A.1.2)**	**6–8 course standards (PE.A.1.3)**	**9–12 course standards (PE.A.1.4)**
1. Combines shapes, levels, directions, pathways, and ranges into simple sequences. 2. Kicks stationary and rolled balls with strong force while maintaining balance. 3. Adapts movement to changing environmental conditions. 4. Chases, flees, and dodges to avoid or catch others and maneuver around obstacles. 5. Consistently strikes lightweight objects with body parts and with lightweight implements. 6. Knows ways to manage own body weight in a variety of situations (e.g., hanging and climbing and balancing in symmetrical and asymmetrical shapes on a variety of body parts on mats or apparatus). 7. Demonstrates basic locomotor skills (e.g., hop, walk, run, jump, leap, gallop, skip, and slide). 8. Uses an overhand throwing pattern with accuracy. 9. Knows various techniques for catching thrown objects.	1. Knows various techniques for throwing or catching different objects. 2. Knows how to design and modify sequences that show changes in direction and speed. 3. Knows how to demonstrate functional patterns of striking, dribbling, volleying, throwing, and catching in dynamic situations. 4. Understands that games consist of people, boundaries, equipment, purpose, and rules that all interrelate during game play. 5. Knows how to create, explore, and devise game strategies.	1. Combines skills competently to participate in a modified version of team and individual sports, demonstrating mature patterns of manipulative skills (e.g., proper catching techniques). 2. Uses basic offensive and defensive positioning while playing a modified version of a sport. 3. Designs and performs folk and square dance sequences. 4. Knows basic skills and safety procedures to participate in outdoor sports.	1. Demonstrates competency or proficiency in self-selected activities.

Figure 5.7   Example of elementary, middle, and high school course standards designed-down from one program standard at the state level.

Reprinted, by permission, from Florida Department of Education, 1996. [Online] Available: http://www.firn.edu/doe/curric/prek12/frame2.htm.

Unit Standards

Once course-level standards have been developed, it is usually up to the teacher to develop *unit* standards or goals that move the students toward achieving the course standards. (This may also be completed at the district level, depending on the leadership and organization in the district.) Through the process of defining unit standards, you develop a fairly detailed idea of what it is you want students at various grade levels to achieve in that unit. This can especially highlight the progression of learning among different grade levels for that particular unit, which cannot be done at the course level (too broad of a picture) or lesson level (too narrow of a picture). This progression indicates if instruction is realistic and on-track to meet the desired, higher-level course standards.

For an example of unit standards, see figure 5.9, developed by Brubaker for one of his course standards from figure 5.8 (personal communication, August 24, 2001). Note that there are numerous concepts and skills, each specific to different units in his curriculum, that students need to master if they are to achieve the respective course standard. These unit standards cover grades 3 and 4. Brubaker combined these two grades to facilitate his planning (just as many teachers cluster grades 1 and 2 together, 5 and 6, and so on). In the designing-down process, teachers typically spend most of their time developing unit and lesson standards.

Demonstrates competency in many movement forms and proficiency in a few movement forms	
4th	Performs a lead pass to a moving partner in a game of keep away Develops, refines, and performs a gymnastics floor routine with another person Strikes a ball with a paddle using mature forehand form Develops, refines, and performs a repeatable dance sequence to 4/4 music
2nd	Throws a small ball to a target using mature underhand form Develops, refines, and performs a gymnastics floor routine Strikes a ball with a paddle using mature underhand form Combines locomotor patterns in time to music or to the sequence of a story
K	Demonstrates critical elements of galloping, sliding, hopping, and skipping Tosses a ball and catches it before it bounces twice Rolls sideways without hesitating or stopping
Applies movement concepts and principles to the learning and development of motor skills	
4th	Accurately identifies three critical elements of forehand striking
2nd	Accurately identifies four characteristics of a mature underhand pattern
K	Demonstrates an understanding of self-space Demonstrates an understanding of general space
Achieves and maintains a health-enhancing level of physical fitness	
4th	Demonstrates an understanding of basic fitness concepts Exhibits a health-enhancing level of physical fitness as defined by FITNESSGRAM
2nd	Sustains activity for longer periods of time in various endurance challenges
Demonstrates responsible personal and social behavior in physical activity settings	
K	Responds to teacher signals for attention Uses equipment safely and properly
Understands that physical activity provides opportunities for enjoyment, challenge, self-expression, and social interaction	
4th	Expresses positive feelings about exercise and physical activity
2nd	Expresses positive feelings about physical activity

Figure 5.8   Example of elementary course standards, designed-down from Brubaker's program standards.

Reprinted, by permission, from Nathan Brubaker. Nathan Brubaker is a doctoral student in pedagogy and former elementary physical educator in Vermont.

Standard: Develops, refines, and performs a gymnastics floor routine with another person.

By the end of grades 3–4, students should be able to

Balancing unit

- Balance in inverted positions using the smallest possible number of bases of support.
- Balance in various positions on large gymnastics equipment (e.g., beams, benches, boxes) using different bases of support, symmetry, and asymmetry.
- Cooperatively balance with others by partially supporting each other's weight.
- Demonstrate dynamic balance on various objects (e.g., stilts, balance boards, cans).

Jumping and landing unit

- Jump off low equipment and move the body into various shapes in flight.

Rolling unit

- Roll, starting and ending in different shapes and using different speeds.

Transferring weight unit

- Smoothly transfer weight from one balance position to another in various ways.
- Transfer weight in a variety of ways from feet to hands with large extensions (e.g., stretching legs wide, torso twisting, rolling, curving feet over to land on one or two feet).
- Transfer weight on large apparatus (e.g., climbing apparatus, bars, benches).
- Transfer weight off or over low equipment (box, bench, beam).
- Use safe methods to recover from unstable weight transfers (e.g., from feet to hands).
- Design, refine, and perform (alone or with a partner) simple sequences involving rolling, weight transfers, balances, and concepts (levels, shapes, directions, speeds).

Figure 5.9 Example of Brubaker's unit standards, designed-down from one course standard.

Reprinted, by permission, from Nathan Brubaker. Nathan Brubaker is a doctoral student in pedagogy and former elementary physical educator in Vermont.

With this in mind, details about the process appear in the next chapter.

Lesson Standards

The last step in the designing-down process is developing *lesson* standards (objectives). This involves defining your unit standards in very specific, realistic terms of what students can achieve in a given lesson. Lesson standards should answer the question, "What did my students really learn today?" They should spell out the focus of your instruction, whether it is related to a physical skill, cognitive concept, or student attitude or behavior.

You may also wish to think of lesson standards or objectives as *learnable pieces*—a specific focus for what students can realistically achieve in a lesson. As George Graham (2001) explains, "'Children will learn to volley a ball' is not only [too] general but unrealistic for 30-minute lessons. [But] 'The children will learn to bend their knees as they receive

Planning is such an individual endeavor; I am always curious to see how teachers go about it. So I asked Nathan Brubaker to share his method of developing course and unit standards. He said he researched curriculum resources to see what was realistic to expect of children at different points in their development; he also attended professional development events and national conferences to learn more about the curriculum and assessment development processes. From here he began to eliminate standards and content that did not mesh with his teaching space, equipment, and setup. He applied his curriculum for a year and then kept some course and unit standards, modified some, and combined others to come up with what he has listed. He also shared his standards with his principal and parents. His experience is a reminder that developing and working with standards takes time, rather like a work in progress. In chapter 6, we'll take a closer look at many of the same processes Brubaker used to develop his curriculum.

real world

and volley a ball' provides a specific guideline for observation" (p. 28). Specifying learnable pieces, or cues (e.g., bending the knees), gives children and you something specific to practice, focus on, observe, and yes, assess.

An example of how learnable pieces have been designed down from Brubaker's unit standards (in this case, for the units of balancing and rolling) is shown in figure 5.10. You'll see that the learnable pieces to be stressed certainly do not look like the strict behavioral objectives we were taught in college; yet, there is no confusion about what students will be working toward achieving in each lesson. These learnable pieces are emphasized as children

Unit: Balancing			
Lesson one	**Lesson two**	**Lesson three**	**Lesson four**
Concepts of balance • It is *harder to balance* when your bases of support are far away from your center of gravity. • The *higher your center of gravity*, the more difficult it is to balance.	**Concepts of balance** • *Counterbalance* involves a wide base of support and parts pushing against each other. • *Countertension* involves a narrow base of support and parts pulling away from each other. • *Symmetrical shape:* If you cut your body in two, each side would look the same.	**Inverted balances** • Keep your *center of gravity* above your bases of support. • *Behind up!* (above your head) • *Asymmetrical shape:* If you cut your body in two, each side would look different.	**Dynamic balances** • Keep your *center of gravity* above your bases of support.

Unit: Rolling		
Lesson one	**Lesson two**	**Lesson three**
Rolling forward • Soft rolls, finish on your feet. **Backward rolling** • Hands by your ears; push up!	**Rolling forward** • Soft rolls, finish on your feet. • Use different speeds. **Backward rolling** • Hands by your ears; push up!	**Resolving rolls** • Use different shapes to begin and resolve (end) rolls. • Hold your beginning and ending shape.

Figure 5.10   Example of lesson outcomes designed-down from unit standards for balancing and rolling, grades 3–4.

Reprinted, by permission, from Nathan Brubaker. Nathan Brubaker is a doctoral student in pedagogy and former elementary physical educator in Vermont.

When working with learnable pieces, it is best to remember the words of wisdom, "less is more." As fellow Florida elementary physical educator Diana Bandhauer once recommended, "Don't be an objective junkie." In other words, pick one or two learnable pieces per lesson. Too many can overwhelm children (even adults—have you tried golf?), but focusing on one objective allows them to direct their entire attention toward that cue. You will find examples of learnable pieces you can use as lesson guides in the various chapters in part III.

When first introduced to this notion of learnable pieces in my master's program with George Graham at Virginia Polytechnic Institute, I recall balking at the idea of addressing only one aspect of a skill in a lesson. I could not imagine being unable to give students individual feedback on any part of their performance that needed improvement. It was mainly through actually doing it (we taught in local elementary schools as part of our program) that I began to realize the importance of one learnable piece at a time. And I saw that by stressing a specific point, it stuck with students. Yes, as the teacher, I heard my lesson's learnable piece hundreds of times in a day (or so it seemed), but I had to remember that each student was in my class for 30 minutes, and so did not hear that particular learnable piece more than a few times (not to mention the number of times they had to hear it before it really sunk in).

receive instruction and go through various activities. Both the learnable pieces shown here, as well as activities and assessments that support them, can be found under the respective skill sections in chapter 10 of this book.

Summary

The standards movement has, for better or worse, begun to reshape the educational scene in our country. It has led to an array of ideals, terms, and processes important for us to understand. Once accomplished, our next challenge is to determine *how* we can use standards—that is, what we do with them—so they can most influence our teaching and students' learning. Our next chapter helps us use the design-down process so we may develop strong unit and lesson standards and, ultimately, strong assessments of these standards.

Chapter 6

Using Standards to Develop Your Curriculum

Now that content (exit) and program standards have been established at the national and most state levels, we are increasingly being asked to demonstrate how we are using them in our planning and teaching. How do we show this? Are these statements that look nice on paper but have little carryover to the classroom? Or can they truly have a positive effect on our curriculum and planning—and therefore our instruction and students' learning?

I believe in the promise of the latter. I have found that reflective teachers who care about their students' learning are more than willing to review and improve their curriculum. Many teachers have already begun tackling the task of working with state standards to refine their physical education curriculum. All too often, however, states and school districts are unable to provide enough resources, support, or direction to committees and individual teachers in this process. This seems especially true for physical educators, who often get short shrift come in-service time. When this happens, physical education teachers are left to answer their own questions about working with standards and their curriculum:

- What do I do with these standards?
- How do they affect my present curriculum?
- Will I have to plan any differrently?
- Is this going to be of any value for my students?

- How do I do all this and teach hundreds of kids, too?

These are valid questions, given the time and effort that we already put into teaching. They become even more important for teachers in states or districts that do not have teams of teachers working together to design-down standards from the exit and program levels—yet who are required to incorporate the standards into their curriculum.

Whether you are an individual teacher or a member of a team working to improve curriculum, you may find answers to your biggest questions in this chapter. You will be introduced to what Leslie Lambert, a former physical education supervisor and current professor, terms the standards-based program design process—that is, the process "of integrating and merging learning goals, curriculum design, instructional design, and assessment design components into a singular, confluent whole" (Lambert, 2003, p. 130). And while this may sound intimidating, the five steps outlined in this chapter will help make it a more manageable task.

Before you begin, though, a few words of caution: Do not expect to race through this process. Curriculum development takes time and patience—so do not be surprised if it takes the entire school year. With this in mind, you may need to put things down and come back to them at a later date; in fact, this may be preferable so that you can mull decisions over. If you are part of a district team

Certainly there are many ways to join your existing curricular units and your state's program (and course) standards. For example, you could look at each curriculum unit (say, basketball, football, or gymnastics) and decide which course standards they help your students to meet. The problem with this approach is that you examine only the standards already incorporated in your curriculum. What you are not doing is considering course standards that your curriculum does not address, or address fully enough to affect students' achievement. The approach I propose does not put the activity first and the standards second; it puts the intent of the standards first and challenges us to offer enough activities in our curriculum to meet these standards. It may not be quick or easy, but in the long run, your curriculum will offer students the best opportunity to gain the concepts and skills they need to be physically educated.

working on curriculum and assessment, good for you—there is strength in numbers. If not, see if you can find a colleague or two to tackle this project with you. Then the work will be not only more enjoyable but also more helpful.

Step One: Define the Content of Your Course Standards

Content delineation is the "process of thoroughly identifying all aspects of a particular subject domain"—that is, a particular subject area (Tienken and Wilson, 2002, p. 46). By sorting out (in writing) the content inherent in all of your course standards, you recognize the scope, or *breadth* and *depth,* of each standard. In other words, you can identify all the skills and concepts that should be taught for students to reach each standard. Do this before setting your unit standards so that your curriculum will accurately reflect the intent of the course standards. The important intent here is to uncover areas in your curriculum that do not address your existing goals at your program and unit levels.

As an example of how to begin the process of content delineation, let's consider one of Florida's physical education course standards for the pre-K–2 level (see figure 5.7 on page 63).

(PE.A.1.1) 1. Combines shapes, levels, directions, pathways, and ranges into simple sequences. (Florida Department of Education, 1996)

What specific concepts do students need to understand by grade 2 to meet this standard? What skills do they need to perform? Because the language in this standard is very straightforward, we can easily discern these skills and concepts:

- Shapes: round, twisted, narrow, wide, bent, symmetrical, asymmetrical
- Levels: low, medium, high
- Directions: up, down, right, left, forward, backward, sideways
- Pathways: curved, twisted, zigzagged, straight
- Ranges: small, large
- Sequences: one skill performed, with a beginning and an ending shape

For some course standards, the descriptive language may make it difficult to interpret. This can be especially true if the standard contains the vague phrases "such as" or "for example." You may also find that the standard's intent is broader than thought at first glance. For an example of when a course standard is not straightforward, let's take the same Florida standards as shown in figure 5.7, this time for the 3–5 grade range.

(PE.A.1.2) 3. Knows how to demonstrate functional patterns of striking, dribbling, volleying, throwing, and catching in dynamic situations.

In this case, the concepts and skills explicitly stated in the standard (striking, dribbling, volleying, throwing, and catching) are easy to list. But perhaps the skill of kicking should be added, because it is a specific type of strike or volley. So if you are unsure whether to include a skill at this step, it is best to list it to be as thorough as possible. This does not necessarily mean that all of these skills or concepts will be covered in your curriculum (you will refine the list later), but you do want to be open to all that the standards can *potentially* address.

The importance of this point is illustrated in the remaining 3–5 course standards section in figure 5.7. Notice that the skill of kicking is not addressed. Does this mean Florida does not think this skill is important to teach? Likely not. Here is when being more specific at this step is beneficial. To help you outline all of the possible content, consult other teachers and curriculum textbooks (see the references section), or refer to part III of this book, which defines the majority of the movement concepts and skills found in the elementary physical education curriculum. As you go through this development process, treat each course standard separately, and at this point do not worry about overlapping content for different standards at different grade levels. This overlap will be addressed later.

As you draw up your course standards, you may find figure 6.1, the standards-curriculum comparison form, to be helpful; I will refer to it throughout the next four steps. (Figure 6.2 illustrates how one could complete the form using Florida's PE.A.1.2.3 standard.) Begin in the left-hand column and list your first course standard for one of your benchmark years or grade ranges (for example, grades 3 to 5) by designating it with a number or abbreviated description. In the next column, list the general movement skill or concept, as defined by the intent of the standard (e.g., kicking or directions). Then, in the next column, list all the specific skills and concepts, singly and by name, that relate to the particular general skill or concept, no matter the grade level. For example, do not simply list kicking; students in elementary school might work on many types of kicks: inside, instep, dribbling, and so on. On the other hand, at this stage in the game do not list all the learnable pieces for each type of kick. This is too much specific information at this step; culling the specific skills and concepts will be addressed later.

Once you begin this step, you will find it takes time. Working in a group helps the process; each group takes a benchmark year,

for example. If your state has only one benchmark year (grade 5, for example), different groups can work on different strands of the standards. Switch your sections once each group finishes, review the work, and refine the list further. After you complete this step for each course standard, tackle the next step in the process.

Step Two: Compare Curriculum Units and Standards

In this step, you will compare the concepts and skills you listed in step one with your present curricular units. This will enable you to see what changes, if any, need to be made to your curriculum.

To begin this step, take your filled-out standards-curriculum comparison form (figure 6.1) for the grade level or range you are working with and list the name of each unit in your curriculum in a column heading across the top of the form (you may need to add pages). Then, for each overall skill and concept you defined in step one, place a check mark in the appropriate unit box to designate that you instruct toward that specific concept or skill for that particular unit.

Write the name of the concept or skill into each checked unit box. This allows you to see at a glance the specific skills or concepts you focus on in each unit for each grade level or range. As you work with your information, you can easily see which of these you cover in each unit and which (if any) you do not. If there is a skill you will not use because it was covered in an earlier grade level comparison form, draw a line through it in the Concept and skill column (see example in figure 6.2) but keep it legible.

One word of caution: Be sure you are marking only the units in which you take instructional time to introduce, address, or teach the content or skills, not those that *imply* that students would be gaining them or where you use (e.g., mention) that concept or skill as a basis for the learning of other concepts or skills. It may be

tidbit

Remember that a benchmark year connotes that learning is taking place in the grades leading up to and including that year. For example, for Florida's 3–5 course standards, mark the units in which the skills and concepts are taught in grades 3, 4, and 5, not just the units from the benchmark year of grade 5.

Grades	School	Teacher								
		Unit								
Course standard	Concept and skill									

Figure 6.1 Standards-curriculum comparison form.

From *Elementary Physical Education Teaching & Assessment: A Practical Guide*, by Christine J. Hopple, 2005, Champaign, IL: Human Kinetics.

Grades 3-5 **School** Derby Elementary **Teacher** Jodi P.

Course standard	Concept and skill		Unit							
			Space awareness	Traveling	Relationships	Ed. gym	Game strategies	Throwing/ catching	Kicking/ punting	Striking
PE.A.1.2.3 Demonstrate functional patterns of striking, dribbling, volleying, throwing, and catching in dynamic situations	Kicking	• inside • instep • dribble • punting							✓ • instep • inside • dribble	
	Volleying	• with different body parts • overhead • underhand • forearm pass								
	Dribbling									
	Catching	• low level • medium • high						✓ • low • medium • high		
	Throwing	• underhand • overhand • Frisbee						✓ • overhand		
	Striking	• with bats • with hockey sticks • with golf clubs								✓ • with bats • with hockey sticks • with golf clubs
	Offense strategies	• create space • lead kick/pass					✓ • create space	✓ • leading pass • create space	✓ • leading kick • create space	
	Defense strategies	• deny space					✓ • deny space	✓ • deny space	✓ • deny space	

Figure 6.2 Sample standards-curriculum comparison form.

tempting to add those check marks and say, "Yes, I do this in that unit," but resist the temptation to mark incidental instructional events. This will paint the most accurate picture of how your curriculum is aligned to the standards, which is your goal.

When you finish step two you will have a deeper sense of the standards and content that are and are not adequately addressed in your curriculum. To best determine this, take a highlighter and mark the unit titles (the upper columns) that do not have corresponding standards or concepts or skills marked for them. Likewise, highlight any concepts and skills that are not included in your units. Addressing these in a future step is important in the design process; if you just ignore the part of the standards that your curriculum does not address, why go through the process?

Step Three: Develop Your Unit Overview

Next you will develop your unit overview by putting all your information from steps one and two together in a form that allows you to easily develop your units and ultimately, your lesson standards and activities for them. This is when you begin to tailor the intent of the standards to your particular school or district.

To begin step three, choose one unit from your completed standards-curriculum comparison form (steps one and two). Using the unit overview form (figure 6.3, with a completed sample form detailed in figure 6.4), in the left-hand column, write the number and description of *all* of the course standards that relate to this unit, as denoted by the check marks you made in step two. In the second column, list any performance indicators relevant to this unit. You may choose to use NASPE, state, or district performance indicators (or standards); you may also (or alternatively) use the performance indicators from part III in this book. Keep in mind that these are not absolutes, but *examples* of what students might do to demonstrate they have achieved a standard. You do not have to show that your students have met each particular indicator, but they do become another resource to guide your thinking in this step.

In the third column, list the specific concepts and skills (again, as determined in step two) that pertain only to this unit and grade level(s). At this point bring in the learnable pieces under each skill or concept (remember, these were not listed in the standards-curriculum comparison form), using part III of this book to assist you as necessary (for example, page 195 lists learnable pieces for the skill of kicking). These will be of help when you begin to design your lesson activities. (One note of caution: Identify the unit name, grade, number of lessons in the unit, your name, and the school's name to help you keep track of what you're doing.)

Next, after looking at the given course standards and performance indicators as well as the concepts and skills for each standard, develop your unit standards (fourth column) by deciding what students in this grade or grade range should learn in this particular unit. The unit standards or goals provide an overall picture of your expectations by the end of the unit.

It will be helpful at this point to begin to "think like an assessor" (Wiggins, 1998, p. 63)—that is, before you determine what the unit goals should be, take a few minutes to think about what you want students to do in order to demonstrate that they have indeed met this unit standard. At some point down the line, you will want to find out if students can show their learning—and the more you figure out up front how they will demonstrate that knowledge and skill, the less you will have to revise your already-written unit goals and standards. Don't worry if you are not yet comfortable with developing assessment tasks; part III contains assessment ideas and even reproducible assessment forms you can use in your units. In fact, you might find it helpful to take a look at the sample performance and portfolio assessment tasks in part III as you work with each skill or concept.

I will share an example of thinking like an assessor. When I was planning my elementary curriculum for my gymnastics unit, I started designing my grades 1 and 2 unit by defining what I wanted students to accomplish (i.e., my unit goal or standard): to develop and perform a simple sequence consisting of one roll, one balance, and one transfer of weight. I knew this learning activity would also become a performance task to assess their achievement of my unit goal (this happened to reflect my state's standards for kindergarten to second grade). With this as my goal, I made sure I taught all the concepts and skills students needed to complete this task.

As another example, in my dribbling unit, I wanted my fifth-grade students to successfully play

Unit _____ **Grades** _____ **Lessons in unit** _____

Course standard	Performance indicators	Concepts and skills	Unit standard/goals	Methods of assessment

Teacher _____ **School** _____

Figure 6.3   Unit overview form.

From *Elementary Physical Education Teaching & Assessment: A Practical Guide,* by Christine J. Hopple, 2005, Champaign, IL: Human Kinetics.

Unit _Kicking_   **Grades** _3–4_   **Lessons in unit** _6_

Course standard	Performance indicators	Concepts and skills	Unit standard/goals	Methods of assessment
_PE.A.1.2.3_ _Demonstrates functional patterns (of striking, dribbling, and so on) in dynamic situations_ _PE.A.1.2.4_ _Understands that games consist of people, boundaries, rules, and so on_ _PE.A.1.2.5_ _Knows how to create, explore, and devise game strategies_ _[Add additional course standards here]_	_NASPE:_ • _Describes the difference in foot placement when kicking a stationary ball, a ball moving away, and a ball moving toward_ • _Designs a new game incorporating at least two motor skills, rules, and strategies_ _[Can also list additional indicators from appendix A of this resource]_	_Inside kick_ • _Kick through the middle of the ball_ • _Inside of foot points to target_ _Instep kick_ • _Kick underneath the ball_ • _Toes follow through to target_ _Dribble_ • _Use insides of feet_ • _Use outsides of feet_ _Punt_ • _Kick hard_ _Leading kick_ • _Kick to where partner will be_ _Create space_ • _Offense: move to open areas to kick and receive ball_ _Deny space_ • _Defense: stay between goal and offense_	• _Show progress toward kicking with a mature form_ • _Control a ball while dribbling with insides and outsides of feet_ • _Understand part of foot to use for selected kicks_ • _Begin to modify kicking performance by using selected concepts (e.g., force, speed, pathways)_ • _Use games strategies when playing in a small-group game_ • _Knows the soccer leagues in the area they can play in_	_Performance_ • _Checklist for dribbling, look for both feet being used and ball being controlled_ _Portfolio task_ • _Part of foot to use_

Teacher _Jodi P._   **School** _Derby Elementary_

Figure 6.4   Sample unit overview form.

a three-on-three game that demonstrated passing, dribbling, and catching skills, as well as the concept of denying and creating space (defense and offense). With this big-picture goal (which reflected state standards), I developed relevant unit and lesson goals and activities. It really does not matter which you develop first, your unit goals and standards or the methods of assessment. Just remember, this is an inexact science.

Most likely, you will at times begin with one and at other times the other. The most important thing is that ultimately, each should reflect the other, and together they reflect the intent of the skills and concepts determined by your course standards.

Once you've completed this task for each curriculum unit, you will want to do this for any units that you need to add to your curriculum. To do this, go back and take a look at any content standards, skills, or concepts from the standards-curriculum comparison form (figure 6.1) that you highlighted as "not included" in any of your present units of instruction. In looking at all of these items together, it is likely similar skills, concepts, and performance indicators can be grouped and addressed in a unit added to your curriculum. For example, you might notice a number of delineated skills related to striking with long-handled implements that were not part of any unit. Seeing this gap in your curriculum, you might decide to add a unit on striking with golf clubs for grades 3 to 5. To do this, you would copy a new unit overview form for this unit and develop it. (And you would add this unit to an empty "unit" column in your standards-curriculum comparison form.)

If you have a few leftover concepts, skills, or performance standards that do not fit into any one unit, add them to existing units they relate to best. Put them on the appropriate unit overview form and revise your standards-curriculum comparison form accordingly. If you find you still have a unit without any (or a few) standards, concepts, or skills, decide whether it should be included in your curriculum at all. These decisions—what to include and what not to—are addressed in the next step.

tidbit

Before you begin revising your unit goals, make a copy of your completed unit overview form and mark up this copy instead of your original completed form. This way, you can always go back to your original for review. Also, be sure to indicate which version is the original. Date both your original and your revisions, to aid in organization.

Step Four: Revise Your Unit Overview

After you complete a unit overview form for each unit in your curriculum, it is time to take a hard look at your unit goals and consider whether they need revisions. For example, maybe there is duplication of skills and concepts (including learnable pieces) at the different grade levels and ranges. Or perhaps there is just too much content for a year. Now you have some questions to answer and decisions to make. For example, knowing you will not have enough time to cover all of the concepts and skills in a particular unit, how do you determine which to delete? Can you drop an entire unit if its concepts and skills are addressed in another unit? How do you make room for units you need to give students a full set of experiences? This is where the going gets tough, because *all* of these skills are important. But something has to give. To make the hard choices, you must do the following:

- Determine how much curricular time you have.
- Apply some critical questions, or *content screens.*

Determine Available Curricular Time

I cannot recall ever hearing a committed elementary physical education teacher say, "I've got so much time with my students, I'm running out of things to teach them." Generally, it is, "So much to teach, so little time." The constraint of instruction time, in fact, is one of the most frustrating, albeit critical, factors we have to contend with as elementary physical educators.

Most state standards are written at the "optimal" level—that is, they assume you see students enough times during the week to accomplish the standards. (For some teachers, that may be three lessons per week; for others, maybe more.) But there is (or should be) a big difference between what can be taught in one day a week versus three or five days a week; there is no doubt that only one or two days of instruction a week will severely limit the students' experience. And while state departments of education expect students to achieve all the standards, we teachers know that time constraints may hamper our efforts. In fact, Marzano and Kendall (1998) suggests that the largest impediment to the implementation of standards is the overabundance in the quantity of standards.

One tool to help you define your curricular priorities is to figure out exactly how much time you have to teach the concepts, skills, and units in your curriculum. To determine this, use a simple variation of University of Virginia professor Luke Kelly's instructional time formula (Graham, 2001). Figure 6.5 is a worksheet showing how to use this formula.

First, multiply the number of weeks of school (36) by the number of days per week you see your students. This gives you the total number of class periods you (in theory) see your students in a school year. Subtract 10 percent of this number from it; this will account for instruction time lost to those things that just happen: school programs, book fair in the gym, field trips, snow days, and so on. Your result is the number of lessons you realistically have with your students during a school year. (You can also use figure 6.5 to determine the number of hours per year you have with students.) By now, you likely have an astounded look on your face, because the real amount of time you see students is not much at all, when you get down to it.

Next, use figure 6.6 to determine how many lessons you can allot to each unit. In the left-hand column, list all your units. In the next column, estimate the number of lessons you need for each of these units. (Look at your unit overview form, especially your unit goals, to determine this.) Keep a running total of the number of lessons; this total

should not exceed your total number of available lessons per year as indicated by figure 6.5. You may have the difficult task of cutting out content and skills—all are important. If your total is over your limit, don't worry . . . we have one more tool to help in this process.

Apply Content Screens

A variety of criteria and questions called *content screens* can help us make tough decisions about what to include in our curriculum. Just like when panning for gold, what is not useful is thrown away; what is precious is kept. So it is with the concepts, skills, and units in your curriculum. By running your information (and thoughts) through a theoretical screen, your answers become clearer (see figure 6.7 for an illustration of this concept). With all of your information in front of you for reference, use the following screens, or criteria, to help you determine which concepts, skills, and units to keep and delete. (You can add to this list with other criteria.) As you decide to delete or add skills or concepts, make these changes on a copy of your original unit overview form.

1. What movement concepts or skills represent a big idea with enduring value beyond the classroom (Wiggins and McTighe, 1998)? In other words, will the skill or concept be important for children to know as adults? Is it so important to the understanding of other skills or concepts that without it, future understanding or achievement will suffer? For example, I think most elementary physical education teachers agree that performing the basic locomotor movements is of primary importance. They are central in a variety of games and dance, gymnastics, recreation, and everyday life activities for both children and adults. In contrast, being

1. Multiply number of lessons/week × 36 weeks in school year = _____ gross lessons/year = A
2. Multiply A × 10% = _____ lessons/year = B
3. Subtract B from A = _____ net lessons/year for that grade level = C

To convert into hours of instruction/year:

4. Multiply C × the number of class minutes/period = _____ total min/year = D
5. Divide D by 60 minutes/hour = _____ hours/year of instruction for that particular grade level

Figure 6.5   Form to determine time allotment per year, by grade level.
Adapted from G. Graham 2001.

Unit	Number of lessons	Running total (not to exceed _____ lessons/year)
Teacher _____ School _____ Grade _____		

Figure 6.6   Form to determine number of lessons per unit.

From *Elementary Physical Education Teaching & Assessment: A Practical Guide*, by Christine J. Hopple, 2005, Champaign, IL: Human Kinetics.

able to play a game of regulation basketball by grade 5 is not as necessary. As mentioned earlier, the more often a concept or skill is included in the standards, the more weight it has as a big idea for students to master.

2. What movement concepts or skills reside at the heart of our discipline (Wiggins and McTighe, 1998)? In other words, what is so important in our discipline that it *must* be taught? What are the skills and concepts integral to physical education that will not be covered in students' other classes? Are there concepts or skills in our standards that may be taught in other disciplines? For example, classroom teachers cover a number of health concepts in their science units. Perhaps these concepts can be addressed there and not through our curriculum. This does not mean we would take them off our list; I would suggest that you add another unit to the standards-curriculum comparison form, noting that the unit is Mrs. Smith's health unit, for

example. As another example, in my old school district, every third-grade student received swimming lessons during the school year; this was not done during my instructional time, but yet, this unit certainly addressed a number of physical education standards. Therefore, it would be important to add this aquatics unit to the earlier two forms. In determining what concepts or skills are taught elsewhere, you would need to communicate with classroom teachers.

3. How many movement concepts or skills is enough? If a standard includes a large number of concepts and skills, you (and other teachers) may be able to decide, "If we teach *half* of the total number of these, we can still help students achieve the intent of the standard."

4. What movement concepts and skills are worth fighting for? As Larry Satchwell, a former national elementary teacher of the year, asks, What is so important to you as a teacher that you are

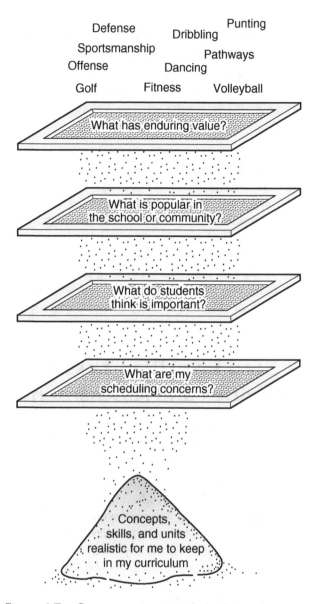

Figure 6.7   Content screens to help determine which skills and concepts to use and delete.

not willing to compromise on it, even if it is not included or heavily stressed in the standards? What are you willing to fight for? For example, perhaps you have a unit (i.e., multiple lessons) pertaining to the annual field day. This may not be instructional time per se, but you feel it is very important—and you are not willing to give it up in your curriculum. No doubt, you have other examples that are unique to your situation.

5. Is the wording of the standard open in nature? Does the statement contain phrases like "such as" or "for example"? If so, these vague terms suggest

that some, but not all, of the concepts and skills should be in the curriculum. For example, given the amount of time you have, you might decide to include only the underhand throw, overhand throw, kick, and dribble for students in kindergarten through second grade. Other skills, such as striking and volleying, may have to be deleted from the curriculum altogether (something we hate to do, but sometimes necessary), or it may be covered in grades 3 to 5. By including some of the skills, you still are helping students work toward the standard, and you can justify why all the skills may not be included.

6. What is popular in the community? When I taught in Virginia, a large percentage of my students played youth soccer year-round. I had two choices: I could stress soccer in my program from kindergarten through fifth grade so that all students had a good chance to learn, or I could cover the basics, given that most students learned the skills elsewhere. I chose the latter. In doing this, I decided to use my curricular time (two days a week) to introduce students, especially those in the upper grades, to less familiar skills (such as golf). In my situation, I think this was the better choice.

7. What do students think is important? This is one of the most overlooked but perhaps one of the most important screens. Many times, we teach what we like (or do not teach what we do not like), without paying attention to what the students like. Or we assume they like an activity when, in fact, they may not. Survey students at the beginning of the year, asking them what they'd like to learn in the upcoming year. Better yet, give it to them at the end of the year, when things are fresh in their minds. Use their feedback as you plan for the upcoming year.

8. How does the facility affect what can be taught? There's no doubt that teaching soccer, for example, is difficult when the only space is a small blacktop area. Dribbling and basketball are almost impossible to teach *without* one. And having no indoor space can make instruction pretty tough. There may be ways to get around a lack of facilities, and you should explore all available options. For example, if your school is near community tennis courts, get permission to use them. Sometimes you might encounter limitations you cannot get around. The important thing is to explore available options.

My hunch is that experienced teachers perform the steps of screening their content, allotting time per unit, and developing their unit standards simultaneously. Their approach is not linear, performing one step and then the next. Because each step affects the others, I'd bet that teachers flip back and forth, building on one step to the next to arrive at their final yearly plan. (I know I did.) Veteran teachers will tell you that planning is an inexact science—which is partly, I think, what makes it so difficult.

When there are none, you have ample justification for excluding an activity from your curriculum.

9. What equipment is available? A lack of appropriate equipment certainly limits how you work with your students. For example, it would be impossible to teach striking with short-handled implements if you did not have rackets or paddles. Explore every option before you officially cross an activity off your list. Perhaps you can post a donations box by your gym for parents to drop off old or outgrown equipment. Make a plea to your school's parent organization. Buy only enough equipment for one station, or learning center, and add some each year. If none of this is feasible, you maybe be justified in dropping this content from your curriculum.

10. What are the scheduling concerns? Having two classes to teach at a time certainly affects class content. So, too, does a schedule that is not conducive to setting up and organizing teaching space. Team teaching, especially with a teacher who may use different techniques from you, can also present certain difficulties. With these complications, you may find you cannot teach particular concepts and skills. First search for ways to counter the situation; involve your principal, if appropriate; or problem-solve to find alternative ways to present activities. If you decide to exclude a specific concept or skill, it is important that you can justify it.

Once you've put your skills, concepts, and units through the screens, you should be able to make some other decisions on the amount of content you can realistically cover in your curriculum. No doubt, you will need to go back and revise the number of lessons devoted to some of your units; be sure to make the changes on your forms. Depending on what you have decided, you may need to revise your unit goals and possibly the concepts and skills on both the unit overview and standards-curriculum comparison form. In some cases, you may decide to delete a unit altogether for a particular grade level (you may decide to keep it for another grade level, so students still get some instruction in its skills and concepts).

Although this step is time-consuming, once you finish you will have unit overview and comparison forms that reflect your lesson plans for the upcoming year. Certainly, you will want to refer to these forms in subsequent years, revising them to match your situation. (Remember always to work from a copy of your original.) Now you are ready for the final step.

Step Five: Plan Lesson Activities and Assessments

Instructional calibration is the technical term for designing lesson activities and constructing assessments that are congruent with the information gained through the process you have just completed (Tienken and Wilson, 2002). This step should be fairly simple. Basically, you are developing standards or objectives and class activities based on the unit development forms you already designed, as well as the alternative assessments to go with them.

Planning Lesson Activities

Undoubtedly, there are as many forms for lesson planning as there are teacher preparation programs in the United States, and I'm sure you have a form that works for you. Figure 6.8 is one example of a lesson format that focuses on standards (figure 6.8 simply shows the elements that should make up a unit or lesson plan). Whether you use this format or another, you should include the standards that give direction and meaning to what takes place in the lessons and in the assessments. While this is not done in traditional lesson planning, it becomes important if your state or district requires an accounting of the standards your curriculum teaches.

Note that the lesson plan shown here does not ask you to specify lesson objectives in the traditional manner; guiding questions and learnable

Teacher _____ **School** _____

Unit _____ **Grade** _____

Number of lessons in the unit _____

Program-Level Content Standards

Choose those applicable to this unit from your state's standards.

_____

_____

_____

Course-Level Content Standards

Choose the designed-down standards for your benchmark year in elementary school.

_____

_____

_____

Unit Standards or Performance Indicators

Identify the unit standards or related performance indicators relative to this unit.

_____

_____

_____

_____

Assessment of This Unit

Briefly identify the type of assessments to be used when assessing learning in this unit—e.g., which P, summative or formative?

Example: (You wouldn't necessarily have this many in one unit): _____

Product—Formative—Lesson 1 _____

Performance—Formative—Lesson 2 _____

Portfolio task—Formative—Lesson 4 _____

Traditional—Selected response—Summative—Lesson 6 _____

Lesson _____ **out of** _____
[add as many as needed per lessons in this unit]

Lesson Activities

Describe lesson activities here.

_____

_____

Learnable Pieces

Include learnable pieces to focus on for each "part" of the lesson, as appropriate.

_____

_____

Assessment Taking Place in This Lesson

Detail type of assessment task; attach copy of it, if applicable; add rubric or answers as needed.

_____

_____

_____

Figure 6.8   Example of a unit and lesson plan focusing on standards.

pieces provide the specific focus for instruction in each lesson. (See figure 5.10 on page 66 for an example of this concept.) Recall that these guiding questions and learnable pieces, in essence, become the lesson objective (i.e., what students can realistically learn during a class). If you compose your own planning form, be sure to leave room at the top for these standards and performance indicators, as well as any assessment measures you intend to use at the end of the lesson. You may find it helpful to keep your unit overview form as a cover sheet for your lesson plans so you can easily refer to it.

When planning your lesson activities, examine a variety of sources, including the "Ideas for Lesson Development" found in part III of this book, for a number of developmentally and instructionally appropriate activities. Don't forget the Internet; Web sites such as PE Central (www.pecentral.org) contain a wealth of lesson activities.

Planning Assessments

Remember back when I asked you to think like an assessor when you were developing your unit goals? If you followed this advice you likely have an idea of an assessment task you can use to measure your students' performance. If not, you may wish to take a look back through part I of this book, at different ideas for assessment in part III, and at a variety of resources such as PE Central and NASPE assessment materials (see the references section). Either way, at this point, add your assessment to the last column on your unit overview form and in your lesson plan. It may also be helpful to detail whether the assessments will be done at the lesson or unit level (you may have to erase or edit the notes you jotted down in this column earlier). And then, you can sit back and breathe a deep sigh of relief, because you've made it through your last step in planning. What comes next is the fun part—teaching your students!

Summary

There is no doubt that the process of using standards to refine your curriculum, teaching, and assessment is a long and tedious journey. You should not expect to complete this process in a few days; you may find yourself working on it over a period of weeks or even months. The good news is that it is always easier once you get this far. From now on, you will be revising what you have already done, instead of coming up with all new ideas. To aid in this process, once you have completed a few units, ask a valued colleague or your principal for comments and thoughts. Share them with others at your state physical education conference. Go to a session on standards and assessment and ask the speakers if they or someone they know would be willing to help. Get on the Internet; visit the PE Central Web site at www.pecentral.org; subscribe to different list-serves that allow you to ask teachers from around the country and world for their input. Through communicating what you are doing in your program and finding out what others are doing in theirs, your curriculum and your students' achievement can only be enhanced. And therein lies the strength and potential of the standards movement in American education . . . used wisely, it can result in the highest standard of all: that our students have learned, and learned well.

Sample Assessment Tasks and Curriculum Ideas

In this part of the guide, you'll find hands-on information and ideas that will help you in the day-to-day planning, implementation, and assessment of your elementary physical education curriculum. My guess is that this is the part of the book that you'll probably spend most of your time working with and poring over!

To make it easier to find information in part III, chapters are grouped by similar skills and concepts from elementary physical education. (You'll find a listing of these chapters and their specific skills and concepts on page 84.) And because you probably organize your year's curriculum differently than I do, I have listed some common units of instruction corresponding to the skills and concepts in these chapters.

For each skill or concept mentioned in the chapters of part III, you'll find several similar elements to use when planning, instructing, and assessing students and your program. These elements are described in more detail now.

Chapter	Possible units
7. Safety and participation	
	Orientation and safety, throughout various units
8. Movement concepts	
Body awareness	Rhythms or dance, tumbling or gymnastics, locomotor skills
Space awareness	Rhythms or dance, tumbling or gymnastics, games, locomotor skills
Effort	Rhythms or dance, tumbling or gymnastics, locomotor skills
Relationships	Tumbling or gymnastics, rhythms or dance, throughout various units
9. Locomotor skills	
Locomotor movements	Locomotor skills, traveling
Chasing, fleeing, and dodging	Tag games
Jumping and landing	Jump rope, tumbling or gymnastics
10. Nonlocomotor skills	
Rolling	Tumbling or gymnastics, rhythms or dance
Balancing	Tumbling or gymnastics, rhythms or dance
Weight transfer	Tumbling or gymnastics, rhythms or dance, locomotor skills
11. Manipulative skills	
Dribbling with the hands	Basketball, ballhandling skills, handball
Kicking and punting	Soccer, football
Throwing and catching	Softball, bowling, football, baseball, handball, basketball
Volleying	Volleyball, soccer
Striking with short-handled implements	Net games, tennis, paddleball
Striking long-handled implements	Hockey, softball, golf, baseball, T-ball
12. Health, activity, and fitness	
Introduction to physical activity and physical fitness	Throughout various units
Cardiorespiratory fitness	Tag games, soccer, jump rope, fitness tests
Muscular strength and endurance	Tumbling or gymnastics, tag games, jump rope, fitness tests
Flexibility	Tumbling or gymnastics, rhythms or dance, fitness tests
Training and conditioning	Throughout various units
Healthy habits	Throughout various units

Sample Course Standards

A sample course standard sets the tone for what students should be able to demonstrate with a given skill or concept by the time they leave elementary school. This course standard serves as a guide for planning standards and assessments at the unit and lesson levels.

Learnable Pieces

Gain an overall idea of the skills and concepts in each chapter by reading the list of relevant *learnable pieces* (also known as critical *cues* or *refinements*). You can use these learnable pieces as guides when you design-down to the lesson standards for each of your units. They are also useful for emphasis during instruction. To make them more helpful, you'll find each learnable piece referenced to the grade level or levels where you'll find it described in this guide.

| 110 **ELEMENTARY PHYSICAL EDUCATION TEACHING & ASSESSMENT** |

Sample Course Standard	Space Awareness	
By the end of elementary school, students should be able to	**Concepts and Skills**	**Learnable Pieces**
• design, refine, and perform dance and gymnastics sequences that focus on the use of one or more of the directions, levels, pathways, extensions, and space concepts.	*Self-, or personal, space*	Space right next to you, out of reach of anyone or anything. (K, 1–2)
	General space	Empty or open space all around you. (K, 1–2)
	Offense	Keep your body between the ball and the defender. (3–4, 5–6)
		Create space by moving to open areas to pass or receive the ball. (5–6)
		Hit the ball to places where opponents aren't standing. (5–6)
	Defense	Deny space by staying between the opponent and intended goal. (5–6)
		Be ready to move. (5–6)
		Partners equally cover the area. (5–6)
	Directions	
	Forward	Your front leads. (K, 1–2)
	Backward	Your back leads. (K, 1–2)
	Sideways	Your side (right or left) leads. (K, 1–2)
	Up	Toward the sky. (K, 1–2)
	Down	Toward the ground. (K, 1–2)
	Pathways	
	Curved	Rounded like a rainbow. (K, 1–2)
	Straight	Like a line or pencil. (K, 1–2)
	Zigzag	Straight lines connected to make sharp points. (K, 1–2)
	Levels	
	Low	Below your knees. (K, 1–2)
	Medium	Between your shoulders and knees. (K, 1–2)
	High	Above your shoulders. (K, 1–2)
	Extensions	
	Near	When your body parts are close to your body. (1–2)
	Far	When your body parts are far from your body. (1–2)

SPACE AWARENESS

Grade Level

You'll find information under each skill or concept organized according to the grade levels of kindergarten, first to second, third to fourth, and fifth to sixth. In keeping with the philosophy of designing-down, these grade levels are presented in reverse order, beginning with fifth and sixth grades and concluding with kindergarten.

Rubric Clues

These give you some ideas for criteria to use as the basis for developing a scoring rubric for each assessment task, one that fits your students and intended standards.

Sample Portfolio Tasks

You will find sample portfolio tasks (some traditional in nature, some alternative) to use for assessing students in almost every skill or concept at the grade levels of 5 to 6, 3 to 4, and 1 to 2, and kindergarten (when appropriate). You'll also find a number of ready-to-use assessment sheets illustrating some of these portfolio tasks.

Movement Concepts 111

GRADES 5 TO 6

Sample Performance Indicators

By the end of grade 6, students should be able to

- purposefully use pathways, levels, directions, and extensions to change the continuity or flow and add variety to a gymnastics or dance sequence; and
- purposefully use general space to create or deny space when developing or using game strategies in a small-group situation.

NASPE Performance Indicators

- Designs a new game incorporating at least two motor skills, rules, and strategies. (3–5, #2, 17)

Sample Performance Task

In groups of three, students create two different running or passing plays in football, incorporating all three of the pathways (straight, curved, and zigzag). Each play should be drawn on paper and practiced, using a football or other preferred object. After each student is familiar with each play, the groups can rotate the passer, receiver, and defender positions.

RUBRIC CLUES

To what extent do students

- use all three pathways?
- run each play correctly so that the pathway they use can be clearly identified?

Sample Portfolio Task

Have students watch an athletic performance on TV, attend a game, or watch a tape of one at school. Have them write down the space awareness concepts athletes used during their performances. What did the athletes do at a high, medium, or low level? What kinds of pathways did they use? Directions? What kind of space did they move in? Have them give examples of how athletes use these concepts.

RUBRIC CLUES

To what extent do students

- show a clear understanding of the different space awareness concepts in their use of examples?

Emphasize	Ideas for Lesson Development
General space *Offense* Create space by moving to open areas to pass or receive the ball. Keep your body between the ball and the defender. *Defense* Deny space by staying between the opponent and intended goal.	- Ask students to compare how space is created or denied in invasion, net, and fielding games. Why is space created or denied? How do team members do this? - See manipulative skills themes (in chapter 11) for further ideas on the use of space in the context of games play. **Belka:** *Advance and Score Soccer* *Advance and Score Basketball*

SPACE AWARENESS

References to Sample Performance Indicators

Relevant sample performance indicators were developed as part of this textbook. These indicators have been reviewed (and approved) by many elementary physical education teachers in the field. The indicators are also found, according to grade level, in appendix A of this text. Many of the performance and portfolio tasks listed can help you determine whether students are on track to meet these expectations. In addition, you can use these indicators as you look to design-down to the unit and lesson levels.

References to NASPE Performance Indicators

You'll find references (when applicable) to the specific performance indicators from the National Association for Sport and Physical Education's *Moving Into the Future: National Standards for Physical Education* resource. Organized by grade range and standard (e.g., "3–5, #5, 3" would refer to grade range 3–5, standard #5, performance indicator 3), these indicators, as well as others not listed here, can be found in appendix B of this book. Many of the performance and portfolio tasks in this book can help you assess whether students have reached these nationally approved indicators of achievement.

Sample Performance Tasks

An example of a performance task to use for assessing students in the skills and concepts is given at the grade levels of 5 to 6, 3 to 4, and 1 to 2, and—when appropriate—kindergarten. Because of the limited writing and verbal ability of kindergartners, as well as how fresh their introduction is to many of the skills and concepts in physical education, few assessments are given for these youngsters. Nor have performance assessments been presented for the cognitive concepts found in the chapter on health and fitness (chapter 12) or all of the concepts in the safety and participation chapter (chapter 7).

Ideas for Lesson Development

Under this heading are kid-tested, ready-to-use ideas you can incorporate into lessons. These ideas may relate to physical skills or (as with the fitness theme) they may be questions for discussion about a specific concept. You will also find helpful hints for making and setting up equipment, as well as cross-references to additional lesson ideas in the popular *Teaching Children* series and PE Central online. These ideas are intended as suggestions for activities to use at various grade levels.

Emphasize

Here you'll find the specific learnable pieces, which can serve as a focus for lesson instruction at the different grade levels. The accompanying Ideas for Lesson Development complement these learnable pieces.

PE Central and *Teaching Children* Series Cross-References

Additional ideas for lesson development can be found on PE Central's K to 2 and 3 to 5 Lesson Ideas Web

---

Movement Concepts | | |

GRADES 5 TO 6

Sample Performance Indicators

By the end of grade 6, students should be able to
- purposefully use pathways, levels, directions, and extensions to change the continuity or flow and add variety to a gymnastics or dance sequence; and
- purposefully use general space to create or deny space when developing or using game strategies in a small-group situation.

NASPE Performance Indicators
- Designs a new game incorporating at least two motor skills, rules, and strategies. (3-5, #2, 17)

Sample Performance Task

In groups of three, students create two different running or passing plays in football, incorporating all three of the pathways (straight, curved, and zigzag). Each play should be drawn on paper and practiced, using a football or other preferred object. After each student is familiar with each play, the groups can rotate the passer, receiver, and defender positions.

RUBRIC CLUES

To what extent do students
- use all three pathways?
- run each play correctly so that the pathway they use can be clearly identified?

Sample Portfolio Task

Have students watch an athletic performance on TV, attend a game, or watch a tape of one at school. Have them write down the space awareness concepts athletes used during their performances. What did the athletes do at a high, medium, or low level? What kinds of pathways did they use? Directions? What kind of space did they move in? Have them give examples of how athletes use these concepts.

RUBRIC CLUES

To what extent do students
- show a clear understanding of the different space awareness concepts in their use of examples?

Emphasize

General space
Offense
Create space by moving to open areas to pass or receive the ball.
Keep your body between the ball and the defender.
Defense
Deny space by staying between the opponent and intended goal.

Ideas for Lesson Development

- Ask students to compare how space is created or denied in invasion, net, and fielding games. Why is space created or denied? How do team members do this?
- See manipulative skills themes (in chapter 11) for further ideas on the use of space in the context of games play.

Belka: *Advance and Score Soccer*
Advance and Score Basketball

SPACE AWARENESS

---

pages (at www.pecentral.org) and in the *Teaching Children* series from Human Kinetics Publishers. The names of specific lesson ideas or learning experiences are referenced according to their sources, which are as follows:

PEC: PE Central's Web site: K–2 or 3–5 lesson ideas (use the search option to easily find the lesson ideas)

(David) Belka: *Teaching Children Games: Becoming a Master Teacher*

(Craig) Buschner: *Teaching Children Movement Concepts and Skills: Becoming a Master Teacher*

(Theresa) Purcell Cone and (Stephen) Cone: *Teaching Children Dance: Becoming a Master Teacher, Second Edition*

(Tom and Laraine) Ratliffe: *Teaching Children Fitness: Becoming a Master Teacher*

(Peter) Werner: *Teaching Children Gymnastics: Becoming a Master Teacher, Second Edition*

I hope you'll find the information in part III helpful and interesting. I encourage you to take from it what is useful to you and your program, adapt it when necessary, and improve it if needed. Have fun!

Safety and Participation

By the end of elementary school, students should be able to

- apply appropriate safety and emergency rules both in and out of physical education class;

- recognize the time, effort, and feelings that are part of participating in activities to improve and maintain physical fitness and skill levels;

- recognize that fun, excitement, and other feelings can be expressed and achieved by participating in physical activities;

- show verbal and physical support of and respect for others while participating in physical activities;

- enjoy the participation and companionship that result from cooperating with a partner or others in physical activities; and

- enjoy feelings of success, improvement, and meeting challenges resulting from positive experiences in physical activity.

Safety and Participation

Concepts and Skills	Learnable Pieces
Rules for safety	There are important rules you need to remember in physical education. (K)
	It is important to wear proper footwear in physical education. (K, 1–2)
	Rules allow everyone to be safe and have fun in physical education. (1–2, 3–4)
	There are some basic first-aid procedures you can perform that can help in an emergency. (5–6)
Cooperating with others	Cooperating involves working together and helping others. (K, 1–2)
	Cooperation involves giving everyone an opportunity to be involved and to contribute ideas. (3–4, 5–6)
Respecting others	Respect involves communicating with others in a positive manner, being considerate, and listening to what teachers and others have to say. (1–2, 3–4)
Learning about self and others	Everyone has different things they can do well, or have to work harder on, in physical education. (3–4)
	Activities with others can be fun and enjoyable for everyone. (5–6)
	Sports, dance, and other activities are ways to get together and learn about other people. (5–6)
Improving your skills	Everyone has to practice to get better at a skill. (1–2)
	Improving your skills and fitness isn't always easy; it takes time and work. (3–4, 5–6)

GRADES 5 TO 6

Sample Performance Indicators

By the end of grade 6, students should be able to

- work cooperatively with others to participate in or solve movement activities or problems;
- work willingly with others, regardless of ability or other distinguishing qualities, in movement situations;
- solve group difficulties in positive, respectful ways; and
- recognize basic emergency situations and first-aid procedures to deal with them.

NASPE Performance Indicators

- Works productively with a partner to improve performance of a dance sequence by following a detailed diagram of the process. (3–5, #5, 37)
- Accepts the teacher's decision regarding a personal rule infraction without displaying negative reactions toward others. (3–5, #5, 38)
- Recognizes and appreciates similar and different activity choices of peers. (3–5, #5, 40)
- Demonstrates respect and caring for a wheel-chair-bound peer through verbal and nonverbal encouragement and assistance. (3–5, #5, 42)

- Regularly encourages others and refrains from put-down statements. (3–5, #5, 43)
- Interacts with others by helping with their physical activity challenges. (3–5, #6, 47)
- Selects and practices a skill on which improvement is needed. (3–5, #6, 48)

Sample Portfolio Task

Have students reflect, in writing, on an activity or sport in which they think they improved. What did they do to improve? Who helped them to improve? How did they feel as a result of improving? Then have them describe an activity or sport in which they would especially like to improve in the future. What do they think they will need to do to improve? Who can help them improve?

RUBRIC CLUES

To what extent do students

- give responses that show they understand the time and effort it takes to improve?

Emphasize	Ideas for Lesson Development
Rules for safety There are some basic first-aid procedures you can perform that can help in an emergency.	• Visit your local Red Cross Center to pick up materials and programs appropriate to help preteens and teenagers recognize emergency situations and learn what to do in them. See if a representative will serve as a guest speaker for students on a day when you know you will need to be in the classroom. **PEC:** *First Aid Booklet*
Cooperating with others Cooperation involves giving everyone an opportunity to be involved and to contribute ideas.	• *Team Building Through Physical Challenges* and *More Team Building Challenges* by Daniel Midura and Donald Glover are excellent resources for team challenges and cooperative activities. Both are available from Human Kinetics (www.HumanKinetics.com).

PEC: *Cars*
Combine Brains
Ditto-A Cooperative Game
Group Juggling
Geography General Space Team Bowling
Island Hopping
Loop-Da-Hoop
Minefield

People Puzzles
Sneak Attack
Slalom Blindfold
Survivors
The Bus
Through the Quicksand
Titanic Challenge

Learning about self and others
Activities with others can be
fun and enjoyable for everyone.

- Organize a "[your school's name] Friends and Family Plan." Discuss with students sports and activities that are fun for them to participate in with a friend or family member. Encourage students to try one of these activities at least once a week. If they do, have them write about it, draw it, or have a photo taken of them doing the activity with their friend or family; put these up weekly on a bulletin board, or spotlight one or two examples in the school (or your physical education) newsletter.

Sports, dance, and other activities are ways to get together and learn about other people.

- Discuss how people can get together and learn about other cultures through sports and dance. Talk about the role of folk dances in other cultures or how the Olympics brings together people from all over the world. Use excerpts from the Olympics or cultural videos to illustrate your discussion.

- Have your school's media specialist highlight books about the Olympics and other international competitions or athletes from other countries and encourage children to look through, read, and check them out.

- Ask your media specialist to subscribe to magazines such as *Sports Illustrated for Kids* for your school library. You can even let students "check it out" from physical education class (if you purchase it as part of your program, for example).

- Ask students to describe examples of how sports and dances have helped them meet people from the community, and other cities, states, or countries.

- Invite an exchange student at your local high school or in the community to talk with your students about the games, sports, and dances that are popular in his or her native country and even participate with your students in one of these activities.

- Simulate different disabilities at stations around the classroom, and show how individuals with these disabilities can participate in movement situations. For examples: A student navigates a maze in a wheelchair (borrow from a local hospital or medical supply store); one student guides a blindfolded classmate through a cone "course"; students use crutches to learn the difficulties in walking, kicking, and so on; students perform movements to music while wearing earplugs. After students have finished the activities, ask them to reflect on which station was the most difficult, easiest, and so on, then ask why. Discuss common disabilities that students encounter in daily life, and how it is important to respect all people.

Purcell Cone and Cone: *Creative Square Dance*

Improving your skills
Improving your skills and fitness isn't always easy; it takes time and work.

- In the beginning of the school year ask students to write down something they would like to improve on during the coming year (you can do this in conjunction with the portfolio assessment). Use this as a goal; revisit this goal during the year (e.g., once a quarter), asking students to reflect on the progress they are making toward their goals.

- Use personal stories from popular athletes—or your own—to illustrate that getting better at skills or fitness takes time and hard work. Have the media specialist feature books and articles telling stories of people's triumphs (not only in physical achievements).

PEC: *Disability Awareness Lesson*   *Jail House Rock*
Improvisation   *Wheelchair Obstacle Course*

GRADES 3 TO 4

Sample Performance Indicators

By the end of grade 4, students should be able to

- identify movement activities they enjoy doing;
- identify movement activities they would like to improve; and
- work together positively with others in a variety of movement situations.

NASPE Performance Indicators

- Explains how appropriate practice improves performance. (3–5, #2, 16)
- In preparation for a kicking on goal task, arranges soccer equipment safely in a manner appropriate to practice. (3–5, #5, 34)
- Cooperates with all class members by taking turns and sharing equipment. (3–5, #5, 36)
- Assesses and takes responsibility for his or her own behavior problems without blaming others. (3–5, #5, 39)
- During class discussion of various dance forms, shows respect for the views of a peer from a different cultural background. (3–5, #5, 41)

- Interacts with others by helping with their physical activity challenges. (3–5, #6, 47)
- Selects and practices a skill on which improvement is needed. (3–5, #6, 48)

Sample Portfolio Task

Ask students to write about an activity they think they are good at in physical education. How does it make them feel about themselves? Why do they feel that way? What is something they do not do as well, but would like to do better? How can they get better at this activity?

RUBRIC CLUES

To what extent do students

- give responses that reflect an understanding of something they do well?
- understand how to improve at an activity?

Emphasize	*Ideas for Lesson Development*

Rules for safety
Rules allow everyone to be safe and have fun in physical education.

- Make a safety video that you can show to new students who enter the school throughout the year, as well as to younger students at the beginning of the year. Divide students into groups; assign each a piece of playground equipment or a specific situation (fire drill, ball kicked into the road, and so on). Have students write down the safety rules for that situation; review these to make sure they have them correct. With help from your media specialist, parent volunteers, or others in the district or community, videotape each group of students as they present the rules for the particular piece of equipment or situation. After editing, keep a copy available to be sent home for review (and returned) or watched during free classroom time by each new student at the school.

PEC: *Risk Factor Charades*

Cooperating with others
Cooperation involves giving everyone an opportunity to be involved and to contribute ideas.

- After discussing the term "cooperation" and how it involves listening to and allowing others to share their ideas, separate students into small groups (four or five students chosen randomly), and give each group a portion of the gym area. Explain that they will be able to choose any equipment you have set out (include a huge variety: hoops, balls, jump ropes, Frisbees, nontraditional equipment; the more varied, the better!) and they have approximately 15 minutes to develop an activity or game in their area, using the equipment they choose. The rule is that only one person from each group can go to the "equipment locker" at any time and take only what can be carried in one trip. Equipment can be returned or exchanged to the pile. Tell each group that they will have 45 seconds at the beginning for each person to give their input before anyone can actually get equipment; your role is to travel to each group and note how well they are interacting, give ideas for better communication and cooperation, and the like. At the end of the time period, ask each group to quickly show their activity to other groups.

Purcell Cone and Cone: *Birthday Celebration*
PEC: *All Aboard*   *Fairbanks Fast Square*
Combine Brains   *Frogs and Ants*
Cooperative Hoops   *Invent a Game*
Ditto-A Cooperative Game   *Secret Handshake*
Foam Ball Pass Over

Respecting others
Respect involves communicating with others in a positive manner, being considerate, and listening to what teachers and others have to say.

- Discuss how students can work to solve small problems without involving the teacher. Introduce some common problems; talk about how they can be handled individually. Discuss what kinds of problems students should (and shouldn't) try to solve on their own.

- Promote a positive, accepting class attitude. First discuss how everyone can do something well, whether in the classroom or physical education. Then give each student in the class a small piece of paper and a pencil.

Ask them to write their names on one side and fold their papers in half. Put all these into a box or hat. Each student picks a paper and writes something good about the person whose name is on it. Try to have students identify something good that the person does in physical education class; you may need to give them examples (e.g., cooperates well, runs well, makes up good routines). If necessary, allow them to write anything down (they smile nice, they read well, and so on) if they can't think of something specific to physical education. Have each student hand the paper to the other person; then students read their "positive promoter" aloud.

Learning about self and others
Everyone has different things they can do well, or have to work harder on, in physical education.

- Discuss how everyone has strengths and weaknesses, even when it comes to physical activity.
- Ask students to write down one thing they think they can do well in physical education, and one thing they'd like to improve on. Where, outside of school, can they go to improve on this?

> **PEC:** *Potato Head*
> *Time Line (Self-Esteem)*

Improving your skills
Improving your skills and fitness isn't always easy; it takes time and work.

- At the beginning of the year, have students draw a picture of a skill or activity they would like to improve on during the year, either in physical education or after school. Ask them to write a paragraph explaining why they would like to improve in that chosen activity. The pictures and explanations can be posted for a nice display.
- Help children to realize the time it takes to improve on a skill by either inviting people (e.g., parents, local athletes, and so on) in to discuss with students their journey toward improving their skills, or offer students a variety of books to read that highlight a similar theme. Your media specialist may be able to suggest a number of children's books that address this theme.

GRADES 1 TO 2

Sample Performance Indicators

By the end of grade 2, students should be able to

- work cooperatively with a partner in movement activities;
- use equipment safely in movement situations; and
- follow rules identified for safe participation in physical education class.

NASPE Performance Indicators

- Recognizes appropriate safety practices in general space by throwing balls only when others are not in direct line of the throw. (K–2, #2, 13)

- Explains that appropriate practice improves performance. (K–2, #2, 18)
- Follows directions given to the class for an all-class activity. (K–2, #5, 32)
- Handles equipment safely by putting it away when not in use. (K–2, #5, 34)
- Uses equipment and space safely and properly. (K–2, #5, 35)
- Works in a diverse group setting without interfering with others. (K–2, #5, 37)
- Assists a partner by sharing observations about skill performance during practice. (K–2, #5, 39)

- Accepts all playmates without regard to personal differences (e.g., ethnicity, gender, disability). (K–2, #5, 41)
- During class closure, identifies sharing with a partner as a way to cooperate. (K–2, #5, 42)
- Willingly tries new movements and skills. (K–2, #6, 46)
- Continues to participate when not successful on the first try. (K–2, #6, 47)

Sample Portfolio Task

Give students a portfolio sheet that asks them to circle the proper footwear for physical education class (see figure 7.1).

RUBRIC CLUES

To what extent do students

- identify the shoes appropriate for physical education?

Emphasize	Ideas for Lesson Development

Rules for safety
Rules allow everyone to be safe and have fun in physical education.

- Discuss why rules are important in physical education; ask students for input about what they think are important rules to have for class. Relate their suggestions to rules you have in mind. If they haven't thought of a specific rule, give a common scenario and ask for a rule that might be of help in this instance.

- Set up situations that allow students to practice rules. When needed, bring students together and discuss their adherence (or breaking) of the rules. Take a few minutes to discuss why the rules are or aren't working and ask for suggestions on how to improve this.

- Establish stations, and instead of using a signal, use music. When the music stops, have students stop and point to the next station they will be moving to (this gives you a quick comprehension check); when the music begins, they move to the next station.

- Set up a method for equipment care. This idea is especially effective when students are outdoors and have a good distance to the activity area. Once students know the protocol for properly choosing equipment, allow each of them to run to the equipment and (safely) take a piece, then move to a self-space and begin to manipulate the object until you get there and give the signal to stop. As they don't all run at the same speed, this method helps keep them from arriving simultaneously at the equipment, gives them a good warm-up, allows you to walk and talk with students on the way, and is a great way to involve the students in an instant activity.

- Have students line up in two lines (boys and girls, for example). This can cut down on pushing and shoving. Two lines can easily move through the hallways as well. Challenge each line to see if it can do a better job of lining up than the other!

- Pick a student to walk backward in front of the line as the "line conductor." This child can use only hand signals to direct other students in line to move over, stop, or turn. (First graders may not be ready for this at the beginning of the year.) Don't select the first student in line; this helps to cut down on students who rush to head the line. Perhaps choose someone who did especially well that day or showed good cooperation; this offers the chance to reward even "problem" students for good work. Plus, students love to be in charge.

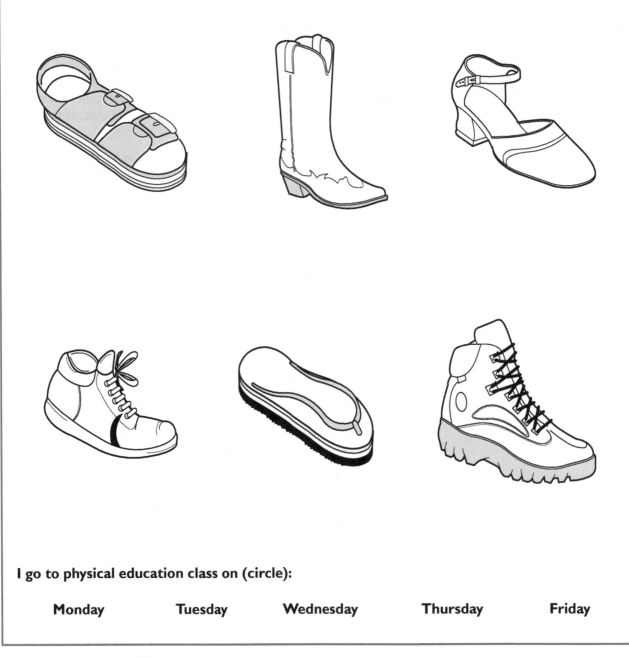

Name _____ **Class** _____

My Best Foot Forward in Physical Education

Circle the shoes that are safe for you to wear in physical education class. Put an **X** on those that are *not* safe to wear.

I go to physical education class on (circle):

| Monday | Tuesday | Wednesday | Thursday | Friday |

Figure 7.1   Portfolio task assessment sheet for safety, grades 1 to 2.

From *Elementary Physical Education Teaching & Assessment: A Practical Guide,* by Christine J. Hopple, 2005, Champaign, IL: Human Kinetics.

- Allow students to run to a selected spot if they have to go quite a distance before they line up, at which point they must walk to get into line. This also helps alleviate some problems of running to be the first in line. Stress—and expect—students to walk to get in line once they pass the designated point.

PEC: *Risk Factor Charades*

Rules for safety
It is important to wear proper footwear in physical education.

- Bring a variety of footwear to class (e.g., sandals, dress shoes, boots, and the like). Ask students to guess which type is most appropriate for physical education. Discuss why.

- Ask for donations of gently used sneakers (in your school newsletter or similar publication). Keep these in a box for use by students who forget their sneakers. After class, shoes can be sprayed with disinfectant, if desired.

- Speak to the school guidance counselor if you suspect that a student doesn't own proper shoes; many times the school can help in a situation such as this.

- Send home the assignment after students complete the portfolio task (figure 7.1). Encourage students to display it on their refrigerators to remind them of the days that they have physical education.

Cooperating with others
Cooperating involves working together and helping others.

- Ask students to discuss helpful behaviors for participating in physical education (e.g., sharing, cooperating, following the rules, taking turns). Ask them to talk about behaviors that hurt others, such as pushing in line, making others feel bad about their abilities, saying no if a person asks you to be a partner, and name-calling. Discuss how both helpful and hurtful behaviors make others feel, and how to respond or take appropriate action (by saying thank you; ignoring the person; telling the teacher if necessary).

- Promote helpful behaviors by giving positive feedback to students who demonstrate them, just as you would when they show proper psychomotor skills.

PEC: *Monsters, Inc.*
Scootermania
Purcell Cone and Cone: *Neighborhood Friendship Streamer Dance*

Respecting others
Respect involves communicating with others in a positive manner, being considerate, and listening to what teachers and others have to say

- Foster cooperative behaviors between students. First, you must put them in situations that require cooperation. Early in the school year, take a day to talk about and practice cooperation to set the tone for what you expect of your students. Working with a parachute is a good example of a fun, cooperative activity that students enjoy.

- Give students positive feedback whenever they show cooperative behaviors, especially those who tend to be difficult. When you give feedback, don't overdo it, and always be sincere.

Improving your skills
Everyone has to practice to get better at a skill.

- Ask students to draw a picture of themselves playing at an activity or skill in which they would like to get better. Question them on what it takes to get better (practice). Discuss with them how playing after school, at recess, and the like are different ways to improve on a skill, and how much time this will take. (A good way to "frame" it is to point out that instead of watching a show on television, one could go outside and play for that amount of time.)

- Discuss with students how physical education class can also help them to improve on their skills. Organized sports and playing with parents and friends are additional ways to get better at something.

- Discuss how people (no matter what their age is) rarely do something "just right" the first time they try something new. If something is difficult at first, keep practicing.

KINDERGARTEN

Sample Performance Indicators

By the end of grade K, students should be able to
- follow rules identified for safe participation in physical education class.

NASPE Performance Indicators

- Follows directions given to the class for an all-class activity. (K–2, #5, 32)
- Uses equipment and space safely and properly. (K–2, #5, 35)
- Invites a peer to take his or her turn at a piece of apparatus before repeating a turn. (K–2, #5, 38)
- Displays consideration of others while participating on the playground. (K–2, #5, 43)

Emphasize

Rules for safety
There are important rules you need to remember in physical education.

Ideas for Lesson Development

- Establish a "quiet" signal. Have students talk as much as they want; see how quickly they stop when you give the signal (e.g., a drum or tambourine beat, your raised hand).

- Establish a "stop" signal. Determine how quickly students can stop moving their bodies or body parts in their self-space at the signal.

- Teach that one signal means "go" and two signals mean "stop." Have the students move throughout general space and stop at the signal; "trick" them by pretending to give a signal or giving two to go instead of one.

- Introduce your special "safety alert" signal for use in emergencies. Have students practice responding to it when they are working with equipment or playing on the playground. Bring them back in and discuss how they did; practice responding to the signal if needed. Occasionally revisit this throughout the school year, making sure the students know it is a practice run, not a real one.

- Explain "self-space" by having the students pretend that there is a bubble around each of them (their self-space), and that they must stay in their own bubble while they line up, not breaking anyone else's bubble.

- Take care of equipment by setting up stations with various pieces of equipment. Have students practice putting the pieces away correctly at your signal.

- Stagger the timing when students put away equipment. Create categories (such as all those who have on jeans, blue clothing, high-top tennis shoes, and so forth) and have students put their equipment away when their category is called. Try tricking boys by calling out "girls with shorts on," "boys with shorts on," "girls with dresses on," then "boys with dresses on."

It is important to wear proper footwear in physical education.

- Bring a variety of footwear to class (e.g., sandals, dress shoes, boots, and the like). Ask students to guess which type is most appropriate for physical education class. Discuss why.

- Ask for donations of gently used sneakers (in your school newsletter or similar publication). Keep these in a box for use by students who forget their sneakers. After class, shoes can be sprayed with disinfectant, if desired.

- Speak to the school guidance counselor if you suspect that a student doesn't own proper shoes; many times the school can help in a situation such as this.

Cooperating with others
Cooperating involves working together and helping others.

- Discuss the concept of cooperation; use activities, such as a parachute, to help demonstrate how everyone must work together.

PEC: *Monsters, Inc.*
Purcell Cone and Cone: *Neighborhood Friendship Streamer Dance*

Movement Concepts

By the end of elementary school, students should be able to

- design, refine, and perform dance and gymnastics sequences, either with or without partners, that focus on the use of body shapes and body movements.

Body Awareness

Concepts and Skills	Learnable Pieces
Body parts	
	Arms (K, 1–2)
	Head (K, 1–2)
	Legs (K, 1–2)
	Elbows (K, 1–2)
	Knees (K, 1–2)
	Others (K, 1–2)
Body shapes	
Angular	Make your body bend or point. (K, 1–2)
Curved	Be round like a tire. (K, 1–2)
Twisted	Turn part of your body one way and part of it another way. (K, 1–2)
Narrow	Stretch so you're long and skinny! (K, 1–2)
Wide	Stretch arms and legs out to the sides! (K, 1–2)
Symmetrical	If you cut your body in two, each side would look the same. (1–2, 3–4)
Asymmetrical	If you cut your body in two, each side would look different. (1–2, 3–4)
Body movements	
Swing	Make big, free movements with your body parts. (K, 1–2)
Sway	Make small movements side to side or front to back. (K, 1–2)
Twist	Move part of your body one way, and move part another way. (K, 1–2)
Turn	Spin like a top! (K, 1–2)
Bend and Curl	Close up your body. (K, 1–2)
Stretch	Stretch your body parts away from your middle. (K, 1–2)

Concepts and Skills	Learnable Pieces
Body movements	
Shake	You're shivering! (K, 1–2)
Rise	Move away from the ground. (1–2)
Sink	Move slowly toward the ground. (1–2)
Push	Move it [object] away from you. (1–2)
Pull	Move it [object] toward you. (1–2)

GRADES 5 TO 6

Sample Performance Indicators

By the end of grade 6, students should be able to

- design, refine, and perform dance or gymnastics sequences in a small group that focus on using different body shapes and body movements.

NASPE Performance Indicators

- Develops and refines a gymnastics sequence (or creative dance sequence) demonstrating smooth transitions. (3–5, #1, 7)
- Works productively with a partner to improve performance of a dance sequence by following a detailed diagram of the process. (3–5, #5, 37)

Sample Performance Task

Ask students to design, refine, and perform a movement sequence with two or three other students. The sequence must last at least 48 counts of music with a 4/4 meter, have a definite beginning and ending, and be performed with props, if desired. The students may choose the music, with approval by the teacher. When performing the sequence, students are asked to demonstrate at least three different body movements and three different locomotor movements, while matching their partners' movements.

RUBRIC CLUES

To what extent do students

- demonstrate the required number of body and locomotor movements in the sequence?
- demonstrate a definite beginning and ending?
- design the sequence so it lasts for the minimum number of counts?

- smoothly perform (with a minimum of breaks in timing) the sequence to the beat of the music and with the partners?

Sample Portfolio Task

Give students an assessment sheet (see figure 8.1) pertaining to the performance task mentioned previously. Each group will evaluate one other group's routine using the given criteria (e.g., circle which movements are used). Each group member looks for one criterion in the demonstrated sequence (write down in the space who looks at what). After the performance, students collectively decide if the dancing group they watched has met the given criteria by answering the first four questions at the bottom of the sheet. Each person then answers the last question on his or her own. The group then meets with the group they watched and explains what they thought and why. When done, the teacher looks at each person's evaluation sheet to see if the group he or she watched was correctly evaluated.

RUBRIC CLUES

To what extent do students

- correctly evaluate the other group's routine, according to the criterion each is assigned?
- give a sound rationale for the overall rating of the other group's performance?

BODY AWARENESS

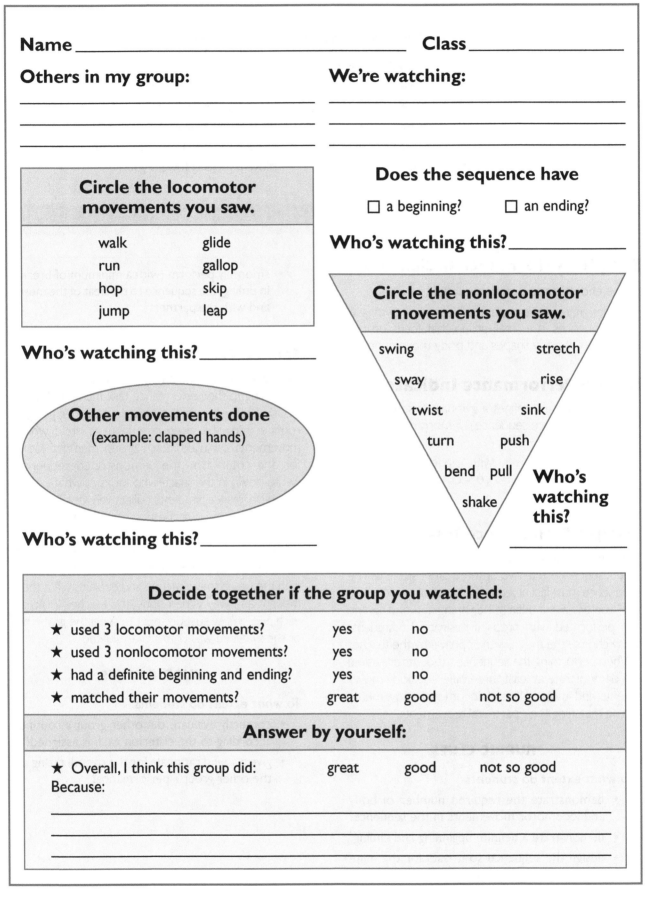

Name _____ **Class** _____

Others in my group:

_____

_____

_____

We're watching:

_____

_____

_____

Circle the locomotor movements you saw.

walk	glide
run	gallop
hop	skip
jump	leap

Who's watching this? _____

Other movements done
(example: clapped hands)

Who's watching this? _____

Does the sequence have

☐ a beginning?   ☐ an ending?

Who's watching this? _____

Circle the nonlocomotor movements you saw.

swing   stretch

sway   rise

twist   sink

turn   push

bend   pull

shake

Who's watching this?

_____

Decide together if the group you watched:			
★ used 3 locomotor movements?	yes	no	
★ used 3 nonlocomotor movements?	yes	no	
★ had a definite beginning and ending?	yes	no	
★ matched their movements?	great	good	not so good

Answer by yourself:			
★ Overall, I think this group did:	great	good	not so good

Because:

_____

_____

_____

Figure 8.1 Sample body awareness assessment sheet, grades 5 to 6.

From *Elementary Physical Education Teaching & Assessment: A Practical Guide,* by Christine J. Hopple, 2005, Champaign, IL: Human Kinetics.

Emphasize	*Ideas for Lesson Development*
The use of specific body shapes and body movements as they pertain to the contexts of games and, especially, dance and gymnastics activities	• Have students design and refine a sequence with two to four other students, using at least two different kinds of body shapes, body movements, and weight transfers. The sequence may include any equipment and music selected by the students. After giving the criteria for the sequence, help students in the process of choosing shapes, movements, and equipment. The sequence should be written down.

• Allow students to use such props as scarves, sheets, and exercise stretch bands (made out of stretchy material, these can be purchased from sports equipment companies) and such equipment as balls for the design and performance of their sequences.

• For additional ideas to teach body awareness concepts, see the themes of effort and relationships later in this chapter, as well as the specific themes under nonlocomotor (chapter 10) and manipulative (chapter 11) skills.

Werner: *See What I Can Do: Partner Task Cards*
Purcell Cone and Cone: *Creative Square Dance*
Bubbles
Dance Maps
PEC: *"Da Da Da" Dynaband Routine*   *Recipe Dance/Making Duets*
Disco Dances   *Swiss Ball Square Dance*
Men in Black Line Dance   *Space Jam Dilemma/Dance*
Macarena   *The Funky Dance*
Macarena Referee Dance   *The Hamster Dance*
Raise the Roof

GRADES 3 TO 4

Sample Performance Indicators

By the end of grade 4, students should be able to

• move the body in the air using various body movements and shapes after jumping off low- or medium-level equipment;

• use different body shapes and body movements to creatively express the various qualities of effort (i.e., force, flow, speed); and

• design, refine, and perform partner or small-group dance and gymnastics sequences that focus on using symmetrical or asymmetrical body shapes.

Sample Performance Task

Ask students to design, refine, and perform a movement sequence with a partner (with or without music or objects). The use of two different body movements, two different body shapes, and two different locomotor movements must be clearly shown in their sequences.

RUBRIC CLUES

To what extent do students

• incorporate the required number of body movements, shapes, and locomotor movements into their sequences?

BODY AWARENESS

- demonstrate a definite starting and stopping shape?
- refine the sequence so they move from one element to another smoothly and without hesitation?

Sample Portfolio Task

Ask students to write down all of the different body movements, shapes, and locomotor movements to be used in their sequence.

RUBRIC CLUES

To what extent do students
- correctly identify the body movements, shapes, and locomotor movements used in their sequence?

Emphasize	*Ideas for Lesson Development*
Body shapes *Symmetrical* If you cut your body in two, each side would look the same. *Asymmetrical* If you cut your body in two, each side would look different.	• Ask the students to balance in a symmetrical shape; then ask them to stretch, bend, or twist into an asymmetrical shape. • Have students use symmetrical shapes in order to move onto and jump off equipment (boxes, benches, and so on). Then mix up the shapes so students move onto equipment with an asymmetrical shape and off equipment with a symmetrical shape. • Have students, with a partner, pick a symmetrical and asymmetrical shape. Each pair must use these shapes to begin and end a sequence; their sequences must also include two locomotor movements and two body movements. They can decide in what order to arrange these movements and what equipment (if any) to use (gymnastics equipment, ropes, scarves, and the like) for dance props. Sequences should be written down and practiced until they can be performed from memory. • Stretch or twist, or bend into a roll. • See the theme of nonlocomotor skills (in chapter 10) for additional ideas.

Werner: *Ready for Takeoff*
        Same, Different
        Taking a Spin
Purcell Cone and Cone: *Dancing Homework Machine*
Buschner: *Twisting, Spinning, and Throwing*
PEC: *Body Shapes With Stretch Ropes*

Emphasize	*Ideas for Lesson Development*
Body movements The use of specific body movements as they pertain to the contexts of dance and gymnastics activities.	• Make up a number of sets of "movement cards" by writing the various body movements on large index cards, tag board, or the like. If desired, additional movements involving only the hands, arms, or head (e.g., snapping fingers, clapping hands, bobbing the head) can be made from a different color card or paper. In groups of three or four, have students choose four cards; they must then use only these movements to develop a movement sequence to music with a strong 4/4 beat. If desired, additional sets of colored cards can be made for locomotor movements, body shapes, and so on, and added for inclusion in the sequence.

> **PEC:** *Add-On Line Dancing*
> *Simply Move with Me*
> **Purcell Cone and Cone:** *Bubbles*
> *Dance Maps*

GRADES 1 TO 2

Sample Performance Indicators

By the end of grade 2, students should be able to

- use different body parts required by different challenges, alone and with a partner;
- mirror the symmetrical or asymmetrical shape of a partner;
- use a variety of bases of support (body parts) to balance on;
- make the different body shapes with and without a partner;
- perform different body movements to a series of beats of varying tempos (i.e., fast or slow);
- make the different body shapes in the air when jumping off the ground or low-level equipment; and
- design and perform simple sequences that focus on body shapes or body movements.

NASPE Performance Indicators

- Discovers how to balance on different body parts, at different levels, becoming "like" a statue while making symmetrical and nonsymmetrical shapes. (K–2, #1, 9)

Sample Performance Task

Call out each of the different body shapes; ask students to demonstrate and hold each shape until the next shape is called out.

RUBRIC CLUES

To what extent do students

- show a correct demonstration of each shape?

Sample Portfolio Task

Ask students to complete figure 8.2 to demonstrate their knowledge of body shapes one can make.

RUBRIC CLUES

To what extent do students

- correctly match the shape (word) with the picture?

BODY AWARENESS

Name _____ **Class** _____

Match the picture of the body shape on the left to the word on the right by drawing a line from the picture to the word.

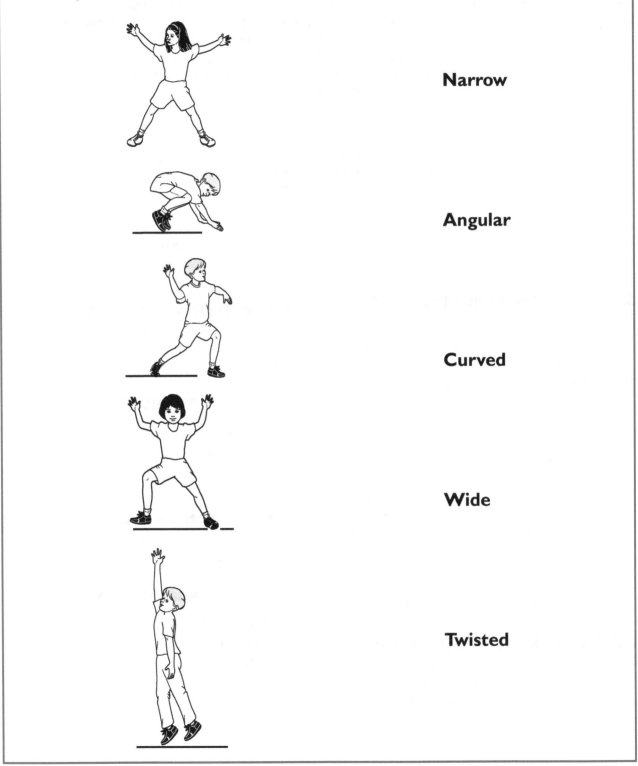

Narrow

Angular

Curved

Wide

Twisted

Figure 8.2   Portfolio task assessment sheet for body awareness, grades 1 to 2.

From *Elementary Physical Education Teaching & Assessment: A Practical Guide,* by Christine J. Hopple, 2005, Champaign, IL: Human Kinetics.

Emphasize	*Ideas for Lesson Development*
Body parts Arms, head, legs, elbows, knees, others	• Have children travel by putting specific body parts on their carpet squares or in their hoops at the signal. • Ask students to balance on specific body parts or on a specific number of bases of support (e.g., three bases, five bases). • Assign travel using specific body parts (two hands and two feet; one hand and one foot; behind and hands). • Make a large cube showing a different body part on each side; have children roll the cube to show the body part they must balance on, touch to a partner, and so forth.

Werner: *Patches and Points*
PEC: *Body Toss*
  Fun With Balloons
  Hula Hoop Twister

Body shapes *Angular* Make your body bend or point. *Curved* Be round like a tire. *Twisted* Turn part of your body one way and part of it another way. *Narrow* Stretch so you're long and skinny! *Wide* Stretch arms and legs out to the sides! *Symmetrical* If you cut your body in two, each side would look the same. *Asymmetrical* If you cut your body in two, each side would look different.	• Students travel and then freeze in a specified shape at your signal. They also can travel to music: Stop the music at intervals, and have the students make shapes to interpret the music. Don't ask them to hold the shape too long; vary how long the music plays. • A partner "molds" the other child into a symmetrical or asymmetrical shape ("Look around you. What do you see that is symmetrical?"). • Students use a jump rope to make the shape of a symmetrical or asymmetrical letter or number; then they shape their bodies into the same letter or number (show letters and numbers on a poster or chalkboard). • Children make a specified shape while they somehow touch a hula hoop with some part of the body. Let them make a shape with a partner while they touch a hoop between them. • Students move over, through, and around a hoop using different shapes. • Students jump off the ground, a box, or tire while they make a specified shape. • Teach that a sequence always starts and ends with a shape. "Make a sequence where you start with a shape, travel, and then end in a different shape." Afterward, ask which shapes the students used. • Relate the different shapes to ones made by athletes in sports. Discuss how a batter in baseball makes a twisted shape, a diver curls up and makes a curved shape, a football wide receiver jumps and makes a stretched shape to catch the ball, and a basketball player uses a wide shape to block a passed ball.

Purcell Cone and Cone: *Neighborhood Friendship Streamer Dance*
  Spaghetti Dance
  Floating Clouds and Rain Showers
Buschner: *Movement Shapes*

BODY AWARENESS

Body movements

Swing
Make big, free movements with your body parts.
Sway
Make small movements side to side or front to back.
Twist
Move part of your body one way, and move part another way.
Turn
Spin like a top!
Bend and Curl
Close up your body.
Stretch
Stretch your body parts away from your middle.
Shake
You're shivering!
Rise
Move away from the ground.
Sink
Move slowly toward the ground.
Push
Move it [object] away from you.
Pull
Move it [object] toward you.

- Perform different body movements to a series of beats in varying tempos (e.g., fast, slow).

- One or two students use different instruments (commercial or home-made) to make a rhythm, while other students use body movements to match the rhythm and sounds. Let all the students get the chance to make a rhythm with the instruments. For example, students shake to maracas, march to the drumbeat, and tiptoe to a triangle.

- Ask the students to make a sequence, starting with a body shape for eight counts, moving by any locomotor movement for eight counts, performing one or more body movements for eight counts (e.g., sink and rise), traveling for eight more counts, and finishing with a different body shape for eight counts. Mark the beat and count out loud for them (i.e., "Make a shape, two, three . . . eight; travel, two, three . . . eight; movement, two, three . . . eight; travel, two, three . . . eight; ending shape, two, three . . . eight.").

Werner: *Sit-Spins*
Purcell Cone and Cone: *The Playground Circus Dance*
PEC: *Monster Mash Dance*
Pata Pata Pat Pat
"This Land Is Your Land" Shaker Routine

KINDERGARTEN

Sample Performance Indicators

By the end of grade K, students should be able to
- make the different body shapes;
- travel while moving in a variety of body shapes;
- use different combinations of body parts to balance on and travel with; and
- move using various body movements.

NASPE Performance Indicators

- Identifies correctly various body parts (e.g., knee, foot, arm, palm). (K–2, #2, 11)

Sample Performance Task

Ask students to put the body part (hands, feet, knees, behind, back, head, shoulder) you call out on their carpet squares.

RUBRIC CLUES

To what extent do students
- put the correct body part on the carpet square?

Emphasize	*Ideas for Lesson Development*
Body parts Arms, head, legs, elbows, knees, others	• Have children strike balloons using specific body parts. • Give them soap bubbles to blow (outside!), then have them break them using specific body parts. • Tell the students to shake (stretch, twist, and so on) specific body parts to a drum signal or other music (alternate fast and slow speeds). • Have students find a partner and touch the same specific body part (e.g., elbow to elbow, knee to knee, back to back) at your signal. **Werner:** *Bunny Hop* *Patches and Points* **Buschner:** *Anatomy*
Body shapes *Angular* Make your body bend or point. *Curved* Be round like a tire. *Twisted* Turn part of your body one way and part of it another way. *Narrow* Stretch so you're long and skinny! *Wide* Stretch arms and legs out to the sides!	• Have youngsters quickly change to the shape that you call out. • Students find a partner, and make the same (mirror) shape at the signal. • Place different objects (e.g., apple, stapler, rubber band, banana, balloon, piece of paper) in a bag. Take one out at a time, asking the students to shape themselves like that object. Move the object (blow up the balloon, stretch the rubber band, and so on) and have them move just like it, imitating its shape. **PEC:** *My Snake* **Purcell Cone and Cone:** *Circus Dance*
Body movements *Swing* Make big, free movements with your body parts. *Sway* Make small movements side to side or front to back. *Twist* Move part of your body one way, and move part another way. *Turn* Spin like a top! *Bend and Curl* Close up your body. *Stretch* Stretch your body parts away from your middle. *Shake* You're shivering!	• The students travel using a specified locomotor movement to a popular song; at the chorus, they stop and move the body using a movement you specify, with a partner, and then they continue traveling when the chorus ends. • The children shake their bodies while moving from a high to a low level; when you give a loud signal, they rise quickly, like a jack-in-the box!

BODY AWARENESS

Sample Course Standard

By the end of elementary school, students should be able to

- design, refine, and perform dance and gymnastics sequences that focus on the use of one or more of the directions, levels, pathways, extensions, and space concepts.

Space Awareness

Concepts and Skills	Learnable Pieces
Self-, or personal, space	Space right next to you, out of reach of anyone or anything. (K, 1–2)
General space	Empty or open space all around you. (K, 1–2)
Offense	Keep your body between the ball and the defender. (3–4, 5–6)
	Create space by moving to open areas to pass or receive the ball. (5–6)
	Hit the ball to places where opponents aren't standing. (5–6)
Defense	Deny space by staying between the opponent and intended goal. (5–6)
	Be ready to move. (5–6)
	Partners equally cover the area. (5–6)
Directions	
Forward	Your front leads. (K, 1–2)
Backward	Your back leads. (K, 1–2)
Sideways	Your side (right or left) leads. (K, 1–2)
Up	Toward the sky. (K, 1–2)
Down	Toward the ground. (K, 1–2)
Pathways	
Curved	Rounded like a rainbow. (K, 1–2)
Straight	Like a line or pencil. (K, 1–2)
Zigzag	Straight lines connected to make sharp points. (K, 1–2)
Levels	
Low	Below your knees. (K, 1–2)
Medium	Between your shoulders and knees. (K, 1–2)
High	Above your shoulders. (K, 1–2)
Extensions	
Near	When your body parts are close to your body. (1–2)
Far	When your body parts are far from your body. (1–2)

GRADES 5 TO 6

Sample Performance Indicators

By the end of grade 6, students should be able to

- purposefully use pathways, levels, directions, and extensions to change the continuity or flow and add variety to a gymnastics or dance sequence; and

- purposefully use general space to create or deny space when developing or using game strategies in a small-group situation.

NASPE Performance Indicators

- Designs a new game incorporating at least two motor skills, rules, and strategies. (3–5, #2, 17)

Sample Performance Task

In groups of three, students create two different running or passing plays in football, incorporating all three of the pathways (straight, curved, and zigzag). Each play should be drawn on paper and practiced, using a football or other preferred object. After each student is familiar with each play, the groups can rotate the passer, receiver, and defender positions.

RUBRIC CLUES

To what extent do students

- use all three pathways?
- run each play correctly so that the pathway they use can be clearly identified?

Sample Portfolio Task

Have students watch an athletic performance on TV, attend a game, or watch a tape of one at school. Have them write down the space awareness concepts athletes used during their performances. What did the athletes do at a high, medium, or low level? What kinds of pathways did they use? Directions? What kind of space did they move in? Have them give examples of how athletes use these concepts.

RUBRIC CLUES

To what extent do students

- show a clear understanding of the different space awareness concepts in their use of examples?

Emphasize	Ideas for Lesson Development
General space *Offense* Create space by moving to open areas to pass or receive the ball. Keep your body between the ball and the defender. *Defense* Deny space by staying between the opponent and intended goal.	• Ask students to compare how space is created or denied in invasion, net, and fielding games. Why is space created or denied? How do team members do this? • See manipulative skills themes (in chapter 11) for further ideas on the use of space in the context of games play. **Belka:** *Advance and Score Soccer* *Advance and Score Basketball*

General space
Offense
Hit the ball to places where opponents aren't standing.
Defense
Be ready to move.
Partners equally cover the area.

Directions, levels, and pathways—as they pertain to movement sequences and game situations

- Discuss with students how, in certain net and volley games (e.g., volleyball, tennis), the objective is to hit the ball where one's partners are not, rather than to where they are. Also, discuss the defensive strategies of being ready to move at all times and covering the area between partners.

- See volleying in the theme of manipulative skills (chapter 11) for further ideas on the use of space in the context of games play.

- Have students form small groups to design, set up, and move through an obstacle course. They can choose what to use from equipment selected or approved by the teacher. The course must incorporate the body moving in at least two different directions, levels, and pathways. When they have completed the course themselves, have students teach it to a group of younger students or to a different group in their class.

- Using the "Passing Patterns" assessment sheet (see figure 8.3), have students work in groups of two or three to develop and practice their own pathway design. If they are working in pairs, one student can be the "thrower" while the other is the "runner"; if they are working in groups of three, you could have one "hiker," one "thrower," and one "runner." Each student should receive the opportunity to practice each role. This activity can later be expanded to help students work on the concepts of offense and defense.

PEC: *The "Hora"–And More*
Purcell Cone and Cone: *Baseball Dance*
Sport Dance
Dance Maps
Action Words

Name _____ **Class** _____

Passing Patterns

The following are examples of pass patterns in football. Keeping in mind the three types of pathways (straight, curved, and zigzag), create your own pathway design and name.

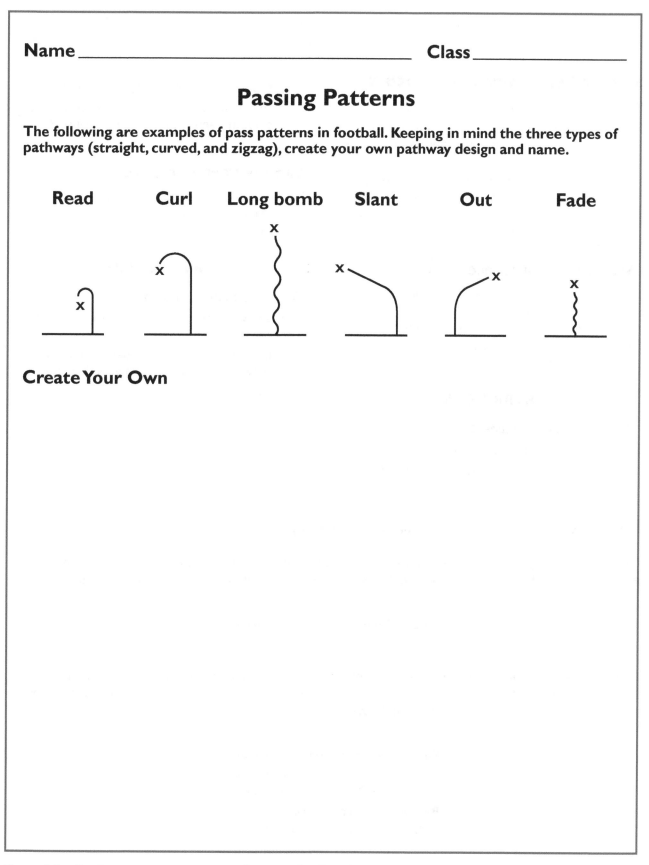

Create Your Own

Figure 8.3   Passing patterns assessment sheet, grades 5 to 6.

Courtesy of Lisa Katilus.

From *Elementary Physical Education Teaching & Assessment: A Practical Guide*, by Christine J. Hopple, 2005, Champaign, IL: Human Kinetics.

GRADES 3 TO 4

Sample Performance Indicators

By the end of grade 4, students should be able to

- change directions and pathways as they move through general space, in order to not collide with others; and
- define, refine, and perform dance and gymnastics sequences that focus on changes in direction, levels, pathways, and extensions (using one or a combination of two at a time).

Sample Performance Task

Students design, refine, and perform a dance or gymnastics sequence with a partner that uses movements in at least two different directions and at two different levels. The sequence must have a definite beginning and ending shape.

RUBRIC CLUES

To what extent do students

- use the required number of levels?
- use the required number of directions?

- show a definite beginning and ending?
- refine the sequence so it can be repeated smoothly and without memory lapses?

Sample Portfolio Task

Ask students to briefly describe and draw how a participant in one activity or sport would use one or more of the different pathways.

RUBRIC CLUES

To what extent do students

- show a clear understanding of the different pathways?
- make a clear connection between the activity they choose and the pathways they use?

Emphasize	Ideas for Lesson Development
Pathways—in the contexts of gymnastics and dance	• Using the floor and their mats, students create an interesting sequence with different pathways. They write it down and teach it to a partner.
	Purcell Cone and Cone: *Dance Maps*
Directions—in the contexts of gymnastics and dance	• Using an appropriate piece of gymnastics equipment (small or large), students find a way to move up to it, on to it, and off it, using the directions of up and down.
	Purcell Cone and Cone: *Action Words* *Baseball Dance* *Dance Maps* **Buschner:** *Directional Gymnastics* **PEC:** *The Old Brass Wagon Hoop Dance*

General space
Offense
Keep your body between the ball and the defender.

- See more "Ideas for Lesson Development" in the themes of chasing, fleeing, and dodging (in chapter 9).

GRADES 1 TO 2

Sample Performance Indicators

By the end of grade 2, students should be able to

- find a self-space in a marked-off area without any prompting;
- purposefully keep out of others' self-space as they travel with or without an object, by changing pathways and using all of the given general space;
- stop and start traveling at a given signal, showing the ability to safely stop in their own self-space;
- travel and change from one direction to another at the signal;
- move a variety of body parts and objects into different levels;
- manipulate different objects through different levels;
- travel and change from one pathway to another at the signal;
- design and perform simple sequences that focus on changes in direction, levels, pathways, and shapes (using one at a time); and
- travel in different ways while using large and small extensions.

NASPE Performance Indicators

- Travels forward and sideways, changing directions quickly in response to a signal or obstacle using a variety of locomotor skills. (K–2, #1, 4)
- Identifies correctly body planes (i.e., front, back, side). (K–2, #2, 10)

Sample Performance Task

Provide music, and ask students to move to it throughout a large marked-off area while they use a variety of locomotor and nonlocomotor movements as you call them out, and avoid bumping into others or leaving the boundaries.

RUBRIC CLUES

To what extent do students

- keep a self-space as they move throughout the area?
- not follow others' pathways as they move through general space?
- move to the open areas and throughout the whole area, not only in a circular fashion?

Sample Portfolio Task

Give students a copy of figure 8.4. Ask them to color the part of the child's body that is at a low level in a red crayon, the part of the body that is at a medium level in blue crayon, and that part of the body that is at a high level in green crayon. (If desired, any of the additional assessment sheets that follow for grades 1 and 2 could be substituted for this specific assessment sheet; the remaining sheets can be used as homework or in class.)

RUBRIC CLUES

To what extent do students

- correctly identify, through coloring, the different levels?

Name _____ Class _____

What's Your Level?

What part of the body is at a low level? Color it red.
What part of the body is at a medium level? Color it blue.
What part of the body is at a high level? Color it green.

Figure 8.4   Portfolio task assessment sheet for space awareness, grades 1 to 2.

From *Elementary Physical Education Teaching & Assessment: A Practical Guide,* by Christine J. Hopple, 2005, Champaign, IL: Human Kinetics.

Emphasize	*Ideas for Lesson Development*

Self-space
Space right next to you, out of reach of anyone or anything.
General space
Empty or open space all around you.

- Have students move through general space. Little by little, move in the boundaries of the area; when students are crowded, move them back out. Discuss what happened. Which was easier, to move in or to move out? Make three different boundaries—one large, one medium, one small—and have children play with a ball in each of them. Which was easier? Harder? Why?

- Trees in the Forest: Six to eight students each have a hoop inside the boundaries. Other youngsters travel with a specified movement; they try to get as close as possible to the self-space of the "trees" without being touched. Trees try to reach as far as possible, although one foot (root!) must stay inside the hoop at all times. When students get caught, they trade places with the trees. Discuss the limits to self-space and the difference between self-space and general space.

- Give students figure 8.5; have them demonstrate their understanding of self- and general space by marking in the appropriate information.

> **Buschner:** *Staying at Home*
> *Painting Movement Pictures*
> **PEC:** *Cross Over*   *On The Move*
> *Far Away*   *Snake Scramble*
> *Locomotor Hello's*   *Spaceship Tag*

Directions
Forward
Your front leads.
Backward
Your back leads.
Sideways
Your side (right or left) leads.
Up
Toward the sky.
Down
Toward the ground.

- Give a signal for students to move in a different, specified direction (you may also want to specify the locomotor movement).

- Use one large, or a few small, parachutes, and have the students move in different directions to counts of eight (forward eight, backward eight, sideways eight, down eight, up eight). Call out the beats to a drum or other music. (Just for fun, have students move the parachute up and down together to try to get a beanbag through the hole in the middle of the parachute.)

> **PEC:** *Directions Boogie*
> *Magic Ball*
> *The Chicken Dance*
> *The Rainbow Game*
> **Purcell Cone and Cone:** *The Playground*

Name _____ **Class** _____

Today we learned about space awareness. In the space provided below, draw 5 Xs with a lot of self-space. Try to use all the space provided in the box.

Below there are students playing, but they are too close together! Use arrows to show how you would spread them out so that they will be using all the general space in the gym.

What could happen if the students stay close together?

_____

_____

Figure 8.5 Portfolio task assessment sheet for general and self-space, grades 1 to 2.

Reprinted, by permission, from Cory Pike.

From *Elementary Physical Education Teaching & Assessment: A Practical Guide,* by Christine J. Hopple, 2005, Champaign, IL: Human Kinetics.

Pathways
Curved
Rounded like a rainbow.
Straight
Like a line or pencil.
Zigzag
Straight lines connected to make sharp points.

- Use a chalking machine for lining football and softball fields (if available) to make large pathways on the grass.

- Give students assessment sheets (figures 8.6 or 8.7); for homework or as additional assessment options have them draw straight, curved, and zigzag pathways as described.

- Hand out 5- × 8-inch or 8.5- × 11-inch cards with pathway maps marked on them. After making the pathway, students trade maps with another student.

- Treasure Hunt: Use different pathways to connect about six stations. Draw these pathways on the chalkboard, a poster board, or directly onto the floor. Ask the students to do something at each station with an object or to enhance fitness. When it is time to change stations, they must follow a partner to the next station, properly following the given pathway.

- Students use chalk to draw a (straight) pathway on the blacktop. They then use other pathways to connect it to another person's pathway and move on the whole pathway. Ask them what kind of pathway they are using— while they are moving—to check their understanding.

- Write letters and numbers on the board. Students copy a letter or number that uses a specific pathway you call out by manipulating a jump rope (beaded ones work best for this). Have two or three students work together to "write" a three-letter word made up of straight, curved, and zigzag pathways.

- Have students draw out a pattern using two or all three of the pathways. Have them draw this pattern on the blacktop, and then move on it.

- See if students can dribble a ball or move a Wiffle ball with a hockey stick along different pathways.

Purcell Cone and Cone: *Spaghetti Dance*
Buschner: *Trails and Roads*
PEC: *Scooter Pathways*
          Skiing Pathways

Levels
Low
Below your knees.
Medium
Between your shoulders and knees.
High
Above your shoulders.

- Have a variety of objects to manipulate at different levels: Ask students to catch a yarn ball with a scoop at a high (medium, low) level, dribble a ball at the different levels, roll a ball to a partner, and so forth. Don't tell them the level; after they have performed the action, ask which level they used, as a check for comprehension.

- Have students make up simple sequences, requiring them to use at least two different levels. The sequence should have a definite beginning and ending.

Purcell Cone and Cone: *Ocean Waves and Swimmers*
                          The Playground
                          Circus Dance

Name _____ **Class** _____

Help Shaver find his way to the mailbox by connecting the dots. Then circle the straight pathways, put an **X** through the zigzag pathways, and put a square around the curved pathways. Remember, a pathway is the trail an object takes as it travels from one place to another.

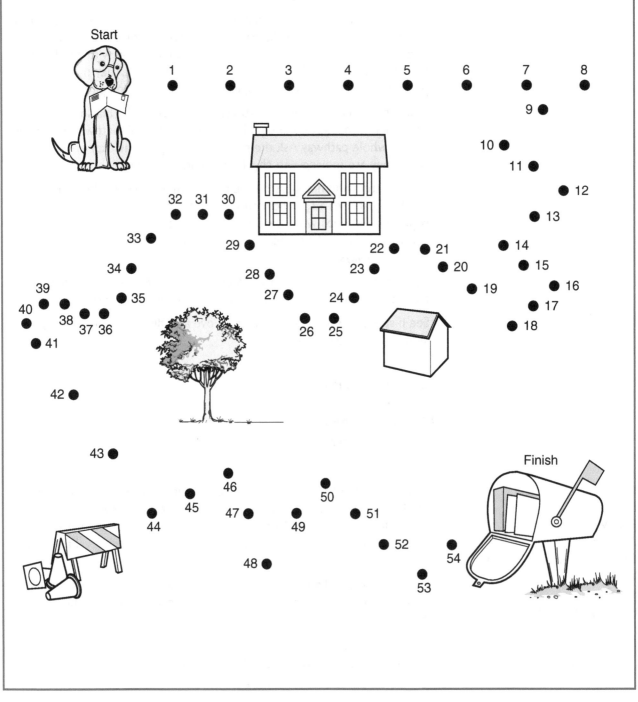

Figure 8.6 Portfolio task assessment sheet for pathways, grades 1 to 2.

Courtesy of Danielle Collier.

From *Elementary Physical Education Teaching & Assessment: A Practical Guide,* by Christine J. Hopple, 2005, Champaign, IL: Human Kinetics.

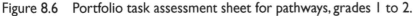

Name _____ **Class** _____

Draw a line to get Tina the Turtle to the star.

1. **Get Tina there in a curved pathway.**

2. **Get Tina there in a zigzag pathway.**

3. **Get Tina there in a straight pathway.**

Draw a pattern that shows a curved pathway in it.

Connect the dots to see how Henry gets back into his room, and write on the line what pathway he took.

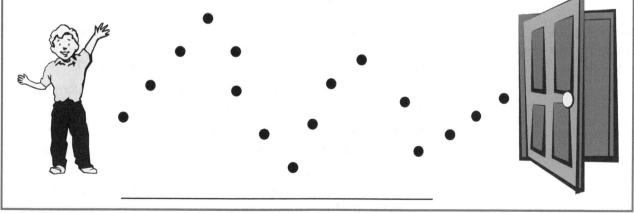

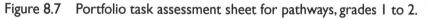

Figure 8.7   Portfolio task assessment sheet for pathways, grades 1 to 2.

From *Elementary Physical Education Teaching & Assessment: A Practical Guide,* by Christine J. Hopple, 2005, Champaign, IL: Human Kinetics.

Extensions
Near
When your body parts are close to your body.
Far
When your body parts are far from your body.

- Balloon Sequence: Blow up an imaginary or real balloon to show near and far; have body parts get farther away from the middle of the body as the balloon expands. Let the balloon go; this movement becomes the second part of the blowing-up sequence. If you wish, have students add a "run, jump, land (without noise)" sequence to imitate the balloon moving quickly before it stops.

Purcell Cone and Cone: *Balloons*

KINDERGARTEN

Sample Performance Indicators

By the end of grade K, students should be able to

- show the boundaries or limits to their self-space, when alone or when using equipment;
- find a self-space on their own in a large marked-off area, with little or no prompting;
- move away from others when traveling in general space;
- travel in general space, starting and stopping in response to a signal;
- move a variety of ways in different directions;
- put a variety of body parts and objects into different levels; and
- move on straight, curved, and zigzag pathways.

Sample Performance Task

Allow students to choose a piece of equipment (ball, streamer, beanbag, and the like) and ask them to take it to a space inside the boundaries where they can move it safely.

RUBRIC CLUES

To what extent do students

- find a self-space on their own to move to and in, out of reach of anyone or anything?

Emphasize	*Ideas for Lesson Development*
Self-space Space right next to you, out of reach of anyone or anything.	• Use hoops or carpet squares to help students define their self-space. • Have students explore the boundaries or limits to their self-space, or personal space, alone and with equipment, such as streamers and balls. Have them use all the space.
General space Empty or open space all around you.	• Students move, at a signal, to touch the boundary of their areas (you can mark the areas with a cone, or indicate to the children that they should stand on the line that "connects each cone like a dot-to-dot"). • Students stand in their hoops or squares and throw a yarn ball to the space "where nobody is" (general space). • Students travel to music using the locomotor movement you call out; they each find a carpet square or hoop (self-space) when the music stops. • Students travel to the beat of the drum and freeze when it stops. They check to see how close they are to other people. Or, play music and have students stop when the music stops (use different durations to keep up their interest).

PEC: *Mr. Tape*   *Spaghetti-O Cans*
My Backyard   *The Three Little Pigs*
Soap Bubbles

Directions
Forward
Your front leads.
Backward
Your back leads.
Sideways
Your side (right or left) leads.
Up
Toward the sky.
Down
Toward the ground.

- Students travel to music in general space in the direction you call out. (You may also call out a movement, for example, "skip forward.") Periodically call out a new direction and movement. For a "breather," have students stop and pat their heads, slap their knees, clap their hands, or do some other action to the music. For a variation, call students to get a partner and perform the movement in the specified direction.

Purcell Cone and Cone: *The Playground*

Pathways
Curved
Rounded like a rainbow.
Straight
Like a line or pencil.
Zigzag
Straight lines connected to make sharp points.

- Put gymnastics chalk on the floor and have the students walk through it, using their bare feet to make a pathway. Provide damp sponges for cleanup.

- Give students large pieces of chalk; have them draw small straight, curved, and zigzag pathways on the blacktop (after they've learned about them).

- Use chalk to make large straight, curved, and zigzag pathways on the blacktop (or have the students draw them), but now have students travel, using different locomotor movements, throughout the (marked-off) area. At the signal, call out a pathway, which they must find and move on. Encourage them to keep moving until they find a pathway that is open.

Buschner: *Trails and Roads*

Levels
Low
Below your knees.
Medium
Between your shoulders and knees.
High
Above your shoulders.

- On a large body shape posted on a bulletin board, illustrate where the different levels are.

- Have students listen for the music to stop and then put the specified body part into a particular level (e.g., behind—middle; feet—high; whole body—low).

- Have children put a hula hoop at the different levels in relation to their bodies. Challenge them to move it as you direct them (hand and neck—high; waist—medium; foot—low).

Purcell Cone and Cone: *The Playground*
                              Ocean Waves and Swimmers

SPACE AWARENESS

Sample Course Standard

Effort

By the end of elementary school, students should be able to

- design, refine, and perform dance or gymnastics sequences that vary in one or more of the effort concepts of force, flow, and speed (rhythm).

Concepts and Skills	Learnable Pieces
Speed	
Fast	Like a rabbit! (K, 1–2)
Slow	Like a turtle! (K, 1–2)
Acceleration	Speed up. (1–2, 3–4)
Deceleration	Slow down. (1–2, 3–4)
Force	
Strong	Make your muscles tight. (1–2, 3–4)
Light	Make your muscles relaxed. (1–2, 3–4)
Flow	
Bound	You can stop quickly and be very controlled. (3–4, 5–6)
Free	It is hard to stop the movement, which is very smooth and fluid. (3–4, 5–6)
	Smooth transitions. (5–6)

GRADES 5 TO 6

Sample Performance Indicators

By the end of grade 6, students should be able to

- use the qualities of force, flow, and speed to creatively express feelings, ideas, and actions of the self, others, or groups of others;
- design, refine, and perform gymnastics or dance sequences that show smooth transitions between movements that vary in elements of force, flow, and speed (rhythm); and
- manipulate objects (e.g., kick, throw) using varied amounts of force, flow, and speed appropriate to the given situation.

NASPE Performance Indicators

- Develops and refines a gymnastics sequence (or creative dance sequence) demonstrating smooth transitions. (3–5, #1, 7)
- Demonstrates correct pattern for the polka step (hop-step-together-step). (3–5, #1, 10)
- During class discussion of various dance forms, shows respect for the views of a peer from a different cultural background. (3–5, #5, 41)

Sample Performance Task

Using pedometers or a stopwatch, students should track on eight different occasions the amount of time it takes them to complete, and how many steps are included in one mile (1.6 km) (or longer distance) (see figure 8.8).

RUBRIC CLUES

To what extent do students

- complete the given task for the specified number of times?

Sample Portfolio Task

Using the data gained from the performance task mentioned previously, students should graph their time for each of the miles and answer the accompanying questions.

RUBRIC CLUES

To what extent do students

- correctly graph their times and answer the questions?

Name _____ Class _____

On eight different occasions, use your pedometer or a stopwatch to keep track of how long (and how many steps) it takes you to cover the distance of one mile (1.6 km). Use the chart below to log your information.

	Date	Time	Steps		Date	Time	Steps
1.				5.			
2.				6.			
3.				7.			
4.				8.			

Use the graph below to plot your data.

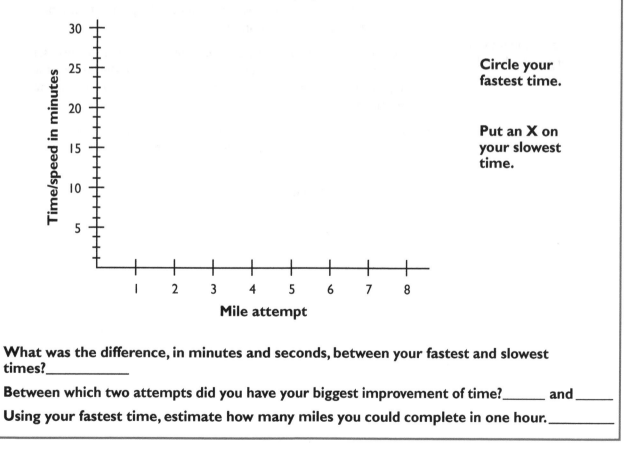

Circle your fastest time.

Put an **X** on your slowest time.

What was the difference, in minutes and seconds, between your fastest and slowest times?_____

Between which two attempts did you have your biggest improvement of time?_____ and _____

Using your fastest time, estimate how many miles you could complete in one hour._____

Figure 8.8   Portfolio task assessment sheet for effort, grades 5 to 6.

From *Elementary Physical Education Teaching & Assessment: A Practical Guide*, by Christine J. Hopple, 2005, Champaign, IL: Human Kinetics.

Emphasize	Ideas for Lesson Development
Speed—Fast, Slow, Acceleration, and Deceleration—in the contexts of dance, gymnastics, and games	• Use folk dances that change in speed and require students to accelerate or decelerate their movements (e.g., Seven Jumps, Les Statues). • See the themes of locomotor (chapter 9), nonlocomotor (chapter 10), and manipulative (chapter 11) skills for additional uses of effort concepts. **Purcell Cone and Cone:** *Birthday Celebration*
Force—Strong and Light—in the contexts of dance, gymnastics, and games	• Use various kinds of folk music representing strong or light force. Discuss what kind of force the students think the dance portrays and why. • See the themes of locomotor (chapter 9), nonlocomotor (chapter 10), and manipulative (chapter 11) skills for additional uses of effort concepts. **PEC:** *Modern Dance* **Purcell Cone and Cone:** *Float and Punch*
Flow *Bound* You can stop quickly and be very controlled. *Free* It's hard to stop the movement, which is very smooth and fluid. Smooth transitions.	• Discuss how various sports and movements use different types of flow, including such examples as a gymnast swinging on the bars who uses free flow, a batter swinging the bat who uses a flowing movement, a player bunting in baseball in a bound-flow movement, and a gymnast pushing up to a handstand on the balance beam using bound flow. • Have the students demonstrate movements from different sports, such as examples of free or bound flow, and then work together to put them into a sequence. Use music that is structural or free flowing to go along with their movements. • See the themes of rolling, balancing, and weight transfer (chapter 10) and locomotor skills (chapter 9) for additional uses of effort concepts. **Purcell Cone and Cone:** *Bubbles*

EFFORT

GRADES 3 TO 4

Sample Performance Indicators

By the end of grade 4, students should be able to

- move in a variety of ways that focus on accelerating and decelerating their speed;
- move in various ways using definite contrasts of bound- and free-flowing movements;
- use the specific qualities of force, flow, or speed to creatively express feelings, ideas, and actions through dance and other expressive movement sequences;
- design, refine, and perform dance and gymnastics sequences that focus on changes in force, flow, and speed (rhythm); and
- manipulate objects (e.g., kick, throw) using varied amounts of force and speed.

NASPE Performance Indicators

- Develops a dance sequence (or game) that is personally interesting. (3–5, #6, 49)

Sample Performance Task

Students design, refine, and perform a movement sequence with a partner that uses at least four action

words (e.g., melt, punch, shout, pop) (Graham, Holt/Hale, and Parker, 2004) to express their choice of either light or strong force and bound or free flow.

RUBRIC CLUES

To what extent do students

- use action words that express the concept they chose?
- refine their sequences and perform them without hesitation?

Sample Portfolio Task

Students complete figure 8.9 by listing activities they perform in daily life that require strong or light force.

RUBRIC CLUES

To what extent do students

- identify activities that require the use of strong and light force?
- give an appropriate reason for their preference of one force over the other?

Emphasize	*Ideas for Lesson Development*
Speed *Acceleration* Speed up. *Deceleration* Slow down.	• Students move on mats continuously, alternating between fast and slow movements without stopping to change speed. Have them do one movement (e.g., roll) fast, then slow. • Students move pieces of equipment using fast speed, then move across or over the equipment using slow speed (or vice versa). • Children make three different shapes: The first one is slow and the last one is fast; then they do the opposite—the first one, fast and the last one, slow. (This demonstrates the ability to accelerate or decelerate.)

Purcell Cone and Cone: *Birthday Celebration*

EFFORT

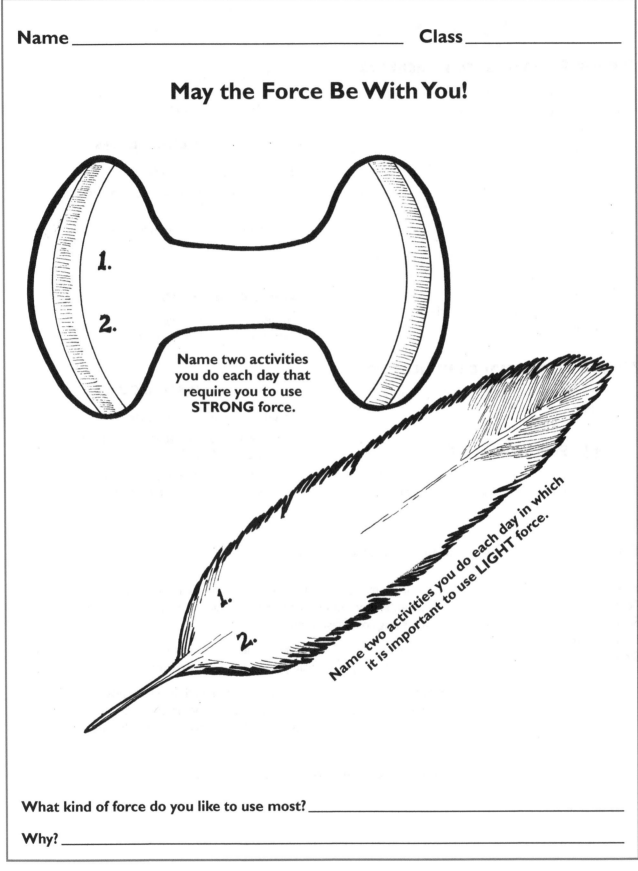

Name _____ Class _____

May the Force Be With You!

1.

2.

Name two activities you do each day that require you to use STRONG force.

1.

2.

Name two activities you do each day in which it is important to use LIGHT force.

What kind of force do you like to use most? _____

Why? _____

Figure 8.9   Portfolio task assessment sheet for effort, grades 3 to 4.

From *Elementary Physical Education Teaching & Assessment: A Practical Guide,* by Christine J. Hopple, 2005, Champaign, IL: Human Kinetics.

Force
Strong
Make your muscles tight.
Light
Make your muscles relaxed.

- Put together snippets of music that convey the qualities of strong or light force. Ask the students to move (with or without a prop) to the music, either while it is playing, or after they have listened to the snippet and you have stopped the music.
- Provide props such as parachutes, rhythm sticks, scarves, and streamers. Students use the props as they work in groups on sequences focusing on speed, force, or flow.

Purcell Cone and Cone: *Float and Punch*

Flow
Bound
You can stop quickly and be very controlled.
Free
It's hard to stop the movement, which is very smooth and fluid.

- Use feathers and bubbles as props for free flow.
- Have students move over their mats in any way that demonstrates free or bound flow.
- Use music (folk, popular, and classical) suggesting the contrasts between free and bound movements. Give students props to use while they move to the music, and have them show free- or bound-flowing movements. Have groups of two or three students make up a sequence of at least 40 counts.
- Show a large card with three locomotor movements on it. Use commas in between the movements to designate a "bound" sequence (students must pause after each movement). Omit the commas to designate one movement after the other without stopping, a "free" sequence. First practice a few together as a class and then give each student a card with the sequence notated. Once the students have completed it, they switch cards with someone else. As they work on their sequences, ask students what kind of flow they are using.
- Discuss how changes in force, flow, and speed are used in dance and gymnastics to add variety to a movement or routine or to express a certain feeling or idea. They are used in games to produce a particular result. Here is an example: In football, the quarterback sometimes wants to throw a fast, deep pass with great force, and at other times a soft touch pass with more control and less force.

Buschner: *Sentence Scrabble*
Purcell Cone and Cone: *Float and Punch*

EFFORT

GRADES 1 TO 2

Sample Performance Indicators

By the end of grade 2, students should be able to

- perform different body movements in time to a signal or music of varying tempos, or speeds;
- manipulate an object in time to a signal or music of varying tempos, or speeds;
- safely change from one speed to another when traveling to a signal or music of varying tempos;
- move in various ways showing definite contrasts of light and strong force;
- express the qualities of light and strong force through a variety of creative dance or gymnastics sequences; and
- express the qualities of fast and slow speed through a variety of creative dance or gymnastics sequences.

NASPE Performance Indicators

- Performs a simple dance step in keeping with a specific tempo (e.g., slow-slow-fast-fast-fast). (K–2, #1, 2)
- Demonstrates clear contrasts between slow and fast movement when skipping (or hopping, galloping, sliding, etc.). (K–2, #1, 3)

Sample Performance Task

Number and arrange three to five crates, boxes, or paper bags holding objects of varying weights. Place them at several different stations; set up enough so that there are no more than five students at one station, or use this one station as one of a number of different stations. Such objects as bowling pins, plastic liter bottles with sand in them, small weights, beanbags, scarves, and Frisbees can be placed in the crates and boxes. Other small pieces of equipment, such as hand weights or large PVC pipes, can also be used outside of a container. Make sure that there is a distinct difference between the weights in the containers, especially between the lightest and heaviest ones. At their stations, students are asked to pick up each container or object, carry it to a designated line, and then carry it back to the starting point. They are then asked to rank the containers at their station along a scale of lightest to heaviest. (This can also be done with the class as a whole.)

RUBRIC CLUES

To what extent do students

- correctly determine the amount of force needed to lift the different objects?
- use the concept of force to explain and justify their answers?

Sample Portfolio Task

Ask students to complete figure 8.10.

RUBRIC CLUES

To what extent do students

- show an accurate understanding of the concepts of force and speed?

Emphasize	Ideas for Lesson Development
Speed *Fast* Like a rabbit! *Slow* Like a turtle! *Acceleration* Speed up. *Deceleration* Slow down.	• Play different excerpts of music, some in a fast tempo and others in a slow tempo. Ask students to travel or move an object (such as a streamer or scarf) in the speed they think the music portrays. • Direct the children, "Show me how you can move fast across your mat. Now go slow." • Have the students travel fast in general space, explaining that when they come to a mat, they are to move slowly across it. Then switch the speeds.

Name _____ **Class** _____

Answer the questions by circling the correct picture.

Speed: Which of the following moves at a _fast_ speed?

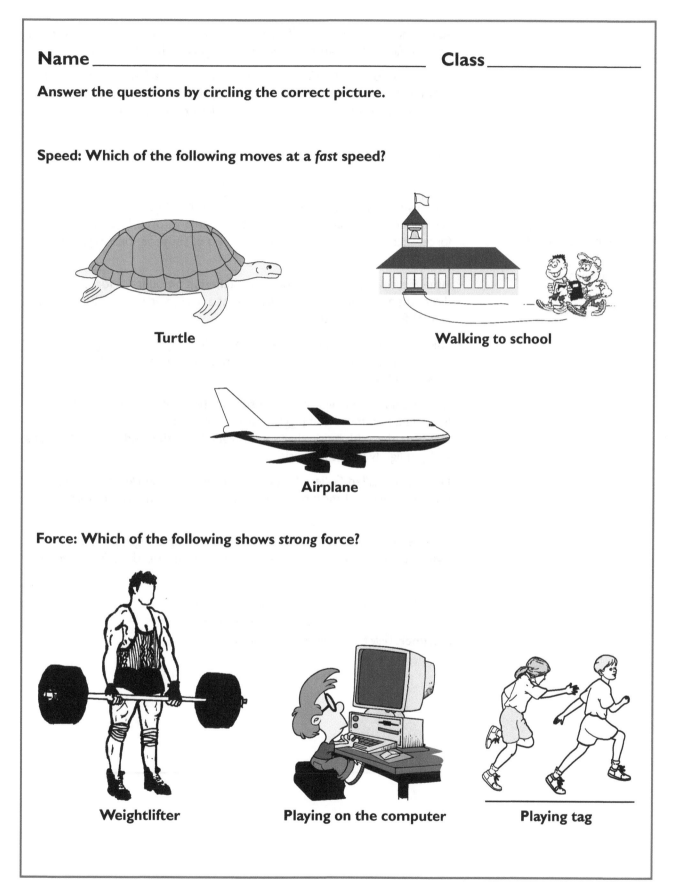

Turtle

Walking to school

Airplane

Force: Which of the following shows _strong_ force?

Weightlifter

Playing on the computer

Playing tag

Figure 8.10 Portfolio task assessment sheet for effort, grades 1 to 2.

- Ask students to move in self-space using different body movements (twist, rise and fall, and so on) to music or to a signal with varying tempos.
- Play a drum or tambourine to give students either a fast or slow speed they must use to travel through general space. Alternate between fast and slow speeds; at times have the signal accelerate or decelerate.

PEC: *Traffic Light Tag*

Force
Strong
Make your muscles tight.
Light
Make your muscles relaxed.

- Say to students, "Show me something in baseball (gymnastics, football, basketball, ice-skating, and so forth) that uses strong force. Show me a light force." Have students perform one or two of these actions together to counts of eight.
- Have the children bounce a ball using different amounts of force as you direct them: "Bounce it so it rebounds at a low (medium, high) level. What kind of force did you use?"
- Ask the students to throw a ball at the wall using strong or light force. Have them discuss which force makes the ball get to the wall faster or slower and why.
- Use forceful-sounding classical music with big, strong clashes. As they listen, children move and juggle scarves like swords, using strong force. Contrast this with music that sounds light. Have the students use balloons and run lightly with this music.
- Use a game called Gallery Statues: The children stand like statues representing strong or light forces. Their partners guess the kind of force they are using.
- Ask the children to travel, then freeze in a strong or light pose at the signal or when music stops (use music that illustrates the different force).

Purcell Cone and Cone: *Floating Clouds and Rain Showers*
Percussion Instrument Dance
Buschner: *Only the Strong and Light Survive*

EFFORT

KINDERGARTEN

Sample Performance Indicators

By the end of grade K, students should be able to

- make fast and slow movements with various body parts;
- travel in various ways at fast and slow speeds; and
- travel and change from one speed to another at a signal.

NASPE Performance Indicators

- Demonstrates clear contrasts between slow and fast movement when skipping (or hopping, galloping, sliding, etc.). (K–2, #1, 3)

Sample Performance Task

Within a large marked-off area, have students travel safely to match both a fast and slow beat.

RUBRIC CLUES

To what extent do students

- move at a speed appropriate for the given beat?

Emphasize	Ideas for Lesson Development
Speed *Fast* Like a rabbit! *Slow* Like a turtle!	• Put up pictures on a bulletin board or chalkboard depicting places where one moves at a slow or fast speed (e.g., the school hallway, a highway, a play area with lots of equipment, a large open yard). Ask the students which speed they should use at each place. • Give a signal and have students move either fast or slow to a new carpet square within a large marked-off area. Give them a second signal that tells them they should be on a square if they're not already there. • Get a slide whistle at a music store (they are inexpensive). Move it slowly; have students move their body parts from a high to a low level slowly. Then play the whistle fast; students move their body parts fast! • Have students move their body parts in their self-space, either fast or slow (for example, hands slow, then fast; head slow, then fast; shoulders slow, then fast; feet slow, then fast; body slow, then fast).

Purcell Cone and Cone: *The Hungry Cat*
Buschner: *Turtles and Rabbits*

EFFORT

Sample Course Standard

Relationships

By the end of elementary school, students should be able to

- design, refine, and perform dance, gymnastics, and small-group games that focus on the use of specific relationships to others and objects.

Concepts and Skills	Learnable Pieces
Relationships to objects or others	Between/inside/outside (K, 1–2)
	Around/through (K, 1–2)
	In front of/behind/beside (K, 1–2)
	Under/over (K, 1–2)
	On/off (K, 1–2)
	Across (K, 1–2)
	Above/below (K, 1–2)
Relationships to partners	
Leading	Moving ahead of a partner. (1–2)
Following	Moving behind a partner. (1–2)
Meeting	Moving toward a partner. (1–2, 3–4)
Parting	Moving away from a partner. (1–2, 3–4)
Matching	In unison; side by side with a partner. (1–2, 3–4)
Mirroring	In contrast; opposite a partner. (1–2, 3–4)

GRADES 5 TO 6

Sample Performance Indicators

By the end of grade 6, students should be able to

- use a variety of relationships with a partner or small group when designing, refining, and performing repeatable dance, gymnastics, or rope-jumping sequences (e.g., behind, beside, mirroring, matching); and
- use a variety of relationships with others in order to play or design a small-group game.

NASPE Performance Indicators

- Develops and refines a gymnastics sequence (or creative dance sequence) demonstrating smooth transitions. (3–5, #1, 7)
- Dribbles then passes a basketball to a moving receiver. (3–5, #1, 8)

Sample Performance Task

Groups of three to five students design, refine, and perform a jump-rope sequence that uses the relationships of meeting, parting, leading, and following. The sequence must last at least 30 seconds and should be performed in 4/4 meter to music of their choice (with teacher's approval, if necessary). It should consist of at least four different jump rope "jumps" or "tricks."

RUBRIC CLUES

To what extent do students

- meet the given sequence criteria?
- refine the sequence so it is repeated smoothly and without hesitation?
- match their movements to the beat of the music?

Sample Portfolio Task

Ask students to describe a situation in a sport or activity (one they participate in, or watch) that uses mirroring (matching, meeting, parting, leading, and following) relationships between players.

RUBRIC CLUES

To what extent do students

- use examples that correctly illustrate the different relationships?

Emphasize	*Ideas for Lesson Development*
Relationships to partners and others—in the contexts of games, dance, and gymnastics activities	• Have students mirror the movement of a partner as they both dribble a ball with their hands and move sideways, as they jog and dribble the ball with their feet, and so forth.
	• Have students dribble and pass a ball back and forth continuously (using the hand or foot) with a partner so that the person receiving the ball doesn't have to stop moving in order to receive it. Discuss how this relates to a leading relationship.
	• Discuss the relationship between an offensive player and a defensive one. How does one person move in relation to the other? Why do they move this way?
	• See other themes for additional activities that use relationship concepts.

Werner: *Me and My Shadow*   *Partner Task Cards*
                    Twins
Purcell Cone and Cone: *Baseball Dance*   *Birthday Celebration*
                    Creative Square Dance   *Partner Dance*
                    Dancing Homework Machine

GRADES 3 TO 4

Sample Performance Indicators

By the end of grade 4, students should be able to

- move in a variety of ways in relation to a partner, either with or without a piece of equipment;
- mirror and match the movements of a traveling partner;
- use matching or mirroring and meeting or parting to design and perform dance or gymnastics sequences with a partner or small group; and
- design, refine, and perform a repeatable sequence with a partner in which the movements of an object (e.g., scarf, ball) are matched as clearly as possible.

Sample Performance Task

Students in small groups are asked to design and perform movement sequences that use matching and mirroring relationships. The movements can be taken from a game or sport, dance, gymnastics, or fitness context. They may use their choice of props and music (with teacher approval, if necessary).

RUBRIC CLUES

To what extent do students

- mirror and match movements to each other?
- refine the sequence until it is performed smoothly and without hesitation?

Sample Portfolio Task

Students write down how well they feel their group worked together and how this affected their performance of the sequence. What was easy about working together? Difficult? What, if anything, would they change about how they worked together?

RUBRIC CLUES

To what extent do students

- put effort into reflecting on the given questions?
- show an understanding of the skills they need to work together with others?

Emphasize	*Ideas for Lesson Development*
Relationships to partners *Meeting* Moving toward a partner. *Parting* Moving away from a partner. *Matching* In unison; side by side with a partner. *Mirroring* In contrast; opposite a partner.	• Students form small groups (three or four students) and make up a sequence to music in which all members of the group do three matching shapes. Locomotor and nonlocomotor movements can be used in the sequence. • Students form small groups, each using an instrument that makes the same kind of sound. (Instruments can be homemade, such as dried beans inside small plastic containers or plastic cartons and wood blocks—bare or covered in sandpaper. Manufactured instruments might be small tambourines, drumsticks, or triangles. See the school music teacher for help.) The students move to match the sound of one group's instruments, then they put these movements together in a sequence. • Students get partners and make up a sequence that includes mirroring or matching and meeting or parting while manipulating an object, such as a streamer, ball, wand, scarf, or jump rope. Specify the duration in counts of the sequence (e.g., 5 actions to sets of 8 to equal 40 beats). Music may be used. For example, students take a count of eight to move toward each other as they dribble a ball, dribble in place for another count of eight, mirror a swaying movement while the ball is held over the head for a count of eight, lead and follow as they dribble along a specific pathway for a count of eight, then dribble in place at a low level for a count of eight.

Purcell Cone and Cone: *Birthday Celebration*   *Partner Dance*
                        Dancing Homework Machine   *Creative Square Dance*
Buschner: *Moving Scarves*
            Name That Movement

GRADES 1 TO 2

Sample Performance Indicators

By the end of grade 2, students should be able to

• move in a variety of ways in relation to a stationary partner or object;

• mirror the shape and movements of a stationary partner; and

• change from a leading to a following position in relation to a partner.

Sample Performance Task

Ask students to find a way, using both the playground equipment and smaller equipment you put out (boxes, hoops, and the like), to demonstrate the relationship (over, under, and so on) that you call out.

RUBRIC CLUES

To what extent do students

• correctly demonstrate the different relationships?

Sample Portfolio Task

Ask students to draw a picture of themselves doing an activity that shows them in relation to an object or other person. They should describe, in writing, what they are doing (e.g., jumping over a rope, moving a hula hoop around a limb, climbing a fence).

<table>
<tr><td colspan="2">**RUBRIC CLUES**</td></tr>
</table>

To what extent do students

- use the correct terminology to explain the relationship?
- interpret a possible relationship?

Emphasize	Ideas for Lesson Development
Relationship to objects or others Between/inside/outside Around/through In front of/behind/beside Under/over On/off Across Above/below.	• Vary your methods of working with the relationship words. For example, sometimes call out a word (e.g., over, behind, above), and other times write each word on a large card. (Help students to recognize the words if needed.) Have the students then move accordingly. • Call out a specific relationship to an object or person. Have students move to a piece of large playground equipment and demonstrate that relationship (i.e., find a way to go around a piece of equipment; move over or under something; freeze beside something). To add activity, have them return to the area near you at the signal before they move to complete the next relationship. Make sure you provide plenty of equipment for students to use (tires, crates, and boxes also can be used). • Have students get partners; one will be the "mover" and the other will be the "freezer." When a relationship word is presented, the mover finds a way to move that way in relationship to the freezer, who must freeze in a shape that allows the mover safe movement. After going through the words, have partners change their roles. • Have a student roll a hula hoop to a partner, who holds it as the student goes over, under, around, and through, moving in as many ways as possible. Then they switch roles. • Place a jump rope on the ground and have students jump over it ("stand with the rope in front of you"), going forward and backward; stand beside it; jump over it; walk on it ("now close your eyes"); race around it; and so forth.
	Werner: *And Away We Go* **PEC:** *You and Me*
Relationships to partners *Leading* Moving ahead of a partner. *Following* Moving behind a partner. *Meeting* Moving toward a partner.	• Students lead or follow a partner through general space; the leading partner gets to decide the movement. On the signal, they switch roles. • Followers stand behind leaders; on the signal, leaders start to run away from their followers. After a head start of five counts, the follower tries to run and safely tag the leader. At the next signal, the follower becomes the leader.

Parting
Moving away from a partner.
Matching
In unison; side by side with a partner.
Mirroring
In contrast; opposite a partner.

• Partners face each other and the follower in each pair mirrors simple movements initiated by the leader. At the signal, they reverse roles.

PEC: Body Shape Fun
  Same and Different
  Shadow Matching

KINDERGARTEN

Sample Performance Indicators

By the end of grade K, students should be able to

• demonstrate a variety of relationships with a stationary partner or object;

• travel while demonstrating a variety of relationships to stationary objects;

• move different objects in a variety of relationships to the self; and

• lead or follow a partner using a variety of locomotor movements.

Sample Performance Task

Ask students to move through an obstacle course in which they have to jump over ropes or low jump-rope hurdles, crawl through mat- or large-box "tunnels," crawl under a table covered by a mat, jump on and off a box, and walk across a balance beam (you can use other "relationship" words in the course, as well). Use pictures to help explain each relationship.

RUBRIC CLUES

To what extent do students

• move using the correct relationship to the object?

Emphasize	Ideas for Lesson Development
Relationships to objects or others Between/inside/outside Around/through In front of/behind/beside Under/over On/off Across Above/below	• Have students put a ball in front of them, behind them, above them, or under them (but not sitting on it!), while in their self-space. • Make up an obstacle course in which students must jump over low rope hurdles, roll across mats, pull themselves under hurdles, walk along jump-rope lines, and crawl through rolled-up mats, standing hula hoops, or foam shapes. Use a variety of equipment and relationships. **Werner:** *And Away We Go* **Buschner:** *Hoops and Me*

Chapter 9

Locomotor Skills

By the end of elementary school, students should be able to

- develop, in a small group, repeatable patterns of one or more locomotor skills into a sequence that is performed to music.

Locomotor Movements

Concepts and Skills	Learnable Pieces
Walk	Heels touch ground first. (K)
	Arms move opposite legs. (K)
Run	Ball of foot touches ground first. (K)
	Arms move opposite legs. (K)
Jump	Bend knees. (K, 1–2)
	Push off, land on balls of feet. (1–2)
	Use both feet. (K, 1–2)
Hop	Bend knees. (K, 1–2)
	Jump, land on ball of foot. (1–2)
	Use only one foot. (K, 1–2)
Gallop	Toe-to-heel. (K, 1–2)
	One foot always chases the other. (K, 1–2)
Slide	Side-together. (K, 1–2)
	One foot pushes the other sideways. (K, 1–2)
Skip	Step-hop. (K, 1–2)
	Kick the beach ball. (K, 1–2)
	Arms move opposite legs. (1–2)
Leap	Bend knees. (1–2)
	One foot to the other. (K, 1–2)
	Land on balls of feet. (3–4)
	Stretch legs wide. (5–6)

GRADES 5 TO 6

Sample Performance Indicators

By the end of grade 6, students should be able to

- run and leap as far and as high as possible;
- run and leap a succession of medium-level obstacles without stopping between;
- design, refine, and perform small-group sequences comprised of even and uneven rhythmic patterns of locomotor movements, body movements, and the use of an object to groups of three or four beats (3/4 or 4/4 time); and
- follow (solo, with a partner, or with a group) given simple patterns of locomotor skills to 3/4 and 4/4 music from various cultures.

NASPE Performance Indicators

- Performs a basic tinikling step to 3/4 time (close, tap, tap). (3–5, #1, 4)
- Demonstrates correct pattern for the polka step (hop-step-together-step). (3–5, #1, 10)

Sample Performance Task

In groups of four, students should design a sequence of locomotor patterns (e.g., moving four steps forward and then four steps backward, or sliding to the left four times and then right four times) and nonlocomotor movements that can be repeated to

music in 4/4 meter (provided or approved by the teacher). The sequence should include at least two patterns of locomotor movements and at least two nonlocomotor movements (done in place). It should be repeatable for at least 64 counts.

RUBRIC CLUES

To what extent do students

- meet the given sequence criteria?
- refine the sequence so partners can perform it smoothly and without hesitation?
- match their movements to the music's beat?
- repeat the sequence for the desired length?

Sample Portfolio Task

Ask students to write out the sequence they designed as part of their performance task.

RUBRIC CLUES

To what extent do students

- correctly write out the steps of their sequence, as performed?
- use correct terminology when describing their sequence?

Emphasize	Ideas for Lesson Development
The use of locomotor movements in the contexts of gymnastics, dance, and game activities **Leap** Stretch legs wide.	• Name different emotions and ask students to express each emotion through a locomotor movement (e.g., happiness as jumping; sadness as walking; joy as leaping). Discuss how folk dances use locomotor movements to express feelings, beliefs, and lifestyles. • Write on a card one pattern of even or uneven locomotor movements that can be done to counts of six or eight (e.g., walk three or four steps forward, then three or four steps backward; step-touch to the right and then to the left three or four times; jog six or eight steps; skip six or eight steps forward; or slide to the right and then to the left three or four times). Students each pick one card and perform the pattern to 3/4 or 4/4 music; then they work with a partner and combine their two patterns (one after the other) to make a sequence. Have them combine their paired sequence with two other students' sequences (again, one sequence

after the other) to make an even larger sequence! Have them write down their sequences. More advanced students can make up their own patterns.

- Let students design their own small-group sequences, which incorporate different locomotor movements and changes in relationships, effort concepts, and so forth (depending on your choice of criteria).

- See Phyllis Weikart's *Teaching Movement and Dance: A Sequential Approach to Rhythmic Movement (4th ed.)* (1998), an excellent resource.

GRADES 3 TO 4

Sample Performance Indicators

By the end of grade 4, students should be able to

- leap a variety of distances, leading with either the right or left leg;

- run and hurdle a succession of low- to medium-level obstacles, using either leg to lead;

- travel and smoothly change directions or movements to music with sets (measures) of three or four beats;

- combine two or more even locomotor movements into a pattern that can be repeated to music with three- or four-beat groupings, such as one, two, three, (four); one, two, three, (four); and so on;

- combine two or more even and uneven locomotor movements into a pattern that can be performed to music with three- or four-beat groupings, such as one and two, three, (four); one and two, three, (four); and so on; and

- combine two or more movement patterns based on sets of either three or four beats into repeatable sequences of traveling, manipulating an object, and space awareness concepts (such as levels or pathways) to a counted-out beat or music.

NASPE Performance Indicators

- Performs a basic tinikling step to 3/4 time (close, tap, tap). (3–5, #1, 4)

- Develops a dance sequence (or game) that is personally interesting. (3–5, #6, 49)

Sample Performance Task

Students work with a partner to design a sequence of four different patterns of locomotor movements. Each pattern should last for eight counts (e.g., slide to the left four times and slide to the right four times, or walk four steps forward and four steps backward). The sequence will be performed two times as a whole to 4/4 music.

RUBRIC CLUES

To what extent do students

- meet the given sequence criteria?

- refine the sequence so both partners can perform it smoothly and without hesitation?

- match their movements to the music's beat?

- repeat the sequence the required number of times?

Sample Portfolio Task

Ask students to complete figure 9.1 to demonstrate their knowledge of how various locomotor movements are used in games and sports.

RUBRIC CLUES

To what extent do students

- correctly identify activities that utilize the various locomotor movements?

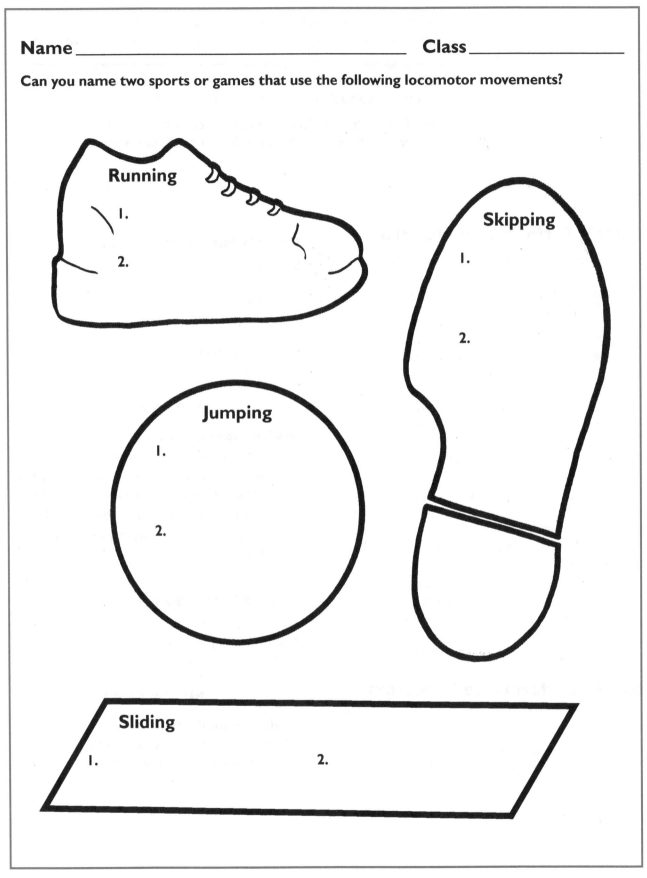

Name _____ **Class** _____

Can you name two sports or games that use the following locomotor movements?

Running
1.
2.

Skipping
1.
2.

Jumping
1.
2.

Sliding
1.   2.

Figure 9.1 Portfolio task assessment sheet for locomotor movements, grades 3 to 4.

From *Elementary Physical Education Teaching & Assessment: A Practical Guide*, by Christine J. Hopple, 2005, Champaign, IL: Human Kinetics.

Emphasize	*Ideas for Lesson Development*
The use of locomotor movements in the contexts of gymnastics, dance, and games activities	• Set up an obstacle course and specify locomotor movements to be done in relation to objects (around, over, between, and so forth). Use jump-rope hurdles, cones, crates, and other equipment. Also let students design their own obstacle courses.

• Give students gymnastics or dance routines that show several different locomotor movements. Here are a few examples: (a) In a group of eight, start in a position that is far apart; move together using a jumping action; show a symmetrical balance; part by using your choice of movement; end in a low-level position. (b) Start at low level; roll to meet or part; show a movement that requires strong force; travel while meeting or parting; end in a position showing a medium and low level. (c) One person must start in high level; travel, showing changes in directions; roll, showing changes in speed; end with one person at a high level.

• Design a sequence, done to counts of eight and using a streamer, in which students show changes in directions and locomotor movements.

> **Buschner:** *Name That Movement*
> **Purcell Cone and Cone:** *Baseball Dance*
> **PEC:** *Simply Move With Me*
>   (see "Jumping and Landing" for additional ideas)

Leap
Land on balls of feet.

• Provide a variety of equipment for students to leap over and across. For instance, use two tug-of-war ropes to make a large V and encourage students to run and leap over whichever part of the rope they feel they can clear. Allow them to change from one part of the rope to another.

> **Buschner:** *Leap for Life*

GRADES 1 TO 2

Sample Performance Indicators

By the end of grade 2, students should be able to

- travel and change from one locomotor movement to another at the signal;
- travel to a signal or music with an even rhythm (walk, run, hop, jump, march);
- travel to a signal or music with an uneven rhythm (slide, gallop, skip);
- perform given or self-designed simple sequences that combine even and uneven locomotor movements into counted-out groups of three, four, or eight beats;
- jump and hop in place while traveling and in relation to an object;
- run and leap, using the favored leg to lead; and,
- design a simple sequence using locomotor and body movements to counted-out beats.

NASPE Performance Indicators

- Skips (or hops, gallops, slides, etc.) using mature form (e.g., step-hops, swings arm, swings knee, shows smooth and continuous motion, shows rhythmical weight transfer, and use of arms). (K–2, #1, 1)

• Demonstrates a smooth transition between loco-motor skills in time to music. (K–2, #1, 5)

Sample Performance Task

Put a cone in four corners of the playing space; attach a number to each cone or to the wall of the corner. Explain that students will move in general space using the locomotor movement you call out; when the music stops, they have to the count of five to move to one of the corners. Roll a die; whatever corner is rolled "wins"; they give a "silent cheer." Everyone moves to a self-space, and you call out a new move-ment. While students are moving, observe them to see if they are using the expected learnable pieces for each movement.

RUBRIC CLUES

To what extent do students
• demonstrate the desired learnable pieces for each locomotor movement?

Sample Portfolio Task

Ask students to match the movement word with a picture showing that movement (see figure 9.2).

RUBRIC CLUES

To what extent do students
• correctly match the movement with the pic-ture?

Emphasize	*Ideas for Lesson Development*

Jump
Bend knees.
Push off, land on balls of feet.
Use both feet.
Hop
Bend knees.
Jump, land on ball of foot.
Use only one foot.
Gallop
Toe-to-heel.
One foot always chases the other.
Slide
Side-together.
One foot pushes the other side-ways.
Skip
Step-hop.
Kick the beach ball.
Arms move opposite legs.
Leap
Bend knees.
One foot to the other.

• Have students travel through general space using the specified locomotor movement. When they come to a crate, box, hurdle, rope, or cone, they leap over it and keep going.

• Students practice traveling and leaping over hoops; with a partner, they put hoops together in a pattern and see how many they can assemble in a row.

• Put four to six "child-designed" hurdles (whose bases insert into a cone) or low and high jump-rope hurdles into a row. Students practice running and leaping over them.

• Ask students to gallop, then slide. Discuss what the differences are between the two movements. Let students walk through each movement if they aren't able to perform it smoothly or rhythmically.

• Have students make up a sequence that involves skipping from one place to another. They should make sure the sequence has a beginning and ending shape.

• Use paper plates on the floor to designate foot placement for different hopscotch patterns. Let students create their own patterns and try other's patterns as well.

• Instruct the children to tap the ground three times with their foot and then slide three times in one direction; they do the same in the other direction. Then they get a rhythm stick and tap it three times on the ground and then slide; they repeat this in the other direction. Then have them put this to 3/4 music with a strong beat.

• Play music with a 4/4 meter. Have the students practice counting the beat and clapping their hands, or tapping their legs or head while standing or sitting. Then ask them to walk, count, and clap in groups of four, making sure they move only one step per beat. Next play a song with a 3/4 meter;

Name _____ **Class** _____

Draw a line from the locomotor movement used in the picture to the word.

Jump

Walk

Run

Hop

Figure 9.2   Portfolio task assessment sheet for locomotor movements, grades 1 to 2.

From *Elementary Physical Education Teaching & Assessment: A Practical Guide,* by Christine J. Hopple, 2005, Champaign, IL: Human Kinetics.

again, have students count and clap along with you to the beat while standing or sitting. Finally, have them move, count, and clap to the beat.

- Mark out an even beat with a drum or tambourine after students have had experience moving with all the different locomotor movements. Ask students to move through general space any way they wish, as long as they can take one movement per beat (walk, run, hop, jump, march). Then, mark out an uneven beat and have them move to it (slide, gallop, skip).

- Have students design an eight-count sequence using locomotor and nonlocomotor movements. Giving a drum beat, have students explore different ways to move to counts of eight while standing still (count it out: move, two, three . . . .eight; switch, two . . . eight; and so on.). The next step is for them to practice moving for eight beats, using any locomotor movement. Then, on counts of eight, have them alternate a nonlocomotor movement they performed earlier with a locomotor movement. Once they can smoothly put together eight counts of nonlocomotor and locomotor movements, progress to using counts of four.

Werner: *And Away We Go*
　　　　　　Landing Pad
Buschner: *Sports Skipping*
Purcell Cone and Cone: *Run, Jump, Hop, and Skip*
PEC: *Clothes on the Line*　　　　*Locomotor Line Tag*
　　　　Dice and Cones　　　　*Locomotor Locomotion*
　　　　Four Corner Cartoon Traveling　　*Locomotor Roll*
　　　　Frog Pond　　　　*Locomotor Treasure Hunt*
　　　　Larger Than Life Line Dance　　*Magician Tag*
　　　　Listen and Move　　　　*One Step at a Time*
　　　　Little Sliders　　　　*Video Game Treasure Hunt*
　　　　Locomotor Go-Fish　　　　*Zesty Kickin' Chicken Dance*
　　　　Locomotor License
(see "Jumping and Landing" for additional ideas)

KINDERGARTEN

Sample Performance Indicators

By the end of grade K, students should be able to

- march in step to a rhythmical (even) beat;
- jump and hop (using both the right and left foot) in place and while traveling;
- gallop forward using a basic or rhythmical galloping pattern; and
- slide sideways using a basic or rhythmical sliding pattern.

NASPE Performance Indicators

- Skips (or hops, gallops, slides, etc.) using mature form (e.g., step-hops, swings arm, swings knee, shows smooth and continuous motion, shows rhythmical weight transfer, and use of arms). (K–2, #1, 1)

Sample Performance Task

To music, have students move around general space, using the locomotor movement you specify (walk, run, and so on). Before students begin to move, identify four to six of them to wear pinnies, crowns, flags tucked in their belt, or other sign. Focus on these students' abilities to move using the learnable pieces for the desired locomotor movements. After the assessment, either have these students give their pinnies to someone else or use them on a different day.

Emphasize	Ideas for Lesson Development

Walk
Heels touch ground first.
Arms move opposite legs.

Run
Ball of foot touches ground first.
Arms move opposite legs.

Jump
Bend knees.
Use both feet.

Hop
Bend knees.
Use only one foot.

Gallop
Toe-to-heel.
One foot always chases the other.

Slide
Side-together.
One foot pushes the other sideways.

Skip
Step-hop.
Kick the beach ball.

Leap
One foot to the other.

- Use an instrument, such as a drum or tambourine, as a signal when working with students on locomotor activities. These instruments are loud enough to be heard over music, and the students love a chance to hit the drum or shake the tambourine! Using a wireless microphone can amplify your instructions so students can hear over the music.

- Have students travel to music using a locomotor movement you call out; when you stop the music, they stop and prepare to move in the next way you call out. As students develop listening and motor abilities, call out the locomotor movement without stopping the music. Intersperse the locomotor with nonlocomotor movements (for instance, every time the chorus comes on, students twist, sway, swing, or the like).

- Students march and clap to the count of eight to the beat of the tambourine, drum, or other 2/4 music. At intervals, they stop and clap the body part you call out (e.g., head, tummy, legs, shoulders) for eight more counts, then begin marching again. Vary the directions and pathways they march. For variety, give four to six students a tambourine to beat as they march. Have them give it to someone else during the "rest stops."

- Students walk in different directions through general space. When they come to a jump rope lying on the ground, they jump over it in the direction they are moving and keep going.

- Have students practice skipping by imagining they are holding a very large beach ball out in front of them. Each time they step, they hit the beach ball with their other knee. This idea (and others) are found in *Teaching Your Wings to Fly* by Anne L. Barlin, 1979.

Werner: *And Away We Go*
  Landing Pad
PEC: *Clothes on the Line*
  Dice and Cones
  Four Corner Cartoon Traveling
  Frog Pond
  Listen and Move
  Locomotor Locomotion

Locomotor Go-Fish
Locomotor License
Locomotor Roll
Locomotor Treasure Hunt
One Step at a Time
Video Game Treasure Hunt

Sample Course Standard	Chasing, Fleeing, and Dodging	
	Concepts and Skills	**Learnable Pieces**
By the end of elementary school, students should be able to	*Chase*	Move quickly! (K, 1–2)
• use locomotor and nonlocomotor skills in order to successfully chase, flee, and dodge others in game situations.		Watch their middle (to see direction they move in). (1–2, 3–4)
		Quick changes (in direction, pathway, speed). (1–2, 3–4)
	Flee	Move quickly! (K, 1–2)
		Quick changes. (1–2)
	Dodge	Quick movements. (1–2)
		Keep on the balls of your feet—be ready! (1–2)
		Quick changes (in direction, pathway, speed). (1–2, 3–4, 5–6)
	Fake	Your head moves one way, your body goes the other. (3–4)
		Quick movements. (3–4)
		Watch their middle. (3–4)

GRADES 5 TO 6

Sample Performance Indicators

By the end of grade 6, students should be able to

- cooperatively devise strategies to keep opponents from reaching a specified area, person, or object; and

- cooperatively play a designed or given small-group game with opponents that involves throwing and catching or other skill themes with dodging, chasing, and fleeing.

NASPE Performance Indicators

- Designs a new game incorporating at least two motor skills, rules, and strategies. (3–5, #2, 17)

Sample Performance Task

Students in small groups of three or four design and play a goal-oriented game in which chasing, fleeing, and dodging are combined with either throwing, dribbling, or kicking in order to move an object or person toward a specified goal area or other person or object. Students may choose boundaries, rules, and objects (balls, Frisbees, and the like) to be used in the game.

RUBRIC CLUES

To what extent do students

- use quick changes in direction, speed, and pathway in order to evade an opponent?

- consistently attempt to create space on offense by moving to open areas so they can receive and move the ball toward a goal?

- consistently deny space on defense by keeping their body between the ball and the intended player or goal?

- cooperate in order to design and play their game?

Sample Portfolio Task

Ask students to give a name to their games and write their rules. They must explain how the skills of either chasing, fleeing, or dodging are used in their games and how they are scored.

Emphasize	Ideas for Lesson Development

Dodge
Quick changes (in direction, pathway, speed)
General space (see "Space Awareness," chapter 8)
Offense
Keep your body between the ball and the defender.
Create space by moving to open areas to pass or receive the ball.
Defense
Deny space by staying between the opponent and intended goal.

- Have two students set up a target (goal area, target on a wall, and so on) in a specified area marked by cones, ropes, or other equipment. One student tries to get a ball to the target by dribbling or throwing without its being stolen by the partner, a defensive player. Discuss how a defensive player denies space and guards a target.

- Set up lanes about 6 to 8 feet (1.8 m to 2.4 m) wide with a goal area at one end. Two offensive players and one defensive player stay in each lane. The offensive players try to get past the defensive player by dribbling with the hands or feet to get the ball to the goal. Discuss what the role of each player is.

- Set up lanes the length of the playing area. One defensive and one offensive player stay in each lane, touching the ball only when it comes into their lane. Discuss how offensive players must work to get open to receive a ball, no matter which lane they are in; discuss the positioning that the defensive player must take.

- Discuss how players on offense sometimes move away from the goal area to get open to pass or receive a ball and that to create space, players do not always stay near the goal area.

Belka: *Runner, Stay Away*
PEC: *Body-Part Tag*   *Quidditch (Harry Potter Style!)*
     Flag Steal   *Sneaker Slap*
     Microorganism Immune System Tag   *Triangle Tag*
     Planet Invasion

GRADES 3 TO 4

Sample Performance Indicators

By the end of grade 4, students should be able to
- travel and dodge stationary opponents; and
- use dodging skills in a small-group situation to avoid a thrown soft, lightweight object.

Sample Performance Task

Set up the Trees in the Forest game (see grades 1–2, page 117) in a marked-off area. Instead of moving from one end line to another, however, students travel and move throughout the area while dribbling a ball with either the feet or hands. As they come to a "tree" standing in a hula hoop (trees can step out of hoop with one foot), they try to dodge the tree and also not lose the ball by positioning their body between the ball and the tree. If the ball is stolen or if the students are tagged, they still keep moving until all observations are made by the teacher. (Have four to six students at a time wear pinnies; observe these students only. After their turn, the students give the pinnies to six other students.)

RUBRIC CLUES

To what extent do students

- use quick changes in direction, speed, and pathway as well as fakes in order to avoid opponents?

Sample Portfolio Task

Ask students to complete figure 9.3 as homework or in the classroom, if possible, to illustrate their knowledge of how chasing, fleeing, or dodging are used in game situations.

RUBRIC CLUES

To what extent do students

- demonstrate a correct understanding of the skills of chasing, fleeing, and dodging?

Emphasize	*Ideas for Lesson Development*

Fake
Your head moves one way, your body goes the other.
Quick movements.
Watch their middle.
Chase
Quick changes (in direction, pathway, speed).
Watch their middle (to see direction they move in).
	• Discuss why faking is used: in order to trick a defender into thinking he or she will move one way, when the intention is to move the other.
	
	• Have paired students start apart and move toward each other in a large marked-off area. When they get close, one partner (the faker) moves first and tries to fake the direction to throw the other person off and avoid being tagged. After three tries, roles are reversed.
	
	Belka: *Partner Tag*
	   Fake and Take
	Buschner: *Dodge and Freeze Tag*
	PEC: *Body-Part Tag*　　　*Planet Invasion*
	   Flag Steal　　　*Sailors and Sharks*
	   Jack Frost Tag Game　　*Take It Home*
	   Microorganism Immune System Tag

Dodge Quick changes (in direction, pathway, speed). **General space (see "Space Awareness," chapter 8)** *Offense* Keep your body between the ball and the defender.	• Set up a Trees in the Forest game similar to the assessment task given earlier. For a variation, let students move from one end line to the other. Students can dribble with the feet instead of the hands. **Belka:** *Merry-Go-Round*

Name _____ Class _____

Chase, Flee, and Dodge!

☆ **What is a game you've seen on TV or in person that used chasing, fleeing, or dodging?**

_____

☆ **What was happening in that game? Why were the players chasing, fleeing, or dodging?**

_____

_____

_____

☆ **What is your favorite game to play that uses chasing, fleeing, or dodging?**

_____

☆ **Why is it your favorite?**

_____

_____

_____

☆ **What is one important thing to remember in order to be a good chaser, flee-er, or dodger?**

_____

_____

_____

Figure 9.3 Portfolio task assessment sheet for chasing, fleeing, and dodging, grades 3 to 4.

From *Elementary Physical Education Teaching & Assessment: A Practical Guide,* by Christine J. Hopple, 2005, Champaign, IL: Human Kinetics.

GRADES 1 TO 2

Sample Performance Indicators

By the end of grade 2, students should be able to

- follow a fleeing partner's pathway to catch or overtake him or her;
- flee from a partner as quickly as possible at a signal;
- travel and change pathways as quickly as possible at a signal;
- travel and change directions as quickly as possible at a signal; and
- quickly perform dodging skills at a signal.

Sample Performance Task

Students organize a two-on-one Dodging Monkey in the Middle game: Two carpet squares placed 10 feet (3 m) apart are used to designate where the two throwers need to stand at or behind, and a small soft (yarn, foam) ball is used for throwing. During the game, the "monkey" uses a variety of dodging skills to avoid being thrown out. Care should be taken that the throwers aim at a low or medium level.

gets three chances to be the "monkey"; at the third hit, they switch places with a "thrower." (Encourage students who stay in the middle for an extended period of time to switch even before they are hit three times.)

RUBRIC CLUES

To what extent do students

- consistently use a dodging skill appropriate to the throw?

Sample Portfolio Task

Ask students to demonstrate their knowledge in writing of chasing, fleeing, and dodging skills by completing figure 9.4.

RUBRIC CLUES

To what extent do students

- correctly identify the skills involved?

Emphasize	*Ideas for Lesson Development*
Dodge Quick movements. Keep on the balls of your feet—be ready! Quick changes (in direction, pathway, speed).	• Students perform the dodging movement that is called out (duck, twist, collapse, roll, stretch, pivot, jump) at the signal. They should get ready for the next call as quickly as possible. • Students travel through general space; at the signal, they perform a dodging movement that is called out and then continue traveling. Discuss the situations in which each movement would be used.
	Belka: *This Way and That Way*
Chase Move quickly! Watch their middle (to see direction they move in). **Flee** Move quickly! Quick changes. **Dodge** Quick movements.	• Students travel through general space; at the signal, they quickly change the direction or pathway they are moving in (specify which of the two they are to focus on). Vary the interval between changes. • Students travel through general space and try to get as close as possible to someone, but quickly change directions and pathways in order to dodge the other child. • Students find partners. One partner is the first "tagger." All students begin to travel throughout a large marked-off area, and each child tries to avoid

Name _____ **Class** _____

Catch Me If You Can!

Which of these pictures show skills you use when you chase, flee, or dodge? Circle them. Then, put an X on the skills you _don't_ use.

Running

Twisting

Standing still

Changing pathways

Ducking

Name one game that uses chasing, fleeing, or dodging. _____

Figure 9.4   Portfolio task assessment sheet for chasing, fleeing, and dodging, grades 1 to 2.

From *Elementary Physical Education Teaching & Assessment: A Practical Guide,* by Christine J. Hopple, 2005, Champaign, IL: Human Kinetics.

being tagged by their tagger partner. When one is tagged (or at the signal), they switch roles. If needed, limit students to using a specific locomotor movement, such as walking.

- Trees in the Forest: Start with about four hoops spread throughout a marked-off area, with a student standing in each hoop. At the signal, remaining students travel from one end of the area to the other, trying not to get caught by the "trees" in the hoops. If they safely reach the other side, they stay at that end until given the signal to go once again. If caught, the student gets a hoop and puts it in the area as well. Start new games often (when about eight or so students are left) to allow all students the chance to be active.

- In pairs, at a signal one partner begins to travel quickly away from the stationary partner. At the next signal (or a count of five) the stationary partner follows and tries to tag the first gently.

- Flag Tag: All students have a flag belt with one or two flags or a flag stuck in their waistband. Using a very large marked-off area, students try to take flags away from all other students while avoiding loss of their own. If a flag is taken, it can be deposited in a specified area; if both flags are taken, the student can still try to capture others' flags. Start the game over when eight or fewer students still have flags. In a variation to make the game more continuous, students can come to the "safe area" to put a flag back on their belt, if both have been taken.

PEC: *Oogedy Boogedy Tag*   *Skunk Tag*
Sailors and Sharks   *Spiders and Flies*

KINDERGARTEN

Sample Performance Indicators

By the end of grade K, students should be able to
- travel and make straight, curved, and zigzag pathways;
- travel around stationary obstacles without touching them; and
- follow the pathway that their partner makes.

Emphasize	Ideas for Lesson Development
Chase Move quickly! **Flee** Move quickly!	• Have students travel throughout the marked-off area using the specific pathway you call out. • Use chalk to make large pathways on a blacktop, or make them on grass using spray paint or line chalk. Students move throughout the area; at the signal, they find the pathway you specify and move on it. Encourage them to keep moving if needed until they find a pathway open. At the next signal, they again travel, waiting until the following signal to find a pathway to move on. Vary the locomotor movements they use.

- Set up cones, boxes, and crates throughout the marked-off area. As students move throughout general space, encourage them to move as close to the objects as possible and move away quickly, without touching them.

- Assign partners to the students; at the signal, one of them runs as quickly as possible toward a long designated line or large area. After the count of three-alligators, the partner runs and tries to catch up with the first child. If the partners meet, they both continue running together to the line or area. After a short rest, the second child gets to run to the opposite line or area, with the first child then trying to catch up to him or her.

PEC: *Gargoyles*
Shadow Tag
Spiders and Flies

By the end of elementary school, students should be able to

- use different jumping patterns to design, refine, and perform a jump-rope routine to music as part of a small group.

Jumping and Landing

Concepts and Skills	Learnable Pieces
Height	Feet (shoulder-width) apart. (1–2)
	Bend hips and knees. (1–2)
	(Push off) balls of feet. (1–2)
	Arms (swing) back to up. (1–2)
	Stretch up high. (3–4)
Distance	Feet (shoulder-width) apart. (1–2)
	Bend hips and knees. (1–2)
	(Push off) balls of feet. (1–2)
	Arms (swing) back to front. (1–2)
	Heels land first. (3–4)
Short jump rope	Bend knees (when pushing off or landing). (1–2)
	Elbows close to body. (1–2)
	Hands down (below the shoulders). (1–2)
	(Push off, land on) balls of feet. (1–2)
	Slow jumps (yield on landing). (1–2)
	Fast jumps (buoyant landing). (1–2, 3–4)
	Jump barely off the ground. (3–4)
	Turn wrist only (to turn rope). (3–4)
Long jump rope	Bend knees. (K, 1–2)
	(Push off, land on) balls of feet. (1–2)
	Slow jumps (yield on landing). (1–2)
	Jump barely off the ground. (1–2)
	Stay in the middle. (1–2)
	Jump when rope is past both shoulders. (1–2)
	Make big circles with arms (to turn rope). (K, 1–2)
	Start near turner (to jump in). (3–4)
	Jump in when rope is on its way up. (3–4)

GRADES 5 TO 6

Sample Performance Indicators

By the end of grade 6, students should be able to

- jump a self-turned rope using as many different types of jumps as possible (e.g., skier, bell);
- perform jumping skills in 3/4 or 4/4 time, using ropes, tinikling sticks, elastic jumping bands, and so forth; and
- design and refine a repeatable routine with a partner or a small group using various jumping skills, other movements, and objects to 3/4 or 4/4 time.

NASPE Performance Indicators

- Performs a basic tinikling step to 3/4 time (close, tap, tap). (3–5, #1, 4)

Sample Performance Task

In groups of three to five, the students design, refine, and perform a jump-rope routine to music of their choice. The routine must contain at least three different types of jumps, two different rope directions, two changes in relationships among group members, and beginning and ending shapes that vary in level. It can be performed to music of the teacher's or students' choice.

RUBRIC CLUES

To what extent do students

- perform a routine that reflects all the criteria?
- refine the routine so all partners can perform it smoothly and without hesitation?
- perform the routine in time with the music?

Sample Portfolio Task

Ask students to jump rope at least four different times in one week (either at home or at recess). Each time, they count the highest number of jumps they can perform in a row without stopping and record this on figure 9.5. At the end of the week, they should answer the given questions.

RUBRIC CLUES

To what extent do students

- complete the assignment?
- correctly answer the questions?

Emphasize	*Ideas for Lesson Development*
The use of jumping in the contexts of dance, gymnastics, and games activities	• Have students practice jumping patterns with tinikling sticks or elastic jumping bands. Discuss the cultural and dance heritage of the activity. (Tinikling is a folk dance from the Philippines, with the sticks originally made from bamboo and the jumper representing wading birds in the rice paddies. See Graham, Holt/Hale, and Parker [2004] for diagrams of various jumping patterns one can use when tinikling.) Allow students in groups to make up different steps to 3/4 and 4/4 music.
	• Use jump-rope videos and materials (see a variety of publishers or equipment companies for items) to introduce students to Double Dutch jump ropes. Allow students to practice in small groups.
	• Set up stations that involve short jump-rope skills along with Chinese jump ropes, tinikling sticks, elastic jumping bands, and Double Dutch ropes (add a water and break station!).
	• Have groups of three or four students take turns jumping for height off of large equipment (tables, benches, stacked mats, and so on.) in order to catch an object thrown to them by another person in the group. If desired, students can perform a safety roll when they land from the jump.

PEC: *Jump-Rope Tag*
Thumbs Up Rope Turning

Name _____ Class _____

Jump for Fun!

Decide how you want to jump rope (forward, backward, skipping, etc.). On four different days, jump rope using your choice of step. Count how many times in a row you can jump without messing up. Record your score below. You may try it many times in one day—write down your *best* score.

Day	Highest number of jumps in a row
1	_____
2	_____
3	_____
4	_____

How many total jumps did you do? _____

What was the difference betwen your lowest number of jumps and your highest number of jumps? _____

Was it easy or hard to jump? Why? _____
_____
_____

What organ has to work very hard when you jump rope? _____

What is one important cue to help you jump well? _____

Figure 9.5   Portfolio task assessment sheet for jumping and landing, grades 5 to 6.

From *Elementary Physical Education Teaching & Assessment: A Practical Guide,* by Christine J. Hopple, 2005, Champaign, IL: Human Kinetics.

GRADES 3 TO 4

Sample Performance Indicators

By the end of grade 4, students should be able to

- jump for distance using a mature form;
- jump for height using a mature form;
- jump a self-turned rope using buoyant landings;
- jump a self-turned rope using at least five different types of jumps (e.g., hop, skip, forward jump, backward jump, skier);
- jump into and out of a turning long rope.

NASPE Performance Indicators

- Jumps vertically to a height of 9 inches (22.9 cm) and lands using mature form (e.g., stands, crouches with arms back and weight on toes, lifts off with hands high, lands on both feet). (3–5, #1, 5)

Sample Performance Task

As a summative assessment of their jumping skills after instruction in jumping and landing, students complete a self-assessment sheet that focuses on their ability to perform a variety of jumping skills (see figure 9.6). Students check off each skill on the sheet that they are able to perform; they then write down the number of times that they can perform that skill in a row without missing. (You may wish to give this to students early in your unit of instruction and allow them to change their score as they improve.)

Sample Portfolio Task

After completing the performance task mentioned previously, ask students to write a paragraph about how well they think they do with their jump-rope skills. Were the skills easy? Difficult? Did they see an improvement over the course of the unit? Can they tell if their endurance has improved as a result of the jumping? Is this something they think they can do at home? How can jumping rope be used to help them stay in shape? Can they think of sports whose athletes jump rope to stay in shape?

Emphasize	*Ideas for Lesson Development*
Short jump rope Jump barely off the ground. Turn wrist only (to turn rope). Fast jumps (buoyant landing).	• Set up stations that focus on different types of jumps (two-foot yielding jumps, skip-step jumps, backward jumps, two-person jumps, and the like). If you wish, intersperse the stations with fitness stations (e.g., sit-ups, jogging around the perimeter). Play music; when the music stops, students stop and prepare to move to the next station. Use the music to signal the move.
Long jump rope Start near turner (to jump in). Jump in when rope is on its way up.	• Groups of three or four students practice jumping into and out of a long jump rope. This can be done as one of many jumping stations or as a separate activity.

JUMPING AND LANDING

Name _____ Class _____

Jump to It!

Check off the jump-rope skills you are able to perform. Write how many times in a row you can do that skill without messing up.

Jump-rope skill	Number of times
☐ Forward	_____
☐ Backward	_____
☐ Criss-cross	_____
☐ Skip step	_____
☐ Bell	_____
☐ Skier	_____
☐ Jump into a turning long jump rope and continue jumping	_____
☐ Other _____	_____
☐ Other _____	_____

Figure 9.6 Performance task assessment sheet for jumping and landing, grades 3 to 4.

From *Elementary Physical Education Teaching & Assessment: A Practical Guide,* by Christine J. Hopple, 2005, Champaign, IL: Human Kinetics.

Height
Stretch up high.
Distance
Heels land first.

- Set up stations to focus on jumping for distance or height: (1) Students measure their vertical jump with a tape measure. (2) Students run up to a jump-rope line, take off on one foot, and land on two; a partner marks the best of three jumps (running long jump). (3) Students jump for distance from a standing position; a partner marks the best jump, and the students measure the distance (standing broad jump). (4) High water, low water: In groups of four with two students holding a long jump rope, the other two students jump, from a standing position, over the rope at a height they instruct the holders to use. If they miss the jump, their next height has to be lower. After five jumps, they become the holders. (5) High jump: Using a line or rope weighted at each end and supported on two standards or a rope held by two holders, the students have the chance to run up to and jump over the rope onto a crash pad.

- Give a small group of students a piece of equipment (carpet squares, hoops, table, bench, mats, ropes, scooters) and a designated area. Ask each group to design a jumping station that will be part of a larger obstacle course, using only their piece of equipment. Once designed, have the class evaluate the safety of each station and judge whether the order of stations "flows" from one to the other. If not, allow them to change the order or revise the station for it to be safer. Once done, students start at different stations and move through the course. (Accompany with fun music!)

> **PEC:** *Jump-Rope Tag*
> *Jumping Numbers*
> *Thumbs Up Rope Turning*

GRADES 1 TO 2

Sample Performance Indicators

By the end of grade 2, students should be able to

- jump and land using a variety of takeoffs and landings in relation to various equipment (e.g. hoops, low hurdles, rope shapes, carpet squares);
- jump a swinging rope with yielding landings;
- jump a self-turned rope both forward and backward with yielding landings; and
- jump a self-turned rope in at least three different ways (e.g., forward direction, backward direction, skip step, fast [buoyant], running skip step).

NASPE Performance Indicators

- Repeats cue words for jumping vertically (e.g., crouch, straighten, land on both feet, and bend knees) and demonstrates/explains what is meant by each. (K–2, #2, 15)

Sample Performance Task

Ask students to jump forward over a self-turned, short jump rope while keeping in their self-space.

RUBRIC CLUES

To what extent do students

- jump repeatedly over the rope without stopping?
- bend the knees when jumping and landing?
- push off of and land on the balls of the feet (rather than flat feet)?

Sample Portfolio Task

Ask students to write to their friend Murgatroid, who is from another planet and has never jumped rope (Graham, 2001). What are some hints that they can give Murgatroid to improve jump-rope skills?

RUBRIC CLUES

To what extent do students

- accurately answer using hints learned in class?
- correctly justify their answers if cues from class are not used?

Emphasize	*Ideas for Lesson Development*
Jump (see "Locomotor Movements," this chapter) Bend knees. Push off, land on balls of feet.	• Spread a variety of low rope hurdles, foam shapes, carpet squares, boxes, and hoops in general space. Students travel throughout the area; at the signal, they find an object to jump over and keep on traveling. If you wish, specify a jumping pattern for them to use. • Make jumping boxes by putting empty vegetable cans (large ones from the cafeteria), bottoms-up, back into their original packing carton. Tape each box securely. Students practice jumping off the box, over the box, and so forth. • Have students (with or without a partner) create different jumps, give them a name (e.g., Michael Jordan jump, SpongeBob jump, Harry Potter jump, Powerpuff Girls jump), and then perform them for the class. • Set up different stations that require students to use a one-to-two jumping pattern, two-to-two pattern, two-to-one pattern, and so on; equipment may be incorporated if desired. • Give partners chalk and allow them to draw their own hopscotch grids on the blacktop.

PEC: *Alligator Alley*   *Jack Be Nimble Jumping*
       Animal Fun   *Jumping Patterns*
       Exploring Shapes   *Shark Attack*
       Hoop Jumper   *Simon*
Werner: *Landing Pad*

Height Feet (shoulder-width) apart. Bend hips and knees. (Push off) balls of feet. Arms (swing) back to up. **Distance** Feet (shoulder-width) apart. Bend hips and knees. (Push off) balls of feet. Arms (swing) back to front.	• Have students practice jumping to reach objects (streamer strips and so on) hung from ropes at different heights. • Blow up small balloons; affix tape to each so that the balloon can stick to the wall. Have students practice jumping for height (standing sideways to the wall) by sticking the balloon to the wall at the highest point of their jump. • Students jump three times for distance from behind a jump rope on the ground. A partner marks the longest distance jumped with an object such as a beanbag or cone. Students switch roles. If you wish, have students measure their longest jumps.

PEC: *Jumping Numbers*

Short jump rope
Bend knees (when pushing off or landing).
Elbows close to body.
Hands down (below the shoulders).
(Push off, land on) balls of feet.
Slow jumps (yield on landing).
Fast jumps (buoyant landing).

Long jump rope
Bend knees.
(Push off, land on) balls of feet.
Slow jumps (yield on landing).
Jump barely off the ground.
Stay in the middle.
Jump when rope is past both shoulders.
Make big circles with arms (to turn rope).

- Have students practice jumping without a rope or over a jump rope lying on the ground to a "buoyant" or "yielding" beat.

- Draw a box on the ground to show where students should stand as they jump over a long rope. Have them practice jumping forward and backward and side to side over a swinging rope.

- Use a drum signal to show the difference between buoyant (fast jumps) and yielding (slow jumps) landings (buoyant—loud, loud, loud beat; yielding—loud and soft, loud and soft, loud and soft beat). See if they can jump to each beat without using a rope and then transfer the yielding for landing when they jump over the long rope.

Buschner: *Knees and Ropes*

KINDERGARTEN

Sample Performance Indicators

By the end of grade K, students should be able to

- jump and land while bending knees;
- jump and land using a two-to-two, one-to-two, and two-to-one jumping pattern; and
- jump a slowly swinging long rope using a two-to-two jumping pattern.

Sample Performance Task

In groups of three (two holders and one jumper), students practice jumping over a slowly swinging long rope. Students practice jumping over the rope using a two-footed jumping and landing pattern (jump off two feet, land on two feet) as many times as possible (at least three times). If you wish, set up a group of stations; you might have two older students as "turners".

RUBRIC CLUES

To what extent do students
- bend the knees when jumping over the rope?
- push off of and land on two feet?
- jump over the rope at least three times without losing their balance?

Emphasize	*Ideas for Lesson Development*
Jump (see "Locomotor Movements," this chapter) Bend knees.	- Each student practices jumping and landing with a variety of takeoff and landing patterns (two-to-two; two-to-one; one-to-two; one-to-one) for jumping over individual low jump-rope hurdles (put ends of jump ropes through holes in the cones), hoops, ropes on the ground, and so forth. - Set up low jump-rope hurdles in a row; students travel up to each hurdle and jump over it with two feet, one foot, or whatever you call out.

- Use a variety of different colored poly spots at one jumping station. Make a diagram showing how many feet each spot is "worth." Arrange the spots in an area, using a variety of the colors and distances between spots. Demonstrate to students how they will jump from one spot to the next, landing with the number of feet the color is "worth." (You can also indicate the number of feet on the spot.)

Werner: *Landing Pad*

Long jump rope
Bend knees.
Make big circles with arms (to turn rope).

- Set up students in groups of three—two turners and one jumper. Have students practice jumping over a swinging (back-and-forth) and twirling (overhead) rope. Students should start by standing in the middle; have the turners count and simultaneously bump the rope against the jumper's foot three times, so jumper starts jumping on the count of three. After five tries, students switch roles.

PEC: *Hoop Jumper*
Jack Be Nimble Jumping
Simon

Nonlocomotor Skills

Sample Course Standard

By the end of elementary school, students should be able to

- with a partner or small group, combine the skills of rolling, balancing, and weight transfer, along with locomotor skills, in order to design, refine, and perform a gymnastics or dance sequence.

Rolling

Concepts and Skills	Learnable Pieces
Rocking	Chin to chest. (1–2)
	Head to knees. (1–2)
	Curved shape—no flat tires! (K, 1–2)
Sideways	Like a pencil (head between arms)! (K, 1–2)
	Tight muscles. (1–2)
	(Begin to) turn from your tummy. (1–2)
Forward	Curved shape—no flat tires! (K, 1–2)
	Chin to chest. (K, 1–2)
	Behind up. (K, 1–2)
	Push with your hands. (1–2)
	Finish on your feet. (3–4, 5–6)
	Soft rolls. (3–4, 5–6)
	Give with your arms. (3–4, 5–6)
Backward	Curved shape—no flat tires! (1–2)
	Head to knees. (1–2)
	Hands by your ears. (1–2, 3–4)
	Push up. (3–4)
	Finish on your feet. (5–6)
	Soft rolls. (5–6)
Aerial roll	Chin to chest. (5–6)
	Give with your arms. (3–4, 5–6)
	Soft rolls. (5–6)
Rolling on equipment	Tight muscles. (5–6)
	Shoulders and body over the equipment. (5–6)

GRADES 5 TO 6

Sample Performance Indicators

By the end of grade 6, students should be able to

- roll smoothly in a forward and backward direction;
- use different shapes to begin and end rolls when rolling in different directions;
- balance in a variety of upright or inverted positions, move smoothly into a roll, then balance again;
- travel, jump over low equipment, land, and roll;
- travel, jump, land, and roll over low equipment (starting the roll with or without hands on the floor);
- jump off the ground or low equipment to catch an object thrown directly to them, land safely, and roll in at least one direction;
- roll forward or backward on low equipment (bench, beam, table); and
- design, refine, and perform repeatable sequences (with a partner or in a small group) involving rolling and other skills.

NASPE Performance Indicators

- Develops and refines a gymnastics sequence (or creative dance sequence) demonstrating smooth transitions. (3–5, #1, 7)

Sample Performance Task

In groups of three or four, students design, refine, and perform a sequence that incorporates rolls of at least two different shapes with at least one balance and one weight transfer. The sequence should incorporate at least two different relationships between partners.

RUBRIC CLUES

To what extent do students
- meet all given sequence criteria?
- refine the sequence so all group members can perform it smoothly and without hesitation?

Sample Portfolio Task

Rolling skills are used in many different sports and activities. Have students describe two different sports or activities that use rolling movements. If possible, they should include pictures showing the rolling movement in the sports they describe. Students should specifically describe why and how the sport or activity uses rolling. Possible examples include football, rhythmic gymnastics, diving, dance, artistic gymnastics (floor or equipment), trampoline, surfing, skateboarding, and swimming (flip turns).

RUBRIC CLUES

To what extent do students
- use knowledge and examples correctly and accurately to explain their answers?

Emphasize	Ideas for Lesson Development
Forward or Backward Finish on your feet. Soft rolls. Give with your arms.	• Encourage students to use different positions (e.g., legs and arms wide, starting from a medium level) to begin and end both forward and backward rolls. Have them connect these shapes into a sequence. • Have students practice moving from a balanced position, in either an upright or inverted position, to a roll and back to a different balanced position. • Write up cards giving different sequences (e.g., handstand, forward roll, and balance on one foot). Make the cards of different levels of difficulty (code by color, for example); let students choose the level they will practice.

- Encourage students to travel to a piece of equipment (box, crate, hurdle, and so on), use a two-footed or spring takeoff to jump over it, land, and roll in any desired direction.

- Assign students to a partner or group and have them take turns throwing a ball (students choose size and weight) to a student who jumps off the ground or low equipment to catch it, then lands and rolls.

PEC: *Rockin' Robin*
Werner: *Partner Task Cards*

Aerial roll
Chin to chest.
Give with your arms.
Soft rolls.

- Encourage students to travel to a piece of low equipment, jump and land in front of it, and roll over it. They may start the roll with or without their hands on the floor.

Rolling on equipment
Tight muscles.
Shoulders and body over the equipment.
Flow (see "Effort," chapter 8)
Free
Smooth transitions.

- Encourage students to roll forward and backward on low equipment, such as a bench, beam, or table.

- Students can make a sequence of moving to the piece of equipment, transferring their weight onto it, rolling on it, and moving off the equipment.

- Discuss how it is necessary to keep the bases of support (hips and shoulders) directly over the equipment in order to not fall off it, and how this requires very tight muscles and control of speed.

GRADES 3 TO 4

Sample Performance Indicators

By the end of grade 4, students should be able to
- roll, starting and ending in different shapes and using different speeds;
- roll forward over a low hurdle, starting with hands on or off the floor;
- jump off low equipment, land safely, and roll; and
- design, refine, and perform (alone or with a partner) simple sequences involving rolling, weight transfers, balances, and movement concepts (levels, shapes, directions, speed).

Sample Performance Task

With a partner, students choose two different rolls to perform consecutively while matching each other. Rolls should show two different body shapes, and there should be a definite beginning and ending.

RUBRIC CLUES

To what extent do students
- match their partner's shapes or rolls?
- include and correctly perform two different rolls?
- refine the sequence to perform it smoothly and without hesitation?

Sample Portfolio Task

Ask students to hypothesize about four objects from home or school that might roll in either a forward, backward, or sideways direction and two that cannot roll at all. Have students verify whether their hypotheses are correct, and, if not, why they think their hypotheses were incorrect.

RUBRIC CLUES

To what extent do students

- hypothesize for four objects that roll and two that do not?
- correctly verify that the objects can or cannot roll?
- give complete explanations for incorrect hypotheses?

Emphasize	*Ideas for Lesson Development*
Forward Finish on your feet.	• Encourage students to roll forward using different beginning and ending positions (e.g., legs wide, body piked). • Discuss how different positions affect a roll. Why is more force needed for some rolls than others? Relate force to the length of the body extension: The longer the extension around which the roll is done, the more force is needed for the roll. • Have students roll forward at a fast and a slow speed. Discuss why one is easier than the other.
Forward Soft rolls. Give with your arms.	• Encourage students to jump off low equipment (e.g., boxes, tires, crates), land, and roll. Some students may try landing and then rolling over a jump-rope hurdle. Emphasize that landings should be "soft." • Have students in pairs design and refine sequences that include rolls, balances, and weight transfers. Require changes in relationships, speeds, pathways, directions, or levels (focus only on one or two of these, depending on how many other criteria you give). **Werner:** *Same, Different*
Backward Hands by your ears. Push up.	• Encourage students to roll backward. An incline mat can be a useful teaching aid for learning to roll—especially in a backward direction. A mat with a slight (not severe) incline may be less threatening to beginning students. Hold to high expectations for student behavior with this, and any, equipment used in gymnastics. **Werner:** *Roll, Roll, Roll Your Body*
Aerial roll Give with your arms.	• Arrange jump ropes and low jump-rope hurdles on the ground for students to practice rolling over. They can start with the hands on the floor on the far side of the hurdle or hands off the floor. • Discuss how giving with one's arms is important to absorb force, especially for starting with hands off the floor.

GRADES 1 TO 2

Sample Performance Indicators

By the end of grade 2, students should be able to

- roll smoothly and consecutively in a sideways direction, with an extended body position;
- rock smoothly and repeatedly back and forth on the back;
- roll forward smoothly;
- roll in at least two different directions;
- starting from a squatting position, rock backward, placing hands in the appropriate position behind;
- jump, land, and roll in at least one direction; and
- design a simple sequence incorporating one roll in any direction, one weight transfer, and one balance.

Sample Performance Task

Ask students to design, refine, and perform a simple sequence that starts with a definite beginning (balanced) shape, ends with a different shape, and has one roll (in any direction) and one weight transfer in the middle.

RUBRIC CLUES

To what extent do students

- show a definite beginning and ending shape in their sequences?
- include and correctly perform one roll and one weight transfer?
- practice the sequence so it can be performed smoothly and without hesitation?

Sample Portfolio Task

Give the students a list of pictured objects: an egg, pencil, ball, box, tire, and toaster (see figure 10.1). Ask them to circle the objects they think can rock or roll if pushed and to cross out the ones they think cannot rock or roll.

RUBRIC CLUES

To what extent do students

- select objects that rock or roll by accurately circling and crossing out their pictures?
- identify correctly a curved shape as the best one for rolling?

Emphasize	*Ideas for Lesson Development*
Rocking Chin to chest. Head to knees. Curved shape—no flat tires!	• Students practice rocking back and forth on their backs and from side to side, while staying in self-space. Encourage them to try rocking hard enough to touch their feet to the ground. • Students transfer their weight from a squatting position onto their backs, then rock back and forth. • Students move from a stand to a low level and rock onto their backs. Encourage them to try to come back up to a squat or stand. **Werner:** *Rock and Roll*
Sideways Like a pencil (head between arms)! Tight muscles. (Begin to) turn from your tummy.	• Students practice rolling sideways in self-space the length of a mat and then rolling first in one direction, then the other. **Werner:** *Balls, Eggs, and Pencils*

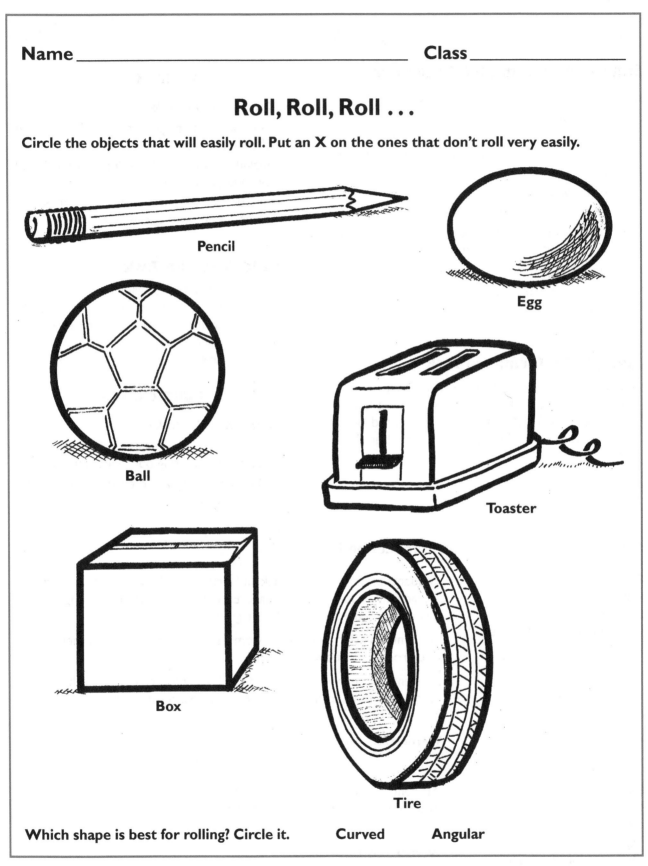

Roll, Roll, Roll . . .

Circle the objects that will easily roll. Put an **X** on the ones that don't roll very easily.

Pencil

Egg

Ball

Toaster

Box

Tire

Which shape is best for rolling? Circle it.   **Curved**   **Angular**

Figure 10.1   Portfolio task assessment sheet for rolling, grades 1 to 2.

From *Elementary Physical Education Teaching & Assessment: A Practical Guide,* by Christine J. Hopple, 2005, Champaign, IL: Human Kinetics.

Forward
Curved shape—no flat tires!
Chin to chest.
Behind up.
Push with your hands.

Backward
Curved shape—no flat tires.
Head to knees.
Hands by your ears.

- Students practice rolling forward at their spaces on the mats, down the mats, and so forth.

- Students practice jumping into the air, landing, and rolling. You should emphasize soft landings!

- Have students practice moving onto their backs and rocking.

- Write simple sequences on large task cards. Let students pick one from the "deck" and work on it. Here are some examples: starting shape, roll, balance, roll, ending shape; starting shape, roll, travel, roll, ending shape; starting shape, roll, weight transfer, roll, ending shape. Let students trade cards with other students or groups. Be sure to discuss the terms with students when you first use them.

Werner: *You've Got It All Backward*

KINDERGARTEN

Sample Performance Indicators

By the end of grade K, students should be able to

- roll sideways consecutively;

- rock back and forth on the back in a curled shape; and
- rock side to side in a curved (curled) shape.

Emphasize	*Ideas for Lesson Development*
Rocking Curved shape—no flat tires!	• In self-space, students practice rocking back and forth and side to side. Encourage them to wrap their arms around their legs as they rock.
Sideways Like a pencil (head between arms)!	• Students practice rolling sideways (log roll) to the right and left in their self-spaces and across mats.
	Werner: *Balls, Eggs, and Pencils*
Forward Curved shape—no flat tires! Chin to chest. Behind up.	• Set up very low (barely off the ground) jump-rope hurdles; encourage students to practice rolling over a hurdle, starting with their hands on one side of the hurdle and their feet on the other side.

Sample Course Standard

By the end of elementary school, students should be able to

- with a partner or a small group, combine the skills of balancing, rolling, and weight transfer, along with locomotor skills, to design, refine, and perform a gymnastics or dance sequence.

Balancing

Concepts and Skills	Learnable Pieces
Base of support	Bases of support are the body parts that hold you up. (1–2)
	A wide base of support is more stable (or better) than a narrow base of support. (1–2)
	It is harder to balance when your bases of support are far away from or outside your center of gravity. (3–4)
	The higher your center of gravity from the ground or equipment, the more difficult it is to balance. (3–4)
	Counterbalance involves a wide base of support and parts pushing against each other. (5–6)
	Counter-tension involves a narrow base of support and parts pulling away from each other. (5–6)
Static	Tight muscles. (K, 1–2, 3–4, 5–6)
	Count to three. (K, 1–2)
	(Eyes) pick a spot. (1–2)
	(Keep the) center of gravity above bases of support. (3–4)
Dynamic	(Keep the) center of gravity above bases of support. (3–4)
Inverted	Tight muscles. (3–4)
	(Keep the) center of gravity above bases of support. (3–4)
	Behind up. (3–4)

GRADES 5 TO 6

Sample Performance Indicators

By the end of grade 6, students should be able to

- balance on low equipment (tables, benches) in positions using a variety of bases of support;
- balance with partners using principles of counterbalance (pushing) and counter-tension (pulling);
- incorporate balance into a small-group designed sequence;
- balance in a variety of shapes while hanging from equipment; and
- balance in an inverted position.

NASPE Performance Indicators

- Develops and refines a gymnastics sequence (or creative dance sequence) demonstrating smooth transitions. (3–5, #1, 7)

Sample Performance Task

Ask students in groups of three or four to design, refine, and perform a sequence with smooth transitions between balanced, held positions and different weight transfers or rolls. The balances should reflect both individual balances and those in which group members support each other in the balance. Using equipment is optional.

RUBRIC CLUES

To what extent do students

- move smoothly from balanced positions to other elements in the sequence?
- meet all the sequence criteria?
- refine the sequence so all group members perform it smoothly and without hesitation?

Sample Portfolio Task

Ask students to describe one situation, not necessarily involving sports or even people, using the principle of counterbalance and one using the principle of counter-tension. They should be able to explain how and why the principle is used in each of these situations. (One example of counterbalance is the structure of a Native American teepee.)

RUBRIC CLUES

To what extent do students

- understand the concepts of counterbalance and counter-tension?
- understand why a specific concept was used?

Emphasize	*Ideas for Lesson Development*

Base of support
Counterbalance involves a wide base of support and parts pushing against each other.
Counter-tension involves a narrow base of support and parts pulling away from each other.
Static
Tight muscles.

- Discuss the principles of counterbalance (pushing against another person or object with a wide base of support) and counter-tension (pulling against each other or an object with a narrow base of support). Discuss and give examples of how each is used.

- Have students balance first in pairs, using the given examples of counterbalance and counter-tension. Can they move while pushing or pulling against each other? Then ask them to try these in groups of three or four. These examples are some of the ways they can try to move: (1) Sitting back to back with the elbows joined, stand up and sit down without moving the feet. (2) Standing face to face with their partner, palms against each other at shoulder level, inch the feet away from the center. How far can they get without falling? This can also be done in a group. (3) Holding their partner's wrists, with the feet close together, can they shuffle the feet sideways and move in a circle?

> **Werner:** *Lean on Me*
> *A Roll by Any Other Name . . .*

Flow (see "Effort," chapter 8)
Free
Smooth transitions.

- Challenge students to select their three favorite balances. By the time you count to 10 slowly, they must do each one, making a smooth transition from one to the other.

- Have students hold a balanced shape, move smoothly into a roll or weight transfer, and move into a different balance. They can then progress to repeating the sequence with a partner or in a small group.

- Have students design sequences in which they move onto a piece of large equipment (e.g., climbing apparatus, beam), travel and balance, and move off the piece, ending in a balanced position.

Werner: *Twins*
Partner Task Cards

GRADES 3 TO 4

Sample Performance Indicators

By the end of grade 4, students should be able to

- balance in a symmetrical or asymmetrical shape on large gymnastics equipment (e.g., beams, tables, benches);
- move smoothly from one balanced position to another in a variety of ways;
- balance on a variety of moving and other balancing objects (e.g., stilts, balance boards) (dynamic balance);
- balance in inverted positions using the least number of bases of support possible;
- balance in a variety of positions using different bases of support and directions when on large gymnastics equipment; and
- cooperatively balance as part of a small group by connecting with or supporting each other's body weight.

NASPE Performance Indicators

- Balances with control on a variety of objects (e.g., balance board, large apparatus, skates). (3–5, #1, 2)

Sample Performance Task

Ask students to design, refine, and perform a simple sequence starting with a balanced symmetrical shape, ending with an asymmetrical shape, and incorporating a roll (any direction) and a weight transfer in the middle. Different bases of support should be used for each of the two balances.

RUBRIC CLUES

To what extent do students

- meet the sequence criteria?
- hold the beginning and ending shapes long enough to be clearly balanced?
- choose skills they can complete with moderate success?

Sample Portfolio Task

Ask students to describe a sport or recreational activity requiring great balance from the player. If possible, the students should find or draw pictures of this activity. Why do they think the activity requires so much balance? What should the player remember to help keep better balance?

RUBRIC CLUES

To what extent do students

- understand the concept of balance?

Emphasize	*Ideas for Lesson Development*
Static (Keep the) center of gravity above bases of support. Tight muscles.	• Challenge students to balance with a partner by connecting body parts or supporting each other's body weight. • Have students form small groups (of three to five), and ask them to perform a balance in which each child is connected to or supporting another child's body weight.

Base of support
It is harder to balance when your bases of support are far away from or outside your center of gravity.
The higher your center of gravity from the ground or equipment, the more difficult it is to balance.

- Challenge students to balance in a variety of body shapes while they hang from large equipment (bars, climbing apparatus, and so on), with different combinations of body parts (hands, knees, ankles).

- Have the students balance a spoon on one finger to experience the concept of center-of-weight (gravity). Discuss why it did or did not fall off, why the spoon could not be balanced in the middle, and so forth.

- Challenge students to balance on a variety of large pieces of equipment (beams, tables, benches, horses) in symmetrical and asymmetrical shapes.

- Challenge students to balance on large pieces of equipment using different bases of support.

- Encourage students to change direction, level, and base of support while they move and balance on equipment, such as on a balance beam. Give suggestions on task cards for balances and traveling movements that demonstrate these changes, and allow students to make up others.

- Have students try moving on the ground or on appropriate pieces of equipment from one balanced position to another without losing balance. Can they move from a symmetrical to an asymmetrical balance? Inverted to upright balance?

- Take photos of the students' balances and display them on a bulletin board. Seeing the results can be great motivation and fun!

Werner: *Statues*   *Shoulder Stand*
         Same, Different   *Copy Cat*
PEC: *Tumbling Dice*

Dynamic
(Keep the) center of gravity above bases of support.

- Allow students to experiment with the concept of dynamic (moving) balance by balancing on such objects as balancing boards, stilts, skateboards, and roller skates.

Inverted
Tight muscles.
(Keep the) center of gravity above bases of support.
Behind up.

- Challenge students to balance in inverted (hips up) positions on the ground or on equipment, using bases of support appropriate to their skill level. Here are examples of how they might do these balances: head, both hands, one foot; both hands, one or both feet; both forearms, one or both feet; head, both hands; hands only; and forearms only.

- Give additional cues for balancing in a handstand position (introduce these to students as appropriate to their skill level): kick feet up high; hips, shoulders, hands in line; and control balance with fingertips.

Werner: *Bottoms Up*
         Statues

GRADES 1 TO 2

Sample Performance Indicators

By the end of grade 2, students should be able to

- balance on different numbers of bases of support;
- balance using a variety of symmetrical and asymmetrical body shapes, either with or without a partner;
- balance using a variety of inverted symmetrical and asymmetrical body shapes;
- balance using different bases of support on low equipment;
- balance while traveling and changing directions and levels on low- to medium-level equipment; and
- design and perform simple sequences involving balancing along with other skills (weight transfers, rolling) or concepts (levels, shapes).

NASPE Performance Indicators

- Discovers how to balance on different body parts, at different levels, becoming "like" a statue while making symmetrical and nonsymmetrical shapes. (K–2, #1, 9)

Sample Performance Task

Call out the numbers of bases of support from one to six ("Can you balance on three body parts? Five?") Have students hold each for a count of three-alligators.

RUBRIC CLUES

To what extent do students

- hold their position long enough to be clearly balanced ?

Sample Portfolio Task

Have students find a picture or photo or draw a picture of someone who is balanced. They should label the bases of support the person is balancing on.

RUBRIC CLUES

To what extent do students

- accurately describe the bases of support in their drawings?

Emphasize	*Ideas for Lesson Development*
Base of support Bases of support are the body parts that hold you up. A wide base of support is more stable (or better) than a narrow base of support.	• Discuss how shapes that are wider or have a wider base of support have more stability. Encourage pairs of students to make a balanced shape and to see if their partners can make them lose their balance by *gently* pressing against them with a hand. Challenge them to make a balance that is not quite as well balanced: Can they hold their position? **Werner:** *Push and Pull*
Static Tight muscles. Count to three.	• Have students travel throughout the marked-off area; at the signal, they each find a carpet square and balance on the number of bases of support that you call out. For more fun, make a large cardboard die and roll it (or let students roll it) to come up with the number. • See if students can balance rhythm sticks on different body parts while making wild shapes. Challenge them to change their shapes without the sticks falling off. **PEC:** *Toy Story Statues* *Seven Jumps* **Purcell Cone and Cone:** *Run, Hop, Jump, Skip*

Static
(Eyes) pick a spot.
Body shapes (see "Body Awareness," chapter 8)
Symmetrical
If you cut your body in two, each side would look the same.
Asymmetrical
If you cut your body in two, each side would look different.

- Discuss the difference between symmetrical and asymmetrical shapes; have students use different bases of support to make them. Challenge them to make inverted symmetrical and asymmetrical balances as well.

- Put out various pieces of low equipment (boxes, crates, low balance beams, tires, benches, sturdy sawhorses). Challenge students to balance on them using various bases of support.

- Challenge students to travel in different directions while on low- to medium-level equipment, such as beams. Encourage them to also change the level they travel in.

Werner: *Same, Different*
Copy Cat

KINDERGARTEN

Sample Performance Indicators

By the end of grade K, students should be able to
- balance on a variety of combinations of body parts;
- travel and stop in balanced positions; and
- follow different pathways while moving forward and sideways on the ground or on low equipment.

Sample Performance Task

Ask students to perform various simple balances (e.g., on one foot, one foot and two hands, two feet and one hand) on their carpet squares, holding them for a count of three.

RUBRIC CLUES

To what extent do students
- hold the balance without falling?

Emphasize

Static
Tight muscles.
Count to three.

Ideas for Lesson Development

- Students travel throughout general space; at the signal, they each find a carpet square and use the specific body part you call out to balance on the square.

- While in self-space, students balance a beanbag on different body parts that you call out. Challenge them to make wild shapes while balancing the beanbag on that body part.

- Students travel throughout the marked-off area; challenge them, at the signal, to freeze in a balanced position as quickly as possible.

- Have students travel forward and backward on large chalk pathways on the blacktop or ground without falling off.

Purcell Cone and Cone: *Run, Hop, Jump, Skip*
Werner: *Patches and Points*

Sample Course Standard

By the end of elementary school, students should be able to

- with a partner or small group, combine the skills of weight transfer, rolling, and balancing, along with nonlocomotor skills, to design, refine, and perform a gymnastics or dance sequence.

Weight Transfer

Concepts and Skills	Learnable Pieces
Rocking, rolling (from one body part to another)	(see "Rolling," this chapter) (K, 1–2)
Feet only (step-like actions with feet)	(see "Locomotor Movements," chapter 9) (K, 1–2)
Feet to hands (step-like actions using hands and feet)	Kick feet up high (for far extensions). (K, 1–2)
	Soft landings. (1–2, 3–4)
	Behind up. (3–4)
	Strong arms. (K, 1–2, 3–4, 5–6)
	Tight muscles. (K, 1–2, 3–4, 5–6)
	Head up (when moving onto equipment). (3–4, 5–6)
	Arms take weight first. (3–4, 5–6)
Spring takeoffs (flight)	Jump from one foot to two feet. (1–2)
	(Push off) balls of feet. (1–2)
	Soft landings. (1–2)

GRADES 5 TO 6

Sample Performance Indicators

By the end of grade 6, students should be able to

- travel and smoothly move into weight transfers from feet to hands;
- travel into a spring takeoff and then transfer weight onto a large apparatus (e.g., bars, beam, vault box);
- transfer weight off low apparatus (beam, bench, table) using a variety of body actions, starting with hands and feet stationary on the apparatus (e.g., stretching, twisting, turning); and
- transfer weight in a variety of ways along low- to medium-level apparatus (beam, benches) in a variety of ways, using changes in directions, levels, speeds, and body shapes.

NASPE Performance Indicators

- Develops and refines a gymnastics sequence (or creative dance sequence) demonstrating smooth transitions. (3–5, 1, #7)

Sample Performance Task

In groups of three or four, students design, refine, and perform sequences that incorporates rolls of at least two different shapes with at least one balance and one weight transfer. The sequence should incorporate at least two different relationships between partners.

RUBRIC CLUES

To what extent do students

- meet all given sequence criteria?
- refine the sequence so all group members can perform it smoothly and without hesitation?

Sample Portfolio Task

Ask students to diagram their sequence. Where will they start? Finish? What pathways will they use? What roll, balance, and weight transfer will they do and where? After they have performed the sequence, ask them to rate and justify their performances on a scale of one to three, three being the best, according to the criteria they diagrammed.

RUBRIC CLUES

To what extent do students
- correctly diagram their sequences?
- show all of the sequence criteria (e.g., two weight transfers)?

Emphasize	*Ideas for Lesson Development*
Flow (see "Effort," chapter 8) *Free* Smooth transitions.	• Challenge students to transfer weight from their feet to hands in a variety of ways on the ground. If a student is advanced enough, add cues for other actions, which might include these: (1) Cartwheel: stretch arms and feet wide; one body part touches ground at a time; hand, hand, foot, foot sequence. (2) Round-off: snap legs together (at top); twist hips; feet land at same time. (3) Handstand: hips, shoulders, hands in line. (4) Walkover: step into the action (for front walkover); kick leading leg over with force; split legs in air. The students must travel smoothly into and out of these weight transfers. • Encourage students to transfer their weight along low- to medium-level equipment (e.g., beam, bench, table) in a variety of ways. You might require changes in levels, speeds, directions, and body shapes. • Ask students to design sequences, alone or in pairs, in which they transfer their weight in order to move *up to, onto, along,* and *off* a piece of equipment.

Werner:	*Clock Face*	*A Roll by Any Other Name . . .*
	Beam Me Up	*Hip Circles*
	Me and My Shadow	*Feet, Hands, Feet*

Emphasize	*Ideas for Lesson Development*
Feet to hands Strong arms. Tight muscles. Head up (when moving onto equipment). Arms take weight first.	• Challenge students to transfer their weight *onto* large equipment (beams, bars, climbing apparatus, vault box) in a variety of ways by springing off from two feet. How many different ways can they find to transfer their weight onto a particular piece of equipment? • Challenge students, starting with their hands and feet on a chosen piece of equipment, to transfer their weight *off* it. A variety of body actions, such as twisting, stretching, and turning, can be used to move off. • Challenge students to move up to and transfer their weight *over* and *on/off* specific equipment of a chosen size and height.

Werner: *Fantasy Flight*
PEC: *Tater' Diggin*

GRADES 3 TO 4

Sample Performance Indicators

By the end of grade 4, students should be able to

- transfer weight from one body part to another (hands, knees, feet) in a variety of ways when on a large apparatus (e.g., climbing apparatus, bars);
- use safe methods to recover from unstable feet-to-hand weight transfers;
- use a variety of body actions to move into and out of a number of weight transfers from feet to hands with large extensions (e.g., stretching legs wide; torso twisting; rolling, curving feet over to land on one or two feet);
- step into weight transfers from feet to hands over low equipment or apparatus (e.g., box, crate, beam);
- transfer weight in various ways off low equipment or apparatus (beam, bench, box) onto floor level, starting with hands on the floor;
- use balances to move smoothly into and out of different weight transfers;
- travel into a spring takeoff and then transfer weight from feet to hands onto low- to medium-level equipment or apparatus (e.g., beam, bench, table, large tire); and
- transfer weight onto low- to medium-level equipment or apparatus by placing the hands on equipment and springing off of two feet (land on hands and feet or knees).

Sample Performance Task

Ask students to design, refine, and perform a simple sequence starting with a balanced symmetrical shape, ending with an asymmetrical shape, and incorporating a roll (any direction) and a weight transfer in the middle. Different bases of support should be used for each of the two balances.

RUBRIC CLUES

To what extent do students

- meet the sequence criteria?
- hold the beginning and ending shapes long enough to be clearly balanced?
- choose skills they can complete with moderate success?

Sample Portfolio Task

At the end of the learning experiences in weight transfer, ask students to complete figure 10.2.

RUBRIC CLUES

To what extent do students

- complete the given questions?

Emphasize	*Ideas for Lesson Development*
Feet to hands Tight muscles. **Flow (see "Effort,"** **chapter 8)** *Free*	• Challenge students to transfer their weight from one body part to another when they are on large equipment (e.g., climbing apparatus, bars, beam). Encourage them to use the hands, knees, and feet to move from one part of the apparatus to another. • Have students demonstrate a balance that allows them to move smoothly into and out of a chosen weight transfer. Have them practice to learn to do it smoothly. • Discuss how weight transfers using large extensions (cartwheels, handstands, and so on) require more force and speed to complete the movement than do movements with small extensions.

Werner: *Cross at the Intersection*   *Clock Face*
                The String Challenge   *A Roll by Any Other Name . . .*
PEC: *Tater' Diggin*

Name _____ Class _____

Transferring My Weight

☆ **My favorite weight transfer is** _____ **because** _____

_____

_____ .

☆ **The easiest weight transfer I can do is** _____

_____

_____ .

☆ **The hardest weight transfer I can do is** _____

_____

_____ .

☆ **My favorite sport or activity that uses weight transfers is** _____

_____

_____ .

☆ **The weight transfer I want to improve the most is** _____

_____

_____ .

Figure 10.2   Portfolio task assessment sheet for weight transfer, grades 3 to 4.

From *Elementary Physical Education Teaching & Assessment: A Practical Guide*, by Christine J. Hopple, 2005, Champaign, IL: Human Kinetics.

Emphasize	*Ideas for Lesson Development*
Feet to hands Behind up. Tight muscles. Head up (when moving onto equipment). Arms take weight first.	• Challenge students to step *into* weight transfers, then move *over* low equipment (e.g., box, crate, beam) by placing their hands on the equipment. If you wish, have them begin by starting on the ground, making a circle on the mat or ground in which they can place their hands. Once they are comfortable with this, they can progress to moving over equipment that is higher off the ground. • Have students practice transferring their weight *onto* low- to medium-level equipment by first placing their hands on the equipment, then springing off both feet to land on it. Encourage them to land on either their knees and feet or feet only. • Encourage students to travel into a spring takeoff, then transfer their weight *onto* low- to medium-level equipment (e.g., beam, bench, table, bar, large tire set in ground). **Werner:** *Ready for Takeoff*
Feet to hands Tight muscles. Soft landings.	• After transferring their weight onto low- to medium-level equipment, such as boxes, tires, beams, and mats, ask students to transfer their weight *off* the equipment in a variety of ways, starting with their hands on the floor. They can use such actions as rolling and pushing their feet off the equipment.

GRADES 1 TO 2

Sample Performance Indicators

By the end of grade 2, students should be able to

- transfer weight from one set of body parts to another in a variety of ways (e.g., twist, turn);
- transfer weight over low equipment (e.g., hurdles, hoops, mats) in a variety of ways, beginning with hands on the opposite side of the hurdle;
- transfer weight from feet to hands in a variety of ways;
- transfer weight from feet to hands, making the legs land in different places around the body;
- transfer weight across a mat in as many ways as possible; and
- transfer weight by traveling into a spring takeoff.

Sample Performance Task

Ask students to design, refine, and perform a simple sequence that starts with a definite beginning (balanced) shape, ends with a different shape, and has one roll (in any direction) and one weight transfer in the middle.

RUBRIC CLUES

To what extent do students

- show a definite beginning and ending shape in their sequences?
- include and correctly perform one roll and one weight transfer?
- practice the sequence so it can be performed without hesitation?

Sample Portfolio Task

Discuss with students the many ways they can transfer their weight, then ask them to draw a picture of their favorite way to transfer their weight.

To what extent do students
- show an example of weight transfer?

Emphasize	Ideas for Lesson Development
Rocking, rolling (see "Rolling," this chapter) Curved shape—no flat tires! **Feet to hands** Strong arms. Tight muscles.	• Ask students to show how many different ways, using low-rope hurdles, hoops, mats, and so forth, they can transfer their weight over the equipment. • Challenge students to move their feet, with their hands on a hoop, to other parts of the hoop. • Set up mats at stations, each with a picture and description of the weight transfer students should use to move across that mat. Examples can include the crab walk, bear walk (hand and foot on the same side of the body move forward at the same time), inchworm (feet stay in place, hands "walk" forward; hands stay anchored, feet "walk" forward), and wheelbarrow (with a partner). Have one mat and station where students can choose a movement (caterpillar, cartwheel, and so on.). Use the stations alone or as part of gymnastics stations, which include rolls and balances as well. • Use jumping boxes, tires, bars, and so forth to challenge students to transfer their weight onto and off the equipment, beginning with their hands on the equipment. **Werner:** *Bunny Hop* / *Rock and Roll*
Feet to hands Strong arms. Soft landings. Kick feet up high (for far extensions).	• Challenge students in self-space to take as much of their weight as possible on their hands. • Have students see if they can make their legs land first in the same place, then in different places, around their body than where they were originally.
Spring takeoffs (flight) Jump from one foot to two feet. (Push off) balls of feet. Soft landings.	• Have students practice transferring their weight by traveling into a spring takeoff (taking off one foot, landing on two feet). Stress the landings; have different equipment available that students can travel up and spring onto (jumping boxes, mats, large tires set in the ground). Have them jump off the object, making different shapes. **Werner:** *Ready for Takeoff*

KINDERGARTEN

Sample Performance Indicators

By the end of grade K, students should be able to

- transfer weight from one body part to another in a variety of ways, using rocking, rolling, and feet-to-hand actions with small extensions; and

- take weight momentarily onto the hands by transferring weight from feet to hands with large extensions.

Emphasize	Ideas for Lesson Development
Rocking, rolling (see "Rolling," this chapter) Curved shape—no flat tires!	• Have students, in self-space, practice transferring their weight from one body part to another by rocking back and forth on their backs and fronts.
Feet to hands Strong arms. Tight muscles. Kick feet up high (for far extensions).	• Students can practice various weight transfers, such as the crab walk, bear walk, and leap frog. • Encourage students to take their weight onto their hands by transferring it from the feet. Challenge them to kick the feet high! • Have a very low jump-rope hurdle or rope on the ground for each student. Challenge them to put their hands on one side of the rope and jump their feet up and over to the other side of the line. They can also start with one hand on each side of the rope and try to move their feet from one side to the other.

Chapter 11

Manipulative Skills

By the end of elementary school, students should be able to

- design and play a small-group game that incorporates the skills of dribbling with the hands, passing, and shooting to keep a ball away from defenders and move it toward a goal area; and

- use the basic offensive and defensive strategies for keep-away games (i.e., creating and denying space) when playing in small groups.

Dribbling With the Hands

Concepts and Skills	Learnable Pieces
Dribbling	Waist high. (K, 1–2)
	Finger pads. (1–2)
	Firm, flexible wrists. (3-4)
	Ball in front, out to side. (3-4)
	Look up. (5-6)
Passing (throwing skill specific to basketball)	Hands to side, behind ball. (3-4)
Bounce pass	Push the ball out and down. (3-4)
Chest pass	Push the ball away from your chest. (3-4)
	Step toward your partner or target. (5-6)
Shooting (throwing skill specific to basketball)	Pushing hand is behind, toward bottom of the ball. (5-6)
	Other hand supports the ball at the side. (5-6)
	Extend arms up and out. (5-6)

GRADES 5 TO 6

Sample Performance Indicators

By the end of grade 6, students should be able to

- dribble while traveling in a group (in a large marked-off area) without touching others or stationary objects;
- dribble and smoothly change from one direction to another without stopping;
- dribble and smoothly change from one speed to another without stopping;
- dribble continuously while stopping and starting traveling at the signal;
- dribble and then throw a leading pass to a moving partner using a chest or bounce pass;
- travel, dribble, and pivot on one foot to begin dribbling in another direction;
- shoot toward an appropriate-height goal from different distances;
- dribble and keep the ball away from an opponent in a one-on-one situation;
- dribble and pass in a small-group keep-away game; and
- cooperate and play a small-group game using passing, receiving, and shooting toward an appropriate-height goal.

NASPE Performance Indicators

- Dribbles then passes a basketball to a moving receiver. (3-5, #1, 8)

Sample Performance Task

In a small group (two-on-two or three-on-three), students are asked to design and play a keep-away game using dribbling, passing, and shooting to keep a ball away from defenders and move it toward a goal area. They may determine their own boundaries and rules except that double dribbling and traveling with the ball are not allowed.

RUBRIC CLUES

To what extent do students

- consistently dribble legally?
- correctly pass the ball to a partner?

If desired, the following also can be assessed during this task:

- try to create space on offense by moving to open areas where they can receive the ball?
- try to deny space on defense by keeping their bodies between the ball and intended player or goal area?
- cooperate and work together in order to play?

Sample Portfolio Task

Students view a basketball game on TV or in person. Ask them to respond to these written questions: (a) What does the person with the ball (offensive player) do when dribbling to keep the ball away from the defensive person? (b) What is one thing a player on offense, without the ball, can do to create space to receive the ball? (c) Name two things a defensive person does to deny space and keep an offensive player from passing the ball to a teammate.

RUBRIC CLUES

To what extent do students

- show they understand the concepts of creating and denying space through their accurate answers and citation of examples?

Emphasize	*Ideas for Lesson Development*
Dribbling Look up.	- Have students dribble while traveling in a group (in a large marked-off area) without touching others or stationary objects. Challenge them to go as fast as possible and control dribbling.
	- Challenge students to travel through general space, moving as close as possible to others without touching them. See how quickly they can move away from others.

- Call out different directions as students move through general space; challenge students to dribble and change direction smoothly without stopping.

- Use a tambourine or drum to mark different speeds for the students while they are dribbling; challenge them to change speed smoothly. Vary the time intervals between changing the speeds.

- Students dribble while they travel through general space and, at the signal, stop traveling but continue dribbling. At the next signal, they begin traveling again.

- Discuss how pivoting means one foot is "glued" to the floor. Have students dribble in any direction and, at the signal, pivot on one foot before dribbling in another direction.

PEC: *Blinking Game*	*Dribbling With Dinosaurs*
Dribble Tip Over	*Dribbling Maze*
Dribbling Beanbag Transfer	*Shadow Dribble Tag*
Dribbling Dance	*Sharks and Minnows*

Passing
Bounce pass or chest pass
Step toward your partner or target.

- Have students practice dribbling, stopping, pivoting, and passing the ball to a partner or target on the wall. Post targets of varying sizes at different heights around the gym for practicing against the wall.

- Have students practice dribbling and throwing a leading pass to a moving partner using a chest or bounce pass. Discuss how a leading pass is thrown where a person will be, not where they are, in order for the receiver not to have to stop for it.

PEC: *Card Sharks Basketball Passing*
Ghostbuster Dribble

Shooting
Pushing hand is behind, toward bottom of the ball.
Other hand supports the ball at the side.
Extend arms up and out.

- Put up different-sized targets on the wall; have students shoot toward one of them at an appropriate height from different distances.

- Set carpet squares in various locations and have students shoot toward wall targets from each one (or choose several they want to shoot from). Discuss how distance affects how they must shoot the ball.

General space (see "Space Awareness," chapter 8)
Offense
Create space by moving to open areas to pass or receive the ball.
Keep your body between the ball and the defender.

- Dribble Tag: Students dribble anywhere within the boundaries, which are the size of half a basketball court or smaller (if students are highly skilled). They try to avoid being tagged by the student designated as "it" and who also is dribbling while moving. If tagged, a student stands and dribbles with the nondominant hand 25 times.

- Students partner up and set up boundaries. The partner on offense dribbles, trying to keep the ball from the defender; the defender tries to maneuver the offense into a position to lose the ball. Allow students to make up additional rules.

DRIBBLING WITH THE HANDS

Defense
Deny space by staying between the opponent and intended goal.

- Have students form small groups (two-on-two, three-on-two, two-on-one); offensive players use dribbling and passing to keep the ball away from defenders. Allow the players to make up their own rules. When it is appropriate, discuss the offensive and defensive strategies of creating and denying space, and why these are important.

- Students in small groups dribble, pass, receive, and shoot toward a goal of appropriate height or some other target.

Belka: *Advance and Score Basketball*
PEC: *Dribbling Tag*   *Rug Rats*
      Rings of Fire Dribbling   *Shark*

GRADES 3 TO 4

Sample Performance Indicators

By the end of grade 4, students should be able to
- dribble a ball in self-space using one, then the other, hand with proper form;
- dribble while moving to the right or left, using the appropriate hand;
- dribble and change direction at the signal;
- dribble and quickly change the pathway they are moving on at the signal;
- dribble and change from one speed to another at the signal;
- dribble while keeping the ball away from stationary opponents; and
- travel, dribble, and chest- and bounce-pass the ball to a stationary partner.

Sample Performance Task

Ask students to dribble and move at a comfortable speed throughout a large marked-off area while avoiding others and keeping control of the ball.

RUBRIC CLUES

To what extent do students
- change the direction and pathway of their dribbling to avoid crashing into others?
- control the ball as they move throughout the area?

Sample Portfolio Task

Ask students to write a letter to a current basketball player of their choice, as if the player is in a slump and having trouble controlling the ball when dribbling. In the letter, they give some hints to help the player get back to great dribbling.

RUBRIC CLUES

To what extent do students
- show they understand how to dribble by using cues they learned during instruction?
- accurately justify their suggestions?

Emphasize

Dribbling
Firm, flexible wrists.
Ball in front, out to side.

Ideas for Lesson Development

- Have third and fourth graders teach you to dribble; do exactly as they say. They'll learn (and remember) the cues much better!
- Have students change the direction they are moving in while dribbling to the one you call out.
- See if students can dribble at the speed you mark by tambourine or drum.

- Have students change from the pathway they are moving on to the one you call out.

- Challenge students to dribble while moving to the right and left, each making sure to dribble with the hand opposite the direction they are moving.

- Have students face you; use hand or verbal signals to indicate the direction they should dribble in (forward, backward, right, left). Then have them get in groups of two or three, with one partner directing the others in the group; rotate so each child gets to be leader.

> **PEC:** *Dribbling Dance*   *Dribbling Maze*
> *Red Light, Green Light Dribbling*   *Dribbling Beanbag Transfer*
> *Dribbling Math Challenge*   *Shadow Dribble Tag*
> *Dribble Tip Over*   *Dribble Frenzy*

General space (see "Space Awareness," chapter 8)
Offense
Keep your body between the ball and the defender.

- Variation of Trees in the Forest (see page 117): Have students dribble from one end of the marked-off area to the other end, trying to avoid being touched by students who are standing in hoops scattered throughout general space. If touched, they dribble in their self-space for a count of 10 before moving on toward the end line.

- Set up a zigzag obstacle course using hoops or tires. Students standing in these hoops try to steal the ball from one student who is moving from one end of the course to the other. Set up enough courses to have about four or five students per course. After students dribble back to the beginning line they rotate into a hoop, and students in the last hoops become the dribblers. Have students also try this dribbling with the nondominant hand.

> **Buschner:** *Dribble Tag*
> **PEC:** *Rings of Fire Dribbling*
> *Rug Rats*
> *Dribbling Tag*

Passing
Hands to side, behind ball.
Bounce pass
Push the ball out and down.
Chest pass
Push the ball away from your chest.

- Have students dribble toward a stationary partner, then chest- or bounce-pass the ball to him or her.

- Have students pair up; one partner dribbles in general space, while the other partner travels away through general space. At the signal, non-dribblers freeze, while dribblers move toward their partners. When they are about 10 feet (3 m) away, the dribblers pass the ball to their partners and they all move again until the next signal.

> **PEC:** *Ghostbuster Dribble*

GRADES 1 TO 2

Sample Performance Indicators

By the end of grade 2, students should be able to

- dribble a ball in self-space using the favored hand;
- dribble a ball in self-space while switching from one hand to the other;
- dribble a ball in self-space at the different levels;
- dribble while slowly traveling in different directions; and
- dribble while slowly traveling on different pathways.

Sample Performance Task

Students continuously dribble the ball, remaining stationary in self-space.

RUBRIC CLUES

To what extent do students

- keep the ball under control in self-space when dribbling?

- dribble continuously using the preferred hand?
- dribble using the finger pads, rather than slapping the ball with their palms?

Sample Portfolio Task

Ask students to draw an outline of their hands on a piece of paper and color in the part of the hand that should touch the ball while dribbling.

RUBRIC CLUES

To what extent do students

- show they understand which part of the hand to dribble with by coloring in the finger pads (top third of each finger)?

Emphasize	Ideas for Lesson Development
Dribbling Finger pads. Waist high.	• Provide a variety of balls for students to dribble: oversize training volleyballs, regular volleyballs, playground balls, junior basketballs. • Have students trade balls with other students while working on continuously dribbling in self-space. • Have students dribble in as many different places around their bodies as possible. • Have students dribble a ball in self-space, practicing first with one hand and then the other. • Challenge students to dribble a ball in self-space while alternating hands. • Have students dribble a ball in self-space at low, medium, and high levels. • Challenge students to dribble while traveling forward and backward, keeping the ball under control. Have them change the direction they are moving in when you signal. • Mark some pathways on the ground; ask students to dribble while following the pathways. Encourage them to go at a speed that is challenging, yet allows them to keep control of the ball.

- Have students practice dribbling in their self-space around their bodies in different places (e.g., behind them) and while making different shapes (e.g., twisted shape, wide shape with legs, and so on). Afterward, have them pick their three favorite shapes to make while dribbling. Using upbeat music, have them make each shape while dribbling for eight counts, changing from one shape to the other and starting over when done with all three. Challenge students to move from one shape to the other without stopping their dribble.

PEC: *Card Sharks Dribble and Catch*   *Monster in the Forest*
      Dribble Frenzy   *Red Light, Green Light Dribble*
      Hula Hoop Dribbling

KINDERGARTEN

Sample Performance Indicators

By the end of grade K, students should be able to

- use two hands to bounce and catch a large playground ball; and
- use two hands to bounce and catch a ball while slowly traveling forward.

NASPE Performance Indicators

- Drops a ball and catches it at the peak of the bounce. (K-2, #1, 7)

Emphasize	*Ideas for Lesson Development*
Dribbling Waist high.	- Have students use two hands to bounce and catch a large playground ball while they stand in self-space. Challenge them to try catching with one hand. - Have students use two hands to bounce and catch a ball while they slowly travel forward. - Challenge students to bounce the ball, clap, then catch the ball, as well as to continuously bounce the ball using two hands.

Sample Course Standard

By the end of elementary school, students should be able to

- design and play a small-group game that incorporates the skills of kicking, passing, receiving, collecting, and punting to keep a ball away from defenders and move it toward a goal area; and

- use the basic offensive and defensive strategies for keep-away games (i.e., creating and denying space) when playing in small groups.

Kicking and Punting

Concepts and Skills	Learnable Pieces
Instep kick	Eyes (focus) on the ball. (K)
	Stand a little behind, to one side (of the ball). (1–2)
	Kick with the shoelaces (the top part of instep). (1–2)
	Kick hard. (1–2)
	Kick underneath the ball. (3–4)
	Toes (follow through) to target. (3–4)
Inside kick	Eyes (focus) on the ball. (K)
	Stand a little behind, to one side (of the ball). (1–2)
	Toes and knee out, like a duck. (1–2)
	Kick through the middle (of the ball). (3–4)
	Inside of foot (points) to the target. (3–4, 5–6)
	Kick to where your partner will be. (5–6)
Dribbling	Little pushes. (K)
	Push, don't kick (the ball). (1–2)
	Keep it close (to you). (1–2)
	(Use) insides (of the feet). (K, 1–2, 3–4)
	(Use) outsides (of the feet). (1–2, 3–4)
	Look ahead. (5–6)
Punting	Hold (the ball at shoulder level). (1–2)
	Step (with the nonkicking leg). (1–2)
	Drop (the ball). (1–2)
	Kick with the shoelaces (the top part of instep). (1–2)
	Kick hard. (3–4)
	Foot to target. (5–6)
Collecting	
Inside of foot	Inside of the foot faces the ball. (3–4)
	Contact the middle of the ball. (3–4)
	Give with the foot—trap an egg! (3–4)
With body parts	Move under the ball. (5–6)
	Give with the body—trap an egg! (5–6)

GRADES 5 TO 6

Sample Performance Indicators

By the end of grade 6, students should be able to

- dribble and change speeds at the signal;
- dribble with a group in a marked-off area without losing control of the ball and while avoiding contact with others or opponents;
- use the inside of the foot to dribble and kick a leading pass to a moving partner;
- punt a ball using a two- or three-step approach;
- punt a ball to targets at varying distances;
- collect a thrown or kicked ball using the thigh and chest;
- defend a goal by catching or deflecting balls kicked to them with appropriate force;
- dribble and pass in an small-game keep-away situation; and
- cooperate to play a designed or given small-group game involving dribbling, passing, kicking, or punting to keep the ball away from opponents and to reach a goal area.

NASPE Performance Indicators

- Designs a new game incorporating at least two motor skills, rules, and strategies. (3–5, #2, 17)

Sample Performance Task

Students form small groups to design and play a game using dribbling, passing, receiving, collecting, and punting to keep a ball away from defenders and move it toward a goal area. Students can determine their own boundaries, rules, and goal area.

RUBRIC CLUES

To what extent do students

- dribble while looking up?
- kick a leading pass to a teammate while playing?

If desired, the following can also be assessed during this task:

- try to create space when on offense by moving to open areas to pass and receive the ball?
- try to deny space when on defense by keeping their body between the ball and the intended player or goal?
- cooperate to play their game?

Sample Portfolio Task

Ask students to show their knowledge related to the skill of kicking by completing figure 11.1.

RUBRIC CLUES

To what extent do students

- give appropriate examples of sports involving kicking?
- show a clear understanding of the kicking cues?

Emphasize	*Ideas for Lesson Development*
Inside kick Inside of foot (points) to the target. Kick to where your partner will be.	• In a small-group game situation, students pass to each other and toward a goal area using the instep of the foot. Allow them to set up their own boundaries, determine their rules, and use a goalie, if they wish. • Discuss how a leading pass is kicked to where a person will be so the person doesn't have to stop moving in order to receive the ball. Pair up the students: Have one person, in a stationary position, kick the ball to a moving partner using a leading pass. After three kicks, they switch roles.

Name _____ **Class** _____

Kicking—What Do You Know?

Name one hint to be a good kicker: _____

What are two games or activities that use kicking?

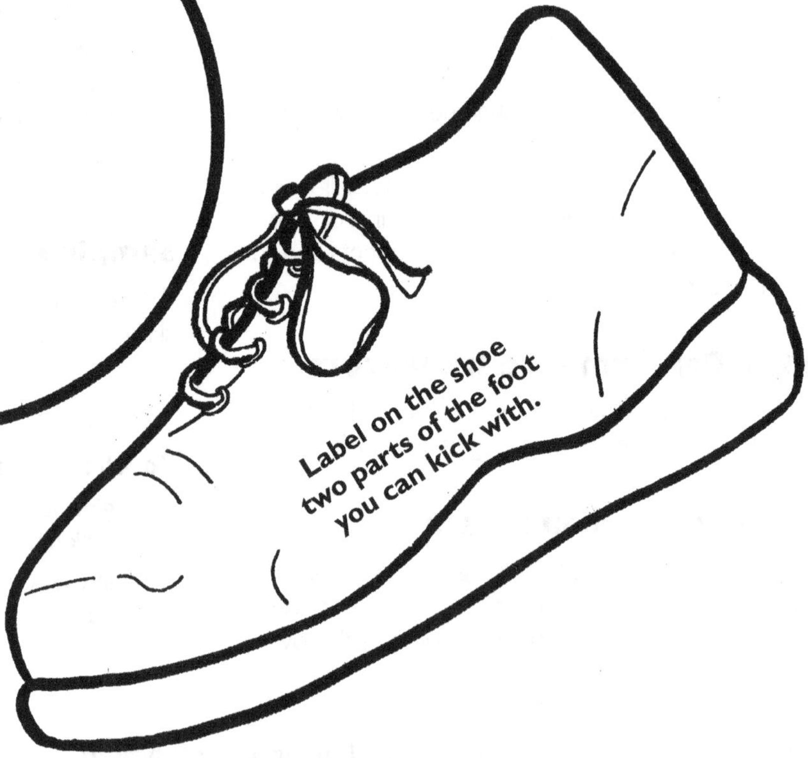

Label on the shoe two parts of the foot you can kick with.

What is the purpose for using these two different parts of your foot to kick?

Part 1 _____ **Use it to** _____

Part 2 _____ **Use it to** _____

Figure 11.1   Portfolio task assessment sheet for kicking, grades 5 to 6.

From *Elementary Physical Education Teaching & Assessment: A Practical Guide,* by Christine J. Hopple, 2005, Champaign, IL: Human Kinetics.

- In a very large, open area, challenge students to keep a ball moving at all times between themselves and a partner. To do this, they should also be moving at all times; thus, they will need to use dribbling and leading passes.

Belka: *Triangle Soccer*
PEC: *Ghostbuster Soccer   Soccer Passing Challenge*
      Soccer Pass Croquet

Dribbling
Look ahead.

- In a large marked-off area, students dribble to the tempo you set by tambourine or drum. See if students can keep up with the speed without losing control of the ball.

PEC: *Obstacle Soccer*

Punting
Foot to target.

- Encourage students to use a two- or three-step approach for punting.

- Put up a net or rope for students to punt a ball over; their partners can catch or retrieve it and punt it back. Slant the rope so students can choose the height at which they punt.

- Pair up the students: One partner hikes the ball to the other, who punts it to targets or zones at various distances.

Collecting
With body parts
Move under the ball.
Give with the body—trap an egg!

- Have one partner toss or gently kick a ball to the other partner at a high level. The receiving partner tries to collect the ball using the chest, thigh, and so forth.

PEC: *Up and Under*

General space (see "Space Awareness," chapter 8)
Offense
Keep your body between the ball and the defender. Create space by moving to open areas to pass or receive the ball.
Defense
Deny space by staying between the opponent and intended goal.

- Allow students to set up a small-group game (two-on-two, three-on-three, four-on-four, three-on-two) and use kicking skills to move a ball toward a goal area. Provide a variety of equipment they can use to set up goals; allow the use of a goalie, if they wish.

Belka: *Advance and Score Soccer*
      Defend the Shot
PEC: *Sharks and Minnows Soccer Style*
      Stock Your Closets

GRADES 3 TO 4

Sample Performance Indicators

By the end of grade 4, students should be able to

- run and kick a ball that is moving slowly toward and away from them, using the instep;
- use the insides or outsides of the feet to slowly dribble the ball;
- dribble while changing pathways and directions at the signal;
- dribble in a group in a marked-off area without losing control of the ball or colliding with others;
- dribble around stationary opponents and avoid losing the ball;
- dribble and then kick the ball to a large target area from a distance of choice, using the instep;
- dribble and then kick the ball to a target or stationary partner while using the inside of the foot;
- use the inside of the foot to collect a ball coming toward them; and
- punt a ball as high and as far as possible.

NASPE Performance Indicators

- Describes the difference in foot placement when kicking a stationary ball, a ball moving away, and a ball moving toward. (3–5, #2, 15)

Sample Performance Task

Students dribble inside a large marked-off area, keeping the ball away from stationary opponents. There should be enough stationary students in the area to challenge the dribblers. If control of the ball is lost, the student retrieves it and continues dribbling.

RUBRIC CLUES

To what extent do students

- keep (or lose) control of the ball?
- keep their bodies between the ball and defender?
- change pathways to elude opponents?

Sample Portfolio Task

Ask students to reflect on what they have learned about kicking by completing figure 11.2.

RUBRIC CLUES

To what extent do students

- demonstrate the ability to correctly kick a ball?

Emphasize	*Ideas for Lesson Development*
Instep kick Kick underneath the ball. Toes (follow through) to target. **Inside kick** Kick through the middle (of the ball). Inside of foot (points) to the target.	• Make large goals for kicking. Crisscross masking tape on a large piece of canvas, spray paint over it, and remove the tape. Hang this canvas over a rope for a great target students can kick a ball to. • Set up different target zones or areas and pair up the students. One partner runs up to and kicks a ball using the instep; the other marks where it lands with a cone. After five kicks, they switch roles. Challenge students to kick to the farthest zone they can. • Place a soccer or playground ball in a ball net suspended from a rope strung between two standards. Students can practice kicking the ball without it going anywhere! • Put up targets and challenge students to kick above them, then below them. Discuss what they had to do differently for each kick (for above, use the instep; for below, use the inside).

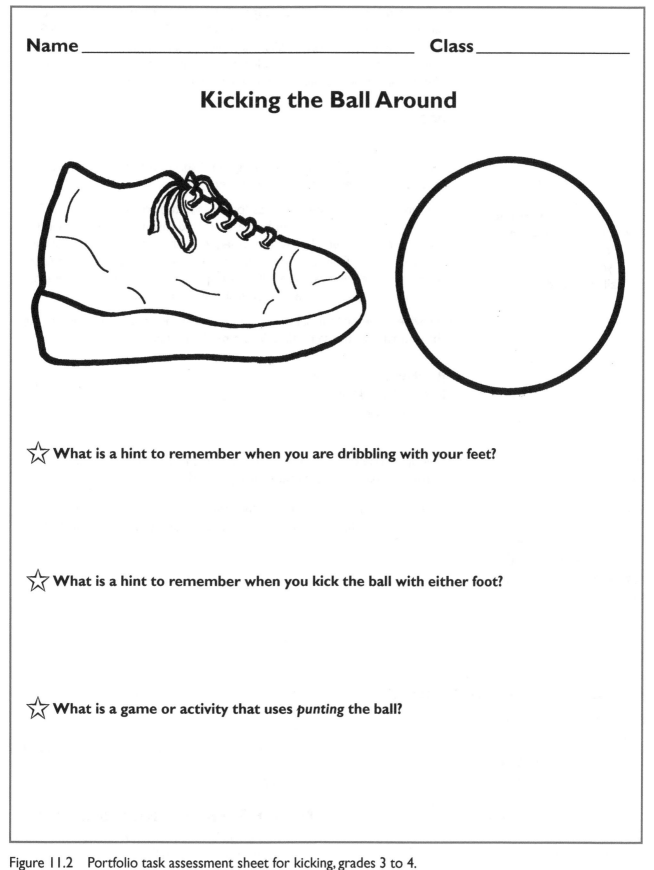

Kicking the Ball Around

Name _____ Class _____

☆ **What is a hint to remember when you are dribbling with your feet?**

☆ **What is a hint to remember when you kick the ball with either foot?**

☆ **What is a game or activity that uses *punting* the ball?**

Figure 11.2   Portfolio task assessment sheet for kicking, grades 3 to 4.

- Allow students to dribble throughout general space and kick to a goal area or target from a distance of their choice. Discuss how distance from the goal affects the type of kick they choose (instep or inside). After many successful trials, have some students play goalies and defend the target. After a short time, goalies should switch roles with dribblers.

PEC: *All-Ball Kickball*

Dribbling
(Use) insides (or) outsides (of the feet).
General space (see "Space Awareness," chapter 8)
Offense
Keep your body between the ball and the defender.

- Have students dribble throughout general space; at the signal, they change pathways or directions (which you specify) as quickly as possible.

- Set up a large marked-off area as for Trees in the Forest (see page 117). Have some students stand in hoops scattered throughout the area; others dribble from one end line to the other, trying not to lose control of their ball to a "tree." Trees get one point each time they cause someone to lose control of the ball, two points if they trap a ball. If students lose control of the ball, they get it back and keep dribbling to the end line.

- Provide three or four balls per child and challenge students to get all the balls moving at the same time in the marked-off area.

Buschner: *Kicking Review*
PEC: *All-Ball Kickball*
    Dot Stops

Punting
Kick hard.

Collecting
Inside of foot
Inside of the foot faces the ball.
Contact the middle of the ball.
Give with the foot—trap an egg!

- Set up a zone or target for each pair. Students punt toward a target while a partner marks the zone; after five punts, they switch roles.

- Students work with a partner: One student passes the ball to the other, who traps it. Challenge them to pass the ball using varied amounts of force.

Belka: *Aim and Go!*

GRADES 1 TO 2

Sample Performance Indicators

By the end of grade 2, students should be able to
- kick a slowly rolling ball by using the instep;
- run up to and kick a stationary ball as far as possible using the instep;
- kick a stationary ball along the ground toward a stationary partner or target while using the inside of the foot;
- dribble and slowly jog while using the inside of either foot;
- dribble and slowly jog around stationary obstacles while using the inside of each foot;
- trap a slowly moving ball rolling toward and away from them, contacting it with the ball of the foot; and
- punt a ball into the air using the instep.

NASPE Performance Indicators

- Taps the ball from foot to foot, shifting weight and balancing the body on the nondribbling foot, while in one location (i.e., not moving). (K–2, #1, 6)

Sample Performance Task

Within a large marked-off area, students travel while dribbling a ball with the feet at a comfortable speed that allows them to show control. If you wish, give pinnies to a small group of students that you will focus on for a time. At the signal, have the students give the pinnies to another group.

RUBRIC CLUES

To what extent do students

- keep (or lose) control of the ball (i.e., keep it close)?
- bump into others or go out of bounds?
- use the inside (or outside) of the foot to dribble, not the toe?

Sample Portfolio Task

Ask students to complete figure 11.3.

RUBRIC CLUES

To what extent do students

- show their understanding of the correct part of the foot to use for dribbling and for kicking a ball into the air?

Emphasize	*Ideas for Lesson Development*
Instep kick Stand a little behind, to one side (of the ball). Kick with the shoelaces (the top part of instep). Kick hard.	• Have students pair up: One student practices running up to and kicking a stationary ball into a marked-off area; the other partner retrieves the ball and places it back for the next kick. After five kicks, they switch roles. • Provide carpet squares or draw a box on the ground. Have students put their nonkicking foot on the bottom left of the box (if they kick with their right leg) before kicking; the ball goes on the upper right-hand corner of the box. • Put large targets (e.g., clowns, animals) on the walls and have the students kick to them. • Place two carpet squares about 8 to 10 feet (2.4 m to 3 m) away from each other. Pair up the students; one partner slowly rolls the ball to the other, the kicker. The roller partner retrieves the ball. After five kicks, they switch roles. If you desire, have the kickers see how many times they can run between the two squares before the rollers return to their square. • Place tug-of-war ropes or two chalk lines on the ground parallel to each other. They should be at a gym-length apart. Students pair up and decide who will kick first. At the signal, the first partner kicks a ball from behind the line, then continues to move to the ball and kick it to see how many kicks it takes to get the ball across the other line. After turning around and dribbling back to the original line, the other partner prepares to kick. Discuss what happens when a player uses great force to kick the ball: How does this make a difference in this activity?
Inside kick Stand a little behind, to one side (of the ball). Toes and knee out, like a duck.	• Have students practice kicking stationary balls along the ground toward a stationary partner or target. If possible, set up large plastic garbage cans, standing hoops, large stacked tin cans, or the like as targets for students to kick toward.

Name _____ **Class** _____

Kick It Up!

On the shoe below, write your name on the part of the foot you should use when you dribble the ball with your feet. Then, with your pencil or a crayon, color in the part you should use to kick the ball far away, up into the air.

Figure 11.3   Portfolio task assessment sheet for kicking, grades 1 to 2.

From *Elementary Physical Education Teaching & Assessment: A Practical Guide,* by Christine J. Hopple, 2005, Champaign, IL: Human Kinetics.

• Have students practice kicking toward their partners using the inside of their feet; the carpet squares that they stand on should be fairly close together. After each kick a partner traps without going off the square, they move their squares back farther. If a pass is missed, they bring the squares close together again and start over.

• Set up six stations, two each of the following: (a) pass the ball back and forth to your partner, using the inside of your foot; (b) dribble around the cones, perhaps racing; (c) take turns defending and kicking toward a goal. Provide enough equipment at each station for all students to be active simultaneously.

PEC: *Inside of the Foot Pass*

Dribbling
Push, don't kick (the ball).
(Use) insides (or) outsides (of the feet).
Keep it close (to you).

• Challenge students to dribble a ball inside a large marked-off area while moving at the fastest speed at which they can control it. At the signal, can they trap the ball before the count of three? (If they cannot, they are dribbling too fast.)

• Put a variety of tires, hoops, crates, and other items in the marked-off area. Challenge students to dribble around the items without touching them.

PEC: *Dribbling 500*

Punting
Hold (the ball at shoulder level).
Step (with the nonkicking leg).
Drop (the ball).
Kick with the shoelaces (the top part of instep).

• Give students a variety of balls to punt (e.g., Nerf balls, playground balls, soft and regular footballs).

• Have students practice punting balls into the air in self-space within a very large area. Challenge them to catch their punts before they touch the ground.

• Hang a rope between standards; challenge children to punt over the rope at the height that most challenges them (a line can also be drawn or taped on a wall). Put up enough ropes so students have sufficient space to safely punt, or use this as one station among a set of kicking or manipulative-skills stations.

KINDERGARTEN

Sample Performance Indicators

By the end of grade K, students should be able to

- walk and "roll" the ball forward, using the inside of either foot;
- kick a large stationary playground ball, using any part of the foot; and
- move up to and kick a stationary ball, using any part of the foot.

Sample Performance Task

Students kick a stationary ball as hard as they can, either from a stationary or running start (they should be facing a marked-off area). Once they kick it, they should retrieve it, replace it on its poly spot or carpet square, and kick again. (Observe at least five trials.)

RUBRIC CLUES

To what extent do students

- consistently make contact with the ball?
- kick, rather than push, the ball with the foot?

Emphasize	Ideas for Lesson Development
Instep kick Inside kick. Eyes (focus) on the ball.	• Have students face a marked-off area and kick a stationary playground ball using any part of the foot; provide a carpet square on which they set the ball after retrieving it. • Challenge students to run up to and kick balls sitting on carpet squares.
Dribbling Little pushes. (Use) insides (of the feet).	• Encourage students to walk and roll balls forward by using the inside of their feet.

Throwing and Catching

Sample Course Standards

By the end of elementary school, students should be able to

- use the skills of throwing and catching in order to design and play a small-group game; and
- use the basic offensive and defensive strategies for keep-away games (i.e., creating and denying space) when playing in small groups.

Concepts and Skills	Learnable Pieces
Underhand throw	Face your target. (K, 1–2)
	Arm (swings) back ("tick"). (K, 1–2)
	Arm (swings) forward ("tock"). (K, 1–2)
	Step with the opposite foot. (1–2)
	Bend the knees as you step. (3–4)
	Point your fingers to the target. (3–4)
Overhand throw	Side (of your body to the target). (1–2)
	Swing (your arm) down, back, and up. (1–2)
	Step (with the opposite foot). (1–2)
	Hand (points straight) up. (K, 3–4)
	Twist your body (as the ball is thrown). (3–4)
	Point (your fingers) to the target. (3–4)
	Throw hard. (3–4)
	Throw ahead of your (moving) target. (5–6)
Frisbees	Twist and untwist your body. (5–6)
	Snap your wrist on the release. (5–6)
Catching	Reach out to the ball. (K)
	Watch the ball. (K, 1–2)
	Thumbs together above your waist. (1–2)
	Pinkies together below your waist. (1–2)
	Move to meet the ball. (3–4)
	Give with your body. (3–4)
	Pull the ball to your body. (5–6)

GRADES 5 TO 6

Sample Performance Indicators

By the end of grade 6, students should be able to

- throw to a partner or at a target, using varying degrees of force and speed;
- throw and catch a Frisbee;
- throw a leading pass overhand to a moving partner using a variety of objects;
- catch objects of different sizes and weights while moving toward a specified area;
- move in order to throw to a stationary partner while being guarded in a small-group keep-away situation; and
- throw and catch in a self-designed or given small-group game to keep the ball away from opponents or to reach a goal area.

NASPE Performance Indicators

- Catches a fly ball using mature form (e.g., has eyes on ball, moves to position, reaches with hands, catches with hands only rather than trapping the ball, and bends elbows to pull ball into chest to absorb force). (3–5, #1, 3)
- Throws a ball overhand to a partner 15 yards away using mature form (e.g., turns side to target, uses T-position [ball held close to and behind

ear], rotates hips and chest toward target, twists, releases, follows through across body) after fielding a ball. (3–5, #1, 9)

Sample Performance Task

Groups of three students each make up three passing plays using throwing, catching, and traveling. Students draw their plays in the dust or on paper before practicing them. After a while, one partner becomes the defender (i.e., two-on-one situation); the partners take turns running and defending the plays.

RUBRIC CLUES

To what extent do students

- throw and catch using correct form (i.e., desired learnable pieces)?

If desired, the following can also be assessed during this task:

- on defense, stays between the thrower and the catcher in position to intercept the ball?

Sample Portfolio Task

Ask students to demonstrate knowledge of throwing and catching by completing figure 11.4.

RUBRIC CLUES

To what extent do students

- show they understand the cues pertaining to throwing and catching?

Emphasize	Ideas for Lesson Development
Frisbees Twist and untwist your body. Snap your wrist on the release.	• Have students practice throwing Frisbees back and forth with a partner. • Set up a Frisbee course using playground equipment, cones inside hoops, and so forth. Frisbees need to go over, between, or under something if possible. If you wish, give each student a map of the course and a scorecard. **Belka:** *Mini Frisbee Golf* **PEC:** *Disc Golf* *Top Saucer* *Frisbee Pop*
Catching Pull the ball to your body.	• Have students throw different objects, using varying degrees of force and speed, to a partner. • Have students work in pairs to throw and catch leading passes. Have one partner start by rolling a hula hoop, while the other tries to throw a ball overhand through it. Have them practice so the catcher doesn't have to stop in order to catch the ball. • Have pairs of students make up and practice different passing plays with one another. If you desire, have them work in groups of three: After practice, one player becomes the defender. If they choose to, they may set up a goal area to move toward after catching. • Set up a large crash pad. Students jump off a box, crate, or other object and stretch to catch the ball, landing on the crash pad. The thrower should toss the ball so that the catcher really has to jump and stretch to catch it. You can use a regular mat instead of a crash pad; students have to roll after catching the ball.

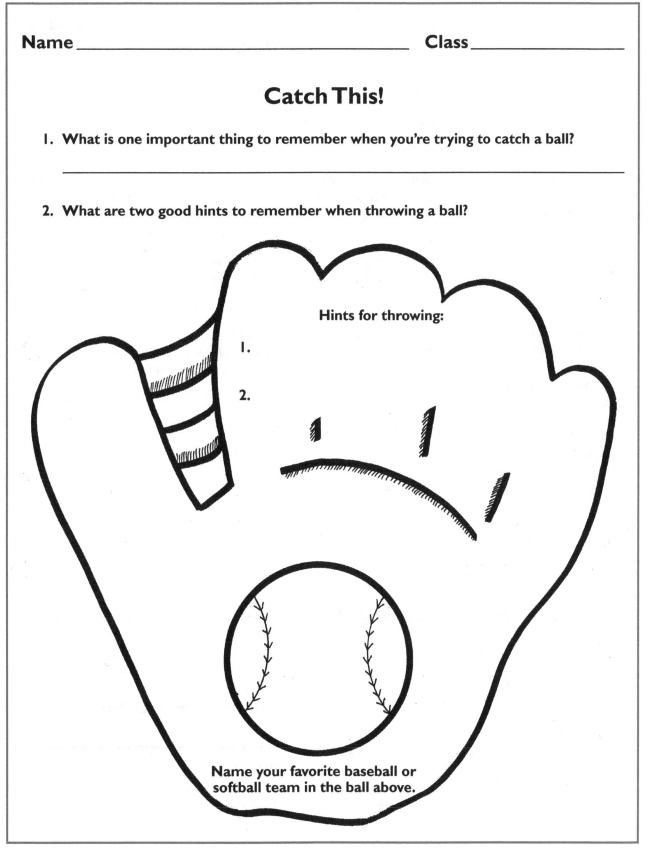

Name _____ **Class** _____

Catch This!

1. **What is one important thing to remember when you're trying to catch a ball?**

   _____

2. **What are two good hints to remember when throwing a ball?**

   Hints for throwing:

   1.

   2.

   Name your favorite baseball or softball team in the ball above.

Figure 11.4   Portfolio task assessment sheet for throwing and catching, grades 5 to 6.

• Set up two-on-two or three-on-three modified Newcombe or deck tennis games, using Geo balls, yarn balls, and so forth. (Don't use volleyballs or students will want to play volleyball!)

Belka: *Over and Under*   *Predict-a-Bounce*
       The Route of It All
PEC: *Throw and Run Challenge*

Overhand Throw
Throw ahead of your
(moving) target. (5–6)

• Demonstrate how a good leading pass allows the receiver to catch the ball without having to break stride. Have students, working in pairs, practice throwing a leading pass, with the thrower stationary.

PEC: *Football Downs*   *The Mystery Passing Game*
       Moving Target Throwing   *Throw to the Cone*

General space (see "Space Awareness," chapter 8)
Offense
Create space by moving to open areas to pass or receive the ball.
Defense
Deny space by staying between the opponent and intended goal.

• In an area about 20 × 3 × 20 feet (6.1 m × 0.9 m × 6.1 m), students use throwing and catching to keep the ball away from opponents and to reach a designated goal area. Have students write down their own rules and boundaries.

PEC: *Football Downs*   *Goalie Game*
       Football Mania   *The Mystery Passing Game*

GRADES 3 TO 4

Sample Performance Indicators

By the end of grade 4, students should be able to

• throw a variety of objects to target areas using a smooth underhand motion;
• throw as far as possible using a smooth overhand motion;
• throw balls of various sizes and weights to an appropriate target or partner using a smooth overhand motion;
• throw, using an overhand motion, so the ball travels in different pathways in the air and covers different distances;
• catch a ball, tossed by themselves or by others, at different levels;

• move in different directions to catch a ball thrown by a partner; and
• move to catch an object in a small-group (two-on-one) keep-away situation.

NASPE Performance Indicators

• Throws a ball overhand and hits a target on the wall (6-foot square centered 4 feet above the ground) from a distance of 40 feet. (3–5, #1, 6)
• Accurately recognizes the critical elements of a catch made by a fellow student and provides feedback to that student. (3–5, #2, 14)

Sample Performance Task

Have students set up a two-on-one keep-away (Monkey in the Middle) game; carpet squares can designate a minimum distance for the two outside partners. Using any types of throws and catching, the outside partners try to keep the ball away from the middle player. If the ball is caught or the "monkey" does not catch the ball after five throws, the middle player trades places with a student on the outside.

RUBRIC CLUES

To what extent do students
- throw using the desired learnable pieces?
- catch using the desired learnable pieces?

Sample Portfolio Task

Ask students to picture themselves in this situation: They are friends with the pitcher of their baseball or softball team. Their friend is having trouble pitching, and the big game of the season is a week away. What are some hints they might give to help the friend pitch better? (Students should designate whether their friend pitches overhand or underhand.)

RUBRIC CLUES

To what extent do students
- show an understanding of the correct cues for either the overhand or underhand throw?

Emphasize	*Ideas for Lesson Development*
Underhand throw Bend the knees as you step. Point your fingers to the target.	• Set up stations for throwing that focus on using the underhand throw. Horseshoes (use stakes and deck tennis rings if you don't have horseshoes), bowling, and a large tic-tac-toe grid (use two different-color beanbags) are just some of the stations you can use.
Overhand throw Hand (points straight) up. Twist your body (as the ball is thrown). Point (your fingers) to the target. Throw hard.	• Discuss various pathways objects can move through in the air. Have students experiment throwing objects so they will move in straight or curved pathways. Discuss how these pathways relate to the object's speed in the air, its "hang" time, the object's weight, and its point of release. Relate these pathways to the way different objects are thrown in different sports (football, baseball, and the like)
	• Set up different-size targets at varying distances from a line. Assign and label a point value for each target, depending upon its distance and size. (Make sure that there are targets of easy, medium, and hard difficulty so all students can gain points). Have students work with a partner to see if together they can reach a predetermined amount of points by the end of the class period; let students choose their target or targets and what objects they want to throw.

Belka:	*Long Toss-n-Guard*	*Hoop Guard*
	Bounce and Field	
Buschner:	*Spring Training*	
PEC:	*Earthball Throw*	*Terminator*
	Catch 100	*Throw Everything*
	Football Frenzy	*Throwing and Catching Medley*
	Freezemania	

Catching
Move to meet the ball.
Give with your body.

- Have students throw and catch to themselves, challenging them to catch at different levels (high, middle, low), move in different directions to catch the object, and stretch or reach to catch.

- Have a partner throw an object of choice to different places around the catcher's body, so that the catcher has to move (forward, backward, right, or left) to catch the ball.

- Have students set up a two-on-one Monkey in the Middle game; stress how the outside partners must move to get open. Discuss what the defensive player should do to catch the object.

Belka: *Trio Keep-Away*
PEC: *Catch 100*
  Terminator

GRADES 1 TO 2

Sample Performance Indicators

By the end of grade 2, students should be able to

- catch a self-tossed yarn or other soft ball;
- catch a softly thrown ball at different levels;
- catch a softly thrown ball at different places around the body;
- throw a variety of objects using an underhand motion;
- throw as far as possible using an overhand motion; and
- throw (underhand) and catch a self-tossed object, using a scoop or other implement.

NASPE Performance Indicators

- Throws a ball underhand using mature form (e.g., places feet together and shoulders square to target, swings throwing arm straight back, shifts weight forward by stepping forward onto opposite foot, rolls ball off fingers, and finishes with throwing arm outstretched toward target). (K–2, #1, 8)

Sample Performance Task

A student will have three chances to throw underhand to a hoop that is propped against the wall or lying on the floor next to the wall. While throwing, a partner will assess whether or not the student stepped with the opposite foot (see figure 11.5). After three throws, students switch roles.

RUBRIC CLUES

To what extent do students

- consistently step with the opposite foot when throwing?

Sample Portfolio Task

Ask students to assess their partner's ability to step with the opposite foot by completing figure 11.5.

RUBRIC CLUES

To what extent do students

- correctly identify/assess their partner's ability to step with the opposite foot?

Name _____ **Class** _____

Each partner gets three underhand throws to the target. Watch your partner throw; if he or she steps with the opposite foot when throwing, mark a smiley face in the circle. If your partner does *not* step with the opposite foot for a throw, mark an **X** in the circle.

Example:

Did step with opposite foot 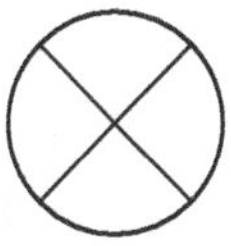   **Did *not* step with opposite foot**

Partner 1's name _____

Partner 2's name _____

Partner 1   ◯   ◯   ◯

Partner 2   ◯   ◯   ◯

Partner 1   ◯   ◯   ◯

Partner 2   ◯   ◯   ◯

Partner 1   ◯   ◯   ◯

Partner 2   ◯   ◯   ◯

Figure 11.5   Performance task assessment sheet for throwing, grades 1 to 2.

From *Elementary Physical Education Teaching & Assessment: A Practical Guide,* by Christine J. Hopple, 2005, Champaign, IL: Human Kinetics.

Emphasize	*Ideas for Lesson Development*

Underhand throw
Face your target.
Arm (swings) back ("tick").
Arm (swings) forward ("tock").
Step with the opposite foot.

- Have students throw either underhand or overhand to a variety of targets. Here are some suggestions:

  - Hang large targets (painted on canvas) 10 to 12 feet (3 m to 3.7 m) from the wall in the gym (so balls won't bounce off the wall, going everywhere!).

  - Place hoops and tires on the ground in a line at progressively farther distances students can throw to.

  - Post each letter of the alphabet on a 12 × 3 × 6-foot (3.7 × 0.9 × 1.8 m) canvas target or area on the wall. Challenge students to spell their names by throwing to the correct letters. You also can arrange letters in the form of a computer keyboard.

  - Paint a calculator on a 5 × 3 × 6-foot (1.5 × 0.9 × 1.8 m) target so students can dial (throw to) 9-1-1 or do easy math problems.

  - Outline batters (boy and girl) on a 5 × 3 × 6-foot canvas, with the strike zone boxed in by a marker. Color in the box with crayon; iron it onto the material.

  - Set up large tin cans in pyramid fashion: Students throw and see how many cans they can knock over.

  - Make scoops out of milk cartons; students can throw underhand and catch yarn and tennis balls in them, either by themselves or with a partner.

PEC: *Bowl-a-Rama*	*Stepping With the Opposite Foot*
Beanbag Tic-Tac-Toe	*The Adventures of Mr. Toss*
Birthday Cake	*Wishing Well*
Catching Animals	

Overhand throw
Side (of your body to the target).
Swing (your arm) down, back, and up.
Step (with the opposite foot).

- Set up targets such as listed earlier (see Underhand throw) for students to throw to.

- Have students hold up hoops in various places around their bodies while partners, using a yarn or other soft ball, try to throw through the hoop. Set a minimum distance for the throws (about 5 feet or 1.5 m). Students accumulate points for each throw that goes through the hoop; after five tries, they switch roles.

- Have students work in pairs, one throwing to the targets and the other giving a point each time the thrower steps with the opposite foot. Partners (evaluators) award another point if the throwers also hit the target. Let students decide the throwing distance.

- Have students pair up and play the Near/Far game: Using an object appropriate to their ability to throw and catch, two students stand close, facing each other. The student tosses the object to the partner, and if caught, the partner takes a step backward. The partner then throws the object back, and if caught, the student takes a step backward. If the catcher misses, drops the object, or has to move more than one step away to catch the object, both students return to their original positions close to one another and begin again. Observe for specific critical throwing and catching elements.

Buschner: *Carnival Throwing*
PEC: *Hail Storm*   *Throwing for Distance*
        Sticker Step Throwing   *Who Let the Frogs Out?*

Catching
Watch the ball.
Thumbs together above your waist.
Pinkies together below your waist.

- Students practice throwing and catching by themselves in self-space. Challenge them to clap one, two, or three times before they catch the ball; twist around and catch it; or add other movements before they catch it.

- Challenge students to throw a ball up and catch it at a high, medium, or low level.

- Challenge students to throw the ball up so they have to catch it at different places around their bodies (catch it on the left side, right side, and so on.).

- Put a clothespin on the shoelaces or a pants leg to remind students which of their feet is the opposite foot!

Buschner: *Egg Catching*
PEC: *Ice Cream "Scoops"*

KINDERGARTEN

Sample Performance Indicators

By the end of grade K, students should be able to
- catch a softly rolled large ball;
- catch a self-tossed yarn or other soft ball;
- throw to a variety of large targets using an underhand throwing motion; and
- throw a yarn or other soft ball using an overhand arm motion.

Emphasize	*Ideas for Lesson Development*

Catching
Watch the ball.
Reach out to the ball.

- Have students get in a straddled sitting position and roll large balls to partners who catch them, using both hands.

- Challenge students to roll and catch a ball both in front of and behind them when standing in a straddled position.

- Have students throw and catch soft objects, such as Nerf balls, yarn balls, and balloons, while they stand in self-space. Challenge them to clap one time before they catch the objects.

Underhand throw
Face your target.
Arm (swings) back ("tick").
Arm (swings) forward ("tock").

Overhand throw
Hand (points straight) up.

- Put up large targets (clowns, animals) for students to throw at using an underhand throw.
- Set up hoops or tires on the ground; allow students to throw soft objects such as beanbags or soft balls toward them from their choice of distance.

- Challenge students to throw overhand to large targets.

By the end of elementary school, students should be able to

- use volleying skills, including the underhand, overhead, and the forearm (bump) pass, when playing or designing a small-group game.

Volleying

Concepts and Skills	Learnable Pieces
Underhand	Bring your arm back. (K, 1–2)
	Step with the opposite foot. (1–2)
	Hit (the ball). (1–2)
	(Use the) heel of your hand. (1–2)
	Point your hand to the target. (3–4)
Overhead	Toss. (1–2)
	Hands above the head—high level. (1–2)
	Push your arms straight. (1–2)
	Step. (3–4)
	Bend the knees. (3–4)
	Hit using the finger pads. (3–4)
	Move under the ball. (5–6)
	Stretch your body up. (5–6)
Forearm (bump) pass	Step (one foot in front). (3–4)
	Bend the knees. (3–4)
	Hands (point) down. (3–4)
	Arms like a paddle. (3–4)
	Move under the ball. (5–6)
	Point toward the target. (5–6)
	Stretch your body up. (5–6)

GRADES 5 TO 6

Sample Performance Indicators

By the end of grade 6, students should be able to

- cooperate in a small group to strike a lightweight ball with various body parts while keeping it off the ground;
- underhand-strike a lightweight ball over a medium-level net or rope (from an appropriate distance);
- overhead-volley a lightweight ball back and forth with a partner across a medium-level net or rope;
- move to forearm-pass or overhead-volley a lightweight ball back to a partner;
- forearm pass a lightweight ball to an area other than the direction it came from;
- forearm pass a lightly tossed lightweight ball back to a partner across a medium-level rope or net;
- use underhand and overhead volleys and forearm passes to cooperatively keep a ball in play over a medium-level net or rope with a partner or a small group; and
- use underhand and overhead volleys and forearm passes in a given or self-designed small-group game.

Sample Performance Task

Students play a small-group game in an area about 20 × 20 feet (6.1 × 6.1 m), using underhand and overhead volleys and forearm passes. Allow students to make up their own rules about the number of hits, height of the net, serving lines, catches, and points.

RUBRIC CLUES

To what extent do students
- consistently volley, either to a teammate or across the net, using the desired learnable pieces for the underhand and overhand volleys and forearm passes?

If desired, the following can also be assessed during this task:
- when on defense, spread out equally to cover an area?
- when on offense, hit the ball where others aren't?

Sample Portfolio Task

Ask students to write down two sports or games that use the skill of volleying, noting when in that sport volleying is used.

RUBRIC CLUES

To what extent do students
- correctly identify the skill of volleying as used in different games or sports?

Emphasize	*Ideas for Lesson Development*
Forearm (bump) pass Move under the ball. Point toward the target. Stretch your body up.	• Challenge students to forearm pass a gently tossed object in a direction other than the one it came from. Thus, the passer must move in order to retrieve the ball. • Have students partner up; the passer gently tosses an object to different places around the other partner, who must move to be in position to forearm pass or overhead-volley the ball back. After five tosses, they switch roles. • Using a net (or a medium-level rope as a net), one student gently tosses the object to a partner, who forearm passes it back to the partner. Challenge them eventually to forearm pass the object back to where the partner is not.
	Belka: *Over Long and Short*
Overhead Move under the ball. Stretch your body up.	• Using a net (or a medium-level rope as a net), students overhead-volley a ball back to the partner who tossed it. As their skills increase, challenge players to volley the ball back and forth.
General space (see "Space Awareness," chapter 8) *Offense* Hit the ball to places where opponents aren't standing. *Defense* Be ready to move. Partners equally cover the area.	• Have students set up and play small-group games that involve using overhead and underhand volleying and bump passing to keep the ball in play as long as possible. • Challenge students to eventually pass to where the defense is not. Allow students to determine the game rules, hits, serve lines, and so forth.

GRADES 3 TO 4

Sample Performance Indicators

By the end of grade 4, students should be able to

- strike a lightweight ball in succession using at least two different body parts, keeping it in self-space;
- strike a lightly tossed lightweight ball back to a partner using a variety of body parts;
- underhand-strike a lightweight ball back and forth across a line or low net to a partner after one bounce;
- overhead-volley a self-tossed lightweight ball to a wall or partner (to an appropriate height, if desired); and
- forearm-pass a lightly tossed lightweight ball back to a partner.

Sample Performance Task

Mark off two large (about 4 feet or 1.2 m) squares adjacent to each other. Students take turns underhand-volleying (striking) an appropriate ball that can be bounced back and forth, always trying to return the ball to the opposite square after one or no bounces. If a ball cannot be returned after one bounce or if it goes out of the square, the other partner starts a new series with an underhand serve.

RUBRIC CLUES

To what extent do students

- consistently volley or strike the ball using the desired learnable pieces of an underhand striking pattern?

Sample Portfolio Task

Ask students to write two hints to remember when volleying?

RUBRIC CLUES

To what extent do students

- show they clearly understand the cues for volleying?

Emphasize	Ideas for Lesson Development
Underhand Point your hand to the target.	• Put up a net against a wall; students can serve or volley to the wall above the net, almost like the real thing! • Challenge students to volley or strike an object using at least two different body parts in succession. • See if students can volley or strike a lightly tossed object to a partner using different body parts. • Put large targets or hoops on the floor on the other side of a low net. Students practice serving the ball underhand, trying to get it to a certain target. If you wish, assign point values to the targets and encourage students to work together with a partner to reach a certain number of points. • Set up a two-square court, or make a low jump-rope net. Students take turns underhand striking an appropriate object back and forth across the line or net to their partners, allowing one bounce before returning it. • Have students form groups of four and set up and volley in a four-square situation.

Belka: *Across the Line*
PEC: *Spotting Good Serves*   *Volleyball 4-Square*
    Volleyball Serve and Catch

Overhead
Step.
Bend the knees.
Hit using the finger pads.

- Set up large targets at varying heights on a wall. Students can practice self-tossing, then overhand-volleying an appropriate object to the targets or a partner.

- Have students practice softly tossing an appropriate object to a partner, who overhead-volleys it back. After five volleys, they switch roles.

PEC: *Upside-Down Dribbling!*

Forearm (bump) pass
Step (one foot in front).
Bend the knees.
Hands (point) down.
Arms like a paddle.

- Have students explore why the various cues are important. For example, ask them what happens when they volley the ball without bending the knees. "Now try it bending your knees, to see the difference." Encourage them to figure out why the ball sometimes flies backward when it is hit: What do the hands have to do when hitting high balls?

- Have students softly toss an appropriate object to a partner, who practices forearm- (bump-) passing it back.

GRADES I TO 2

Sample Performance Indicators

By the end of grade 2, students should be able to

- strike a lightweight ball with at least three different body parts (e.g., knee, foot, elbow), keeping it in self-space;

- underhand-strike a soft, lightweight ball or balloon upward with the hand, keeping it in self-space; and

- travel slowly and underhand-strike a soft, lightweight ball or balloon upward with the hand or other body parts.

Sample Performance Task

Have students set up jump ropes and crates or cones as a low net. Students underhand-volley or strike a soft, lightweight ball back and forth over the jump ropes; partners catch the ball and underhand-strike it back over. Students can stand any distance they choose from the ropes.

RUBRIC CLUES

To what extent do students
- demonstrate the ability to underhand-volley or strike?

Sample Portfolio Task

Ask students to draw a picture of themselves on a piece of paper and label the different body parts they can use to strike or volley a balloon or other soft ball by completing figure 11.6.

RUBRIC CLUES

To what extent do students
- give examples of body parts that are feasible to use for volleying and striking?

Name _____ **Class** _____

Draw a picture of yourself and label the different body parts you use to strike or volley a soft ball.

Figure 11.6   Portfolio task assessment sheet for volleying, grades 1–2.

From *Elementary Physical Education Teaching & Assessment: A Practical Guide,* by Christine J. Hopple, 2005, Champaign, IL: Human Kinetics.

Emphasize	*Ideas for Lesson Development*
Underhand Bring your arm back. Step with the opposite foot. Hit (the ball). (Use the) heel of your hand.	• Give students a choice of balls to use for volleying. Punch balls, heavy-duty balloons, and new lightweight, oversize volleyball trainers make volleying less threatening and more motivating. Allow the students to trade balls to keep up their interest.
	• Discuss how a volley is not a push or slap, but a solid "pop" using the hand or other body part (force is not absorbed by the body part). Challenge students to see how many different body parts they can use to volley a soft, lightweight ball while keeping it in self-space. Challenge them to use their heads, elbows, knees, and feet.
	• Have students experiment with how they must strike the object to make it go up, forward, back over their head, or in any other direction.
	• Have students practice the underhand volley, striking a soft object upward with the hand while keeping it in self-space.
	• Challenge students to travel slowly through general space, striking an object underhand (upward) using their hands. See if they can keep control of the object by taking only one or two steps to get to it.
	• Use a ball that bounces, and have students bounce and then "pop" it upward using the heels of their hands. Challenge them to catch a ball after one bounce or before it bounces at all, then pop it again (the sequence becomes bounce, pop, bounce, catch). They can also try to continuously pop the ball without catching it at all (bounce, pop, bounce, pop). Challenge them to pop the ball upward using different body parts.
	• Set up large targets of varying sizes and heights on a fence or wall. Challenge students to strike an object underhand to the targets, from whatever distance they wish.
	• String up a rope between standards. Pair up the students and have them take turns underhand-striking and catching an object.
Overhead Toss. Hands above the head— high level. Push your arms straight.	• Have students practice overhead volleying and catching with self-tossed lightweight balls or balloons, keeping them in self-space.
	• Set up a low net; students take turns overhead-volleying a self-tossed ball over the net to their partner, who catches and returns it doing the same.

KINDERGARTEN

Sample Performance Indicators

By the end of grade K, students should be able to

- using both right and left hands, continuously push a balloon upward with the hands, keeping it off the ground; and

- using the palm, strike a balloon underhand (upward) continuously.

Emphasize	Ideas for Lesson Development
Underhand Bring your arm back.	• Have students strike a balloon underhand while keeping it in self-space. See if the children can do this with both the right and left hands. • Challenge students to strike balloons with their heads, elbows, knees, and other body parts. • Challenge students to move slowly through general space while they use their hands to keep balloons off the ground.

Sample Course Standard

By the end of elementary school, students should be able to

- use the individual skills of the underhand, forehand, and backhand strikes in appropriate situations; and
- use combinations of underhand, forehand, and backhand strikes in appropriate game situations.

Concepts and Skills	Learnable Pieces
Underhand	Watch the ball. (K)
	Shake hands with the paddle. (K, 1–2)
	Paddle way back. (K, 1–2)
	Firm wrist and elbow. (1–2)
	Hit the ball when it is at a medium level. (1–2)
	Flat racket face (to target). (3–4, 5–6)
	Extend arm. (3–4, 5–6)
Forehand	(Turn your) side to the target. (1–2, 3–4)
	Bring your paddle way back. (1–2, 3–4)
	Firm wrist and elbow. (1–2, 3–4)
	Open the door, close the door (i.e., level swing). (3–4, 5–6)
	Step into the swing. (5–6)
	Paddle to the target. (5–6)
Backhand	Arm across the body. (3–4)
	(Turn your) other side to the target. (3–4, 5–6)
	Step into the swing. (5–6)
	Open the door, close the door (i.e., level swing) (5–6)
	Paddle to the target. (5–6)

GRADES 5 TO 6

Sample Performance Indicators

By the end of grade 6, students should be able to

- repeatedly strike a rebounding ball from a wall with a paddle or lightweight racket using a forehand stroke;
- strike a gently tossed ball from a partner, using a backhand motion;
- repeatedly strike a rebounding ball from a wall using forehand and backhand strokes, moving back to a ready position in between strokes; and
- strike a self-dropped ball with a racket over a low-level line or net to various designated areas, using a forehand stroke.

NASPE Performance Indicators

- Explains the necessity of transferring weight from the back leg to the front leg during any action that propels an object forward. (3–5, #2, 13)

Sample Performance Task

Mark a "het" line on a wall, and have students use forehand and backhand strikes to hit a rebounding ball. Allow students to choose the distance away from the wall, as well as the size of racket. A partner will observe for level swings as they strike (see figure 11.7).

RUBRIC CLUES

To what extent do students
- demonstrate the ability to use a level swing when striking?

Sample Portfolio Task

Ask students to assess a partner's ability to use a level swing when striking by completing figure 11.7. (File task in the portfolio of the person striking the ball, not observer's portfolio, when done.)

RUBRIC CLUES

To what extent do students
- correctly assess their partner's ability to strike using a level swing?

Emphasize	*Ideas for Lesson Development*
Underhand Flat racket face (to target). Extend arm.	• Challenge students to stand in self-space and continuously strike a birdie up into the air using a badminton racket. • Have students pair up; each partner gets on opposite sides of a volleyball-height (or as appropriate) rope or net. The server start from a spot closer to the net and underhand-strikes the birdie over the net to the receiver, who "catches" the birdie with the racket. If the receiver catches the birdie without having to move, the server then takes one step backward and attempts to serve from there. After all five birdies have been served, the students switch roles. **PEC:** *Birdie's Nest*
Forehand Open the door, close the door (i.e., level swing). Step into the swing. Paddle to the target.	• Have students focus on thinking of their arm as a door that doesn't bend—it opens all the way back and stays extended as it "closes." It also moves only horizontally—in one plane—not vertically. • Challenge students to strike a ball rebounding from a wall with their rackets or paddles, using forehand strikes. • Set up a low net; ask students to bounce, then strike a ball toward different targets on the other side of the net. Make sure the targets are large and that they vary in distance and angle from the net. • Encourage students to move into a ready position after each strike, prepared to move to where the ball will be returned. **Belka:** *Three-Court Tennis* **PEC:** *Tennis Videotaping Assessment*

Name _____ **Class** _____

Observe your partner as he or she strikes the ball to the wall with the racket. Every time he or she uses a level swing, put a ✔ in a circle. If he or she *doesn't* use a level swing, use an X in the circle.

I'm watching: _____

○ ○ ○ ○ ○ ○ ○ ○ ○

○ ○ ○ ○ ○ ○ ○ ○ ○

○ ○ ○ ○ ○ ○ ○ ○ ○

○ ○ ○ ○ ○ ○ ○ ○ ○

Total ✓ = _____   Total ⊗ = _____

Rate your partner's use of a level swing:

       Very good   **OK**   **Practice lots more!**

Figure 11.7 Performance task assessment sheet for striking with short-handled implements, grades 5 to 6.

From *Elementary Physical Education Teaching & Assessment: A Practical Guide,* by Christine J. Hopple, 2005, Champaign, IL: Human Kinetics.

Backhand
(Turn your) other side to the target.
Step into the swing.
Open the door, close the door (i.e., level swing)
Paddle to the target. (Use only if appropriate for skill level.)

- Have students focus on thinking of their arm as a door that doesn't bend—it opens all the way back and stays extended as it "closes." It also moves only horizontally—in one plane—not vertically.

- Have a partner gently toss a ball; the "striker" uses a backhand motion to hit the ball.

GRADES 3 TO 4

Sample Performance Indicators

By the end of grade 4, students should be able to

- bounce and then strike a small object to a wall or across a low net using an underhand motion with a lightweight paddle or racket;
- bounce and then strike a small object using a forehand motion with a lightweight paddle or racket;
- strike a small object with a forehand motion using both strong and light force; and
- bounce and then strike a small object using a backhand motion with a lightweight paddle or racket.

NASPE Performance Indicators

- Identifies and demonstrates key elements of a proper grip when holding a racket to perform the forehand strike. (3–5, #2, 12)

Sample Performance Task

Students are to bounce and then use a forehand strike to move a small, lightweight ball toward a large target on the wall or ground. Allow students

to choose the distance from the wall and select their paddle or racket.

RUBRIC CLUES

To what extent do students
- demonstrate the ability to correctly strike with a forehand or backhand swing?

Sample Portfolio Task

Ask students to write letters to their favorite tennis players. Their letters should include an important hint to remember for hitting a forehand strike and a backhand strike.

RUBRIC CLUES

To what extent do students
- show they understand the important cues presented in class?

Emphasize	*Ideas for Lesson Development*
Underhand Flat racket face (to target). Extend arm.	• There are a number of short-handled rackets (shorter than tennis rackets) available to help students develop their striking skills (e.g., paddleball rackets). Using these types of rackets, have students underhand strike toward a wall, using a racket surface that is "flat" (pointing) toward the target. • Students can practice "ups" and "downs," striking a small foam ball while staying in their self-space.

Forehand
(Turn your) side to the target.
Bring your paddle way back.
Firm wrist and elbow.
Open the door, close the
door (i.e., level swing).

- Teach the correct forehand grip by having students place the racket flat on the ground, put the hand flat on the paddle face, and slide it down the handle. For the backhand have students place the racket under the non-preferred arm, then reach over and grab it using the striking hand.

- Set up low jump-rope "nets" with cones or crates, or mark or tape a "net" on a wall. Students can each practice forehand striking a lightweight ball using a paddle or racket to a partner or the wall.

- Place large targets on the wall for students to aim at when striking. Allow them to choose the distance from the target.

- Have students focus on thinking of their arm as a door that doesn't bend—it opens all the way back and stays extended as it "closes." It also moves only horizontally—in one plane—not vertically.

- Pair up students. Have a partner gently toss a soft, lightweight ball to the "striker." Put a hoop or jump-rope circle down in an appropriate place for students to aim at when tossing.

Backhand
Arm across the body.
(Turn your) other side
to the target.

- Have students practice bouncing and striking a soft, lightweight ball using a backhand motion toward a marked-off area, partner, or wall.

- Have a partner drop a ball in the appropriate place for students to backhand it.

GRADES 1 TO 2

Sample Performance Indicators

By the end of grade 2, students should be able to
- strike a small, lightweight ball upward with a hand or lightweight paddle, letting it bounce between strikes (i.e., bounce, strike, bounce);
- continuously strike a small, lightweight ball or balloon upward using a hand or lightweight paddle;
- continuously strike a suspended ball, using a forehand motion, with either a hand or lightweight paddle; and
- bounce then strike a small, lightweight ball using a hand or lightweight paddle.

RUBRIC CLUES

To what extent do students
- demonstrate the ability to bring the paddle way back?

Sample Portfolio Task

Ask students to demonstrate their understanding of cues used to strike by completing figure 11.8.

RUBRIC CLUES

To what extent do students
- show they understand the cues for striking?

Sample Performance Task

Students in their self-space use a foam ('lollipop') paddle to underhand strike a balloon into the air, focusing on keeping the 'paddle way back.'

Name _____ Class _____

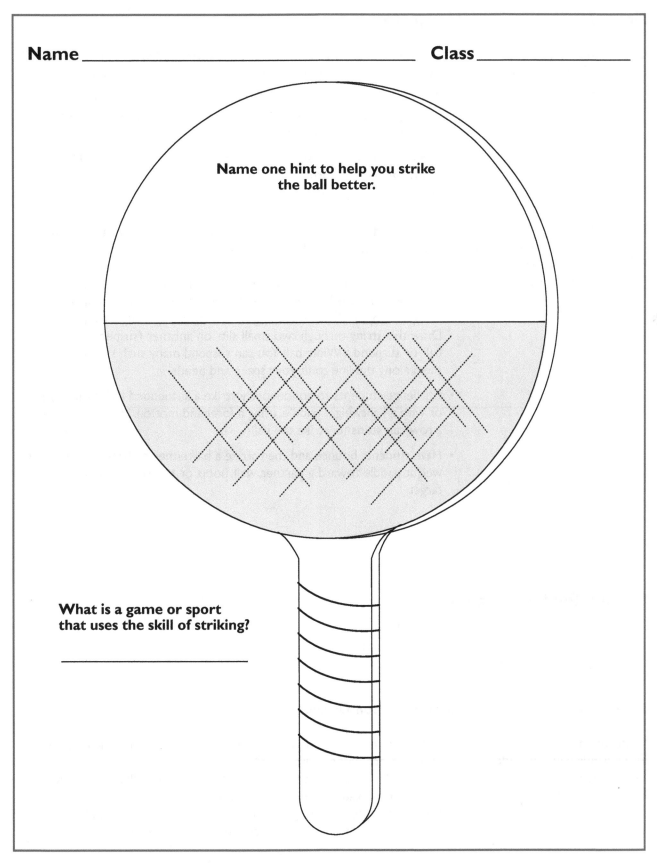

Name one hint to help you strike the ball better.

What is a game or sport that uses the skill of striking?

_____

Figure 11.8   Portfolio task assessment sheet for striking with short-handled implements, grades 1 to 2.

From *Elementary Physical Education Teaching & Assessment: A Practical Guide,* by Christine J. Hopple, 2005, Champaign, IL: Human Kinetics.

Emphasize	*Ideas for Lesson Development*
Underhand Shake hands with the paddle. Paddle way back. Firm wrist and elbow. Hit the ball when it is at a medium level.	• Ask students to stay in self-space while trying to flip a beanbag "pancake" over and catch it on the paddle. Can they travel slowly and do this? • Ask students to stay in self-space while continuously bouncing and then striking a small, lightweight ball upward with a hand or a lightweight paddle (i.e., bounce, strike, bounce, strike). • Challenge students to stay in self-space while continuously striking a small lightweight ball upward. How many times can each hit the ball in a row, before losing control?
Forehand (Turn your) side to the target. Bring your paddle way back. Firm wrist and elbow.	• Prepare and suspend balls in this manner: Cut small slits into the sides of two tennis balls. Use a darning needle to string the balls onto a long piece of line from a weed-trimming machine, and suspend the string between two standards. Add a small (1/2-inch or 1.3 cm) brass ring between the two balls (the two balls will keep the suspended ball you use from moving along the rope). Then, tie a string to the brass ring using a hangman's knot. Draw this string through two small slits on another (suspended) tennis ball, or suspend a Wiffle ball. You can suspend many such sets and move them along the line to fit your space and needs. • Challenge students to continuously strike a suspended ball, either by hand or with a lightweight paddle, using a forehand motion. How many times in a row can students strike the ball? • Have students bounce and then strike a ball either by hand or with a lightweight paddle toward a partner, wall, hoop, or tire set on the ground as a target.

KINDERGARTEN

Sample Performance Indicators

By the end of grade K, students should be able to

• repeatedly strike a balloon upward with a hand or lightweight paddle; and

• repeatedly strike a small suspended ball with a hand or lightweight paddle.

Emphasize	*Ideas for Lesson Development*
Underhand Shake hands with the paddle. Watch the ball. Paddle way back.	• Challenge students to balance a beanbag on a paddle and move through general space without dropping it. • Have students use a hand or lightweight (nylon or "lollipop") paddle to practice repeatedly striking a balloon with an underhand motion. • Challenge students to use a hand or lightweight paddle to underhand-strike underhand a Wiffle ball suspended from a bar or rope.

By the end of elementary school, students should be able to

- strike in appropriate practice situations, using a variety of long-handled implements; and
- use the skills of striking with long-handled implements to play or design small-group games.

Striking With Long-Handled Implements

Concepts and Skills	Learnable Pieces
Batting	Tee in front, side to the target. (K, 1–2)
	Shake hands with the bat, your favorite hand on top. (1–2)
	Twist, untwist (your hips lead). (1–2)
	Stand a bat-length away (from the tee or plate). (1–2)
	Step in the direction of the ball. (3–4)
	Level, stretched stroke. (3–4)
	Extend to the target. (5–6)
Hockey and golf strike	Shake hands with the stick, your favorite hand on top. (1–2)
	Small swings, side to side (hockey only). (1–2)
	Side to the target—ball in front of you. (1–2, 3–4)
	Large swing, side to side (golf only). (3–4)
	Twist, untwist (your hips and shoulders turn). (3–4)
	Hit underneath the ball (golf only). (5–6)
	Extend to the target. (5–6)
Hockey dribble	Use both sides of the stick. (1–2)
	Ball in front of you. (1–2)
	Small taps. (1–2, 3–4)
	Keep it close. (3–4)
	Look up. (5–6)

GRADES 5 TO 6

Sample Performance Indicators

By the end of grade 6, students should be able to

- strike a gently tossed ball using a bat;
- use a hockey stick to control-dribble a ball in a large group and not collide with others or obstacles;
- use a hockey stick to dribble a ball around stationary obstacles without losing control of the ball;

- dribble and then strike a ball to a stationary target or partner, using a hockey stick;
- strike a ball toward large target areas from an appropriate distance using a golf club or hockey stick; and
- design and play small-group keep-away games involving dribbling and shooting with a hockey stick toward a goal area.

Sample Performance Task

Have small groups (three or four students) design and play a small-group game using dribbling and passing with a hockey stick to move a Wiffle ball (you can adjust the type of stick and ball) toward a goal area. Allow students to choose boundaries, size of the goal area, and rules.

RUBRIC CLUES

To what extent do students

- successfully and consistently use the learnable pieces relative to dribbling or passing?

Sample Portfolio Task

Ask students to list all the sports and activities they know that involve the use of striking. Which of these do or would they enjoy playing or learning? How might their experiences in physical education help them be successful in these activities?

RUBRIC CLUES

To what extent do students

- show they understand the skills of striking?

Emphasize	*Ideas for Lesson Development*
Batting Extend to the target.	• Make large target areas (using chalk lines, and the like) and assign each a number of points. Challenge students to strike a ball with the bat toward certain areas and see how many points they and a partner can earn. • Modified striking game: Half of the class is up to bat; the other half is in the field (no out-of-bounds). Give paddles or rackets to half of the fielders. At one time, half of the batters strike and try to run around two cones set up in the field. Each time the group of batters runs around the cones, they get one point. Meanwhile, the fielders without rackets must get the balls to those fielders who do. These fielders try to strike the balls into a large target (9 × 3 × 12 feet, or 2.7 × 0.9 × 3.7 m, on the wall, or a large area set up behind the batters). Fielders can strike from anywhere to get the balls to the target. After all the balls are in the target (or have been hit toward it), the fielders give their paddles to the other half of the fielders to use, and the other half of the batters go to bat. Each person gets to bat twice before fielders and batters switch roles. **Belka:** *300* *Strategy Fielding*
Hockey and golf strike Hit underneath the ball (golf only). Extend to the target.	• Set up zones of varied distances away from a starting line (the "driving range"). Challenge each student to strike a small Wiffle ball for distance toward the zones; a partner can retrieve balls and then switch roles after five strikes. **PEC:** *Battleship* *Hockey Shoot-a-Rama* *Geography Golf* *Horse Hockey*

Hockey dribble
Look up.
General space (see "Space Awareness," chapter 8)
Offense
Keep your body between the ball and the defender.

- Challenge students in a large marked-off area to dribble a Wiffle ball with hockey sticks and change speeds according to the drum or tambourine beat or a signal.
- Put obstacles, such as crates, boxes, and cones, in general space; challenge students to dribble as quickly as possible through general space without colliding with others or with obstacles.
- Modified Trees in the Forest (see page 117): Have defenders stand in hoops spread throughout general space; the other students move through the area, trying not to lose control of the ball.
- Set up an obstacle course with cones, crates, and boxes that students must dribble through; have a large goal set up at the end that they can then strike toward.

PEC: *2-Minute Hockey Challenge*

General space (see "Space Awareness," chapter 8)
Offense
Keep your body between the ball and the defender.
Create space by moving to open areas to pass or receive the ball.
Defense
Deny space by staying between the opponent and intended goal.

- Have students design and play small-group games (two-on-two, two-on-three, three-on-three) that involve dribbling and shooting with a hockey stick toward a goal area. A goal defender can be part of each team. Allow students to determine their own rules, boundaries, and goal size.

GRADES 3 TO 4

Sample Performance Indicators

By the end of grade 4, students should be able to

- strike a softly pitched ball with a bat as far as possible;
- dribble a Wiffle ball with a hockey stick and change directions and pathways at the signal;
- strike a Wiffle ball along the ground to a stationary partner using a hockey stick; and
- strike a Wiffle ball in the air using a golf club or hockey stick.

Sample Performance Task

Students use hockey sticks to strike Wiffle balls toward targets of varied sizes and distances. They choose the targets they wish to strike.

RUBRIC CLUES

To what extent do students
- show they understand the skills of striking with long-handled implements?

Sample Portfolio Task

Ask students to reflect on cues they use in batting by completing figure 11.9.

RUBRIC CLUES

To what extent do students
- show they understand the skills for batting?

Name _____ **Class** _____

What's Your Batting Average?

What's a game that uses striking? _____

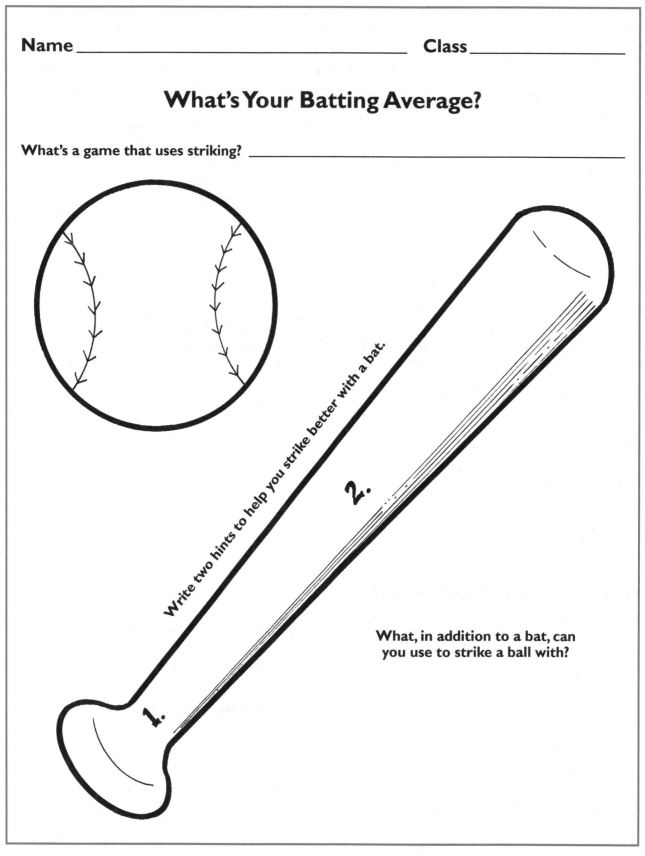

Write two hints to help you strike better with a bat.

2.

1.

What, in addition to a bat, can you use to strike a ball with?

Figure 11.9   Portfolio task assessment sheet for striking with long-handled implements, grades 3 to 4.

From *Elementary Physical Education Teaching & Assessment: A Practical Guide*, by Christine J. Hopple, 2005, Champaign, IL: Human Kinetics.

Emphasize	*Ideas for Lesson Development*
Batting Step in the direction of the ball. Level, stretched stroke.	• Have students take turns hitting off a tee to two partners in the field; after five strikes, they switch roles. Put out a variety of equipment, such as bases, poly spots, and carpet squares, so the students can make up their own games, if they like. • Discuss what makes a good underhand pitch; allow students to practice pitching toward a home plate. Then, in groups of three or four, have students practice the roles of batter, fielder, and pitcher.

Buschner: *Step and Swing*

Hockey strike Side to the target—ball in front of you. Twist, untwist (your hips and shoulders turn).	• Have students stand a distance of choice away from each other and practice striking a Wiffle ball along the ground. Once they can strike the ball close enough that their partners can trap it in one step, challenge them to work from greater distances. • Set up a variety of targets (large tin cans on their sides, hoops, goals) that students can strike toward from a distance they choose. Assign point values to the targets if you wish. • Set up several goals in a large marked-off area. Have partners practice dribbling, then shooting, toward any goal area they wish. Several partners of students can work in the area simultaneously, as long as there is one goal for each pair and the area is large enough to move around safely. If you wish, have students work in groups of three, with one as goal defender. You can specify time limits for them to rotate to the field, as a fielder becomes a goal defender.
Golf strike Side to the target—ball in front of you. Large swing, side to side. Twist, untwist (your hips and shoulders turn).	• Have students strike a small Wiffle ball toward a marked-off area; partners use cones to mark the farthest distance hit. After five strikes, partners switch roles.
Hockey dribble Small taps. Keep it close.	• Encourage students to practice their skills with as many different implements as possible. Many types of long-handled hockey-type sticks are available: Plastic hockey sticks, Pillo-Pollo sticks, and golf sticks or clubs are a few examples. • Have students dribble a Wiffle ball with a hockey-type stick in a large marked-off area and at the signal change the direction, or pathway, they are traveling.

GRADES 1 TO 2

Sample Performance Indicators

By the end of grade 2, students should be able to

- strike a Wiffle ball off a tee with a bat;
- use an underhand swing to strike a Wiffle ball with a hockey stick or golf club; and
- travel slowly in different directions and dribble a Wiffle ball with a hockey stick.

Sample Performance Task

From a tee or large cone, ask students to strike a large Wiffle ball with a plastic bat to a fielder in a large open area.

RUBRIC CLUES

To what extent do students

- demonstrate the ability to contact the ball with the bat?
- use correct hand placement to hold the bat?
- stand in correct relationship to the tee?

Sample Portfolio Task

Ask students to designate the parts of the body that would face the batting tee and the pitcher/fielder when batting by completing figure 11.10.

RUBRIC CLUES

To what extent do students

- designate the side as the correct body part to face the pitcher/fielder and the front as the body part to face the tee?

Emphasize	*Ideas for Lesson Development*
Batting Shake hands with the bat, your favorite hand on top. Tee in front, side to the target. Stand a bat-length away (from the tee or plate). Twist, untwist (your hips lead).	• Stress the protocol when using long-handled implements to students: Always look around to make sure you have plenty of space to swing and always keep your stick at a low level. • Have students practice hitting a Wiffle ball off a tee with a plastic or light-weight bat to a partner who fields. • Allow students, in groups of two or three, to make up their own game when batting. Poly spots and carpet squares can be used as bases. **PEC:** *Cone Baseball*
Hockey strike Shake hands with the stick, your favorite hand on top. Side to the target—ball in front of you. Small swings, side to side.	• Have students practice hitting a Wiffle ball with a hockey-type stick to a hoop on the ground or to some other target, such as foam pins or large plastic bottles slightly filled with sand. • Have two teams stand behind designated lines. On a third line (centered about 12 feet, or 3.7 m, away from each line) set up three or four targets (e.g., large plastic bottles) in front of each student. On the signal, students strike toward their targets. When a team knocks down the targets, they set them up and begin again. This activity can also be done in a small-group situation.

Name _____ Class _____

How Should You Bat?

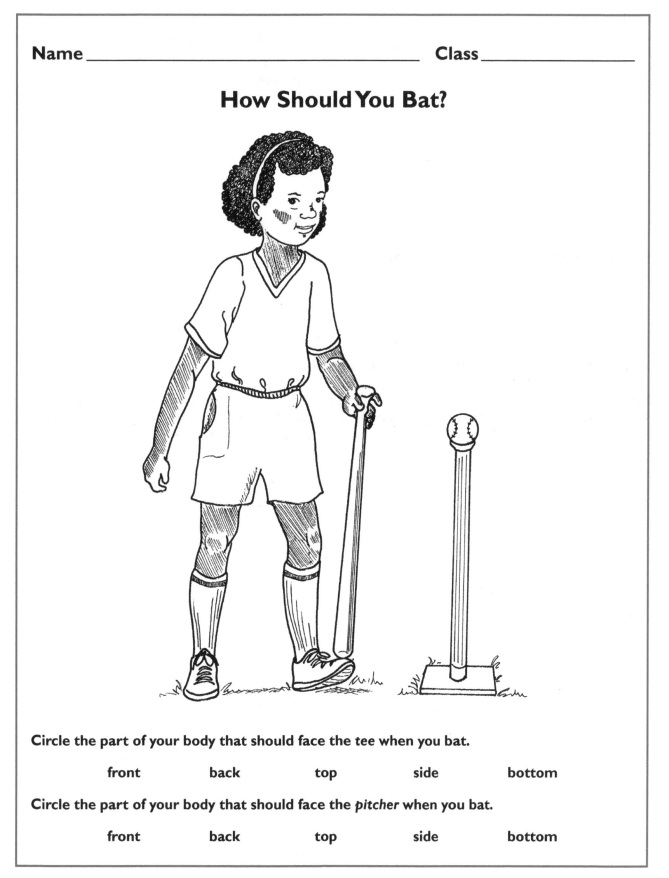

Circle the part of your body that should face the _tee_ when you bat.

        front   back   top   side   bottom

Circle the part of your body that should face the _pitcher_ when you bat.

        front   back   top   side   bottom

Figure 11.10 Portfolio task assessment sheet for striking with long-handled implements, grades 1 to 2.

From _Elementary Physical Education Teaching & Assessment: A Practical Guide,_ by Christine J. Hopple, 2005, Champaign, IL: Human Kinetics.

Hockey dribble
Use both sides of the stick.
Ball in front of you.
Small taps.

- Have students practice dribbling a Wiffle ball with a hockey stick in a marked-off area. Set up a large goal area they can practice striking toward.

- Use paint or chalk to mark off different pathways. Challenge students to dribble their balls on the pathways, moving as quickly as they can while keeping control of the balls.

PEC: *Hockey Highway*

KINDERGARTEN

Sample Performance Indicators

By the end of grade K, students should be able to

- strike a small playground ball off a tee or cone using the hand.

Emphasize	*Ideas for Lesson Development*
Batting Tee in front, side to the target.	• Set up 6-inch (15.2 cm) playground balls on large cones for students to strike, using their hands like bats. Students practice in pairs. Have a partner catch the ball; each batter gets three strikes before they become a catcher.

Chapter 12

Health, Activity, and Fitness

Sample Course Standard

By the end of elementary school, students should be able to

- apply basic concepts of physical activity and physical fitness to as many situations in their daily lives as possible.

Introduction to Physical Activity and Physical Fitness

Concepts and Skills	Learnable Pieces
Being active is important for you and your body.	Being active is good for your body. (K)
	Being active is a healthy habit. (1–2)
	There are many important benefits to being active. (3–4)
You can be active in many different ways.	Playing is a fun way to be active. (K)
	Moving, playing, working, and exercising are ways you can be active. (1–2, 3–4)
	There are many fun ways to become active and fit. (3–4, 5–6)
	It is not always easy to be active. (5–6)
It is important to be physically fit.	Being physically fit means your heart, bones, and muscles are strong and healthy. (1–2)
	Being physically fit means you look good, feel good, and have lots of energy to play and work at home and in school. (3–4)
	The only way to become physically fit is to be physically active. (5–6)
	Being physically fit means you have good aerobic endurance, muscle strength, flexibility, and body-fat levels. (5–6)
Physical fitness tests assess your body's fitness levels.	Fitness tests help you find out how fit your body is and whether you need to improve your activity level. (3–4, 5–6)
	There are other ways to find out how fit you are. (3–4, 5–6)

GRADES 5 TO 6

NASPE Performance Indicators

- Consciously chooses to participate in moderate to vigorous physical activity outside of physical education class on a regular basis. (3–5, #3, 19)
- Participates in organized sport activities provided through local community programs. (3–5, #3, 20)
- Participates in selected activities that develop and maintain each component of physical fitness. (3–5, #4, 25)
- Meets the age- and gender-specific health-related fitness standards defined by FITNESSGRAM. (3–5, #4, 32)
- Identifies his or her strengths and weaknesses based upon the results of FITNESSGRAM testing. (3–5, #4, 33)

- Defends the benefits of physical activity. (3–5, #6, 50)

Sample Portfolio Task

Ask students to describe why they think people are more physically active now or 100 years ago. Why do they think so?

RUBRIC CLUES

To what extent do students

- show their understanding by appropriately using terms and examples?
- use examples to back up their viewpoints?

Emphasize	*Ideas for Lesson Development*
You can be active in many different ways. There are many fun ways to become active and fit.	• Discuss with students the many fun ways they can move, exercise, and be active at home and in school. Ask them for examples: Jumping rope, jogging, dancing, swimming, doing push-ups, throwing and catching, and playing tag are just a few possibilities. • Discuss how gardening, walking, and working around the house or farm help people stay active and physically fit. • Discuss some ways that make exercising more fun, such as exercising with a friend, your pet, parents and siblings, or exercising to music. • Ask students to write down their favorite way of being active and becoming physically fit. Post these on a bulletin board where everyone can see them. • Ask questions to facilitate discussion and review, such as the following: (a) Name some things you like to do that are plain fun. Do you think you get more fit by doing them? (b) What can you do to make exercising more fun? (c) What kinds of things do you like to do to play and be active at home and in school? (d) Does being active mean only participating in sports? What can you do to be active if you don't like to play sports?
You can be active in many different ways. It is not always easy to be active.	• Ask students when they think exercising or being active might be hard: when they have too much homework, when they don't feel good, when the level of exercise is difficult for them, when they are tired, if their neighborhood isn't safe, when they don't have a place to be active, when parents can't take them somewhere. Discuss different ways to deal with these situations, and offer alternatives if appropriate (e.g., Boys Club and Girls Club, Scouts, after-school programs, and the like).

- Let students know that it's okay to not always feel good during or after exercising: Sometimes it does hurt some or make them tired. Discuss the difference between something being hard and hurting a little, versus activity that makes you feel very bad and in pain.

- Discuss how the body has to get used to playing and exercising hard. If people do too much at once, they may not feel well. It's better to start out a little less strenuously!

- Have students write a paragraph for their exercise or class journal that describes feeling good when they were exercising or being active. What made them feel good? Then have them describe a time they didn't feel well when exercising or being active.

- Ask questions to facilitate discussion and review, such as the following: (a) What are some ways you might feel when you're participating in physical activity? Do you think they all are okay? (b) Is exercising always easy? Does it always feel good to exercise? (c) How do you know when you have done too much? (d) What are some ways that you can help yourself not to think that exercising is overly hard?

It is important to be physically fit.
Being physically fit means you have good aerobic endurance, muscle strength, flexibility, and body-fat levels. The only way to become physically fit is to be physically active.

- Discuss with the class that when you're active by moving, playing, working, and exercising, you help yourself become physically fit. Being active is the only way you can become or remain physically fit.

- Ask students who they think is physically fit. Why do they think that? How did this person become physically fit?

- Discuss with students how being fit helps you be the best person you can be; being fit is the way you take care of your body.

- Relate to students how being active helps the body become better, just like doing homework and studying helps the mind become sharper. Being active is a smart way to take care of the body!

- Ask questions to facilitate discussion and review, such as these: (a) What is the only way to become physically fit? (b) What are some ways people, especially on TV, try to make you think you can become physically fit? What ways don't work?

- Ask students to write a private letter about themselves to their portfolio discussing how physically fit they feel. What are some ways they think they are or aren't fit? Can they improve their physical fitness? Would they like you to help them in any special ways? How might they improve their fitness levels, if need be? (Be sure to discuss that there is not a right and a wrong answer: What's important is being honest in the writing.)

Ratliffe: *Health-Related Circuit*
          Shape Up
PEC: *A Spin on Fitness*
          Fitness Pursuit
          Who Wants to be a Fitnessaire?

Physical fitness tests assess your body's fitness levels. Fitness tests help you find out how fit your body is and whether you need to improve your activity level.
There are other ways to find out how fit you are.

- Discuss how the fitness tests students take are ways to discover how fit their bodies are. The tests tell them if they need to be more active to become stronger and healthier.

- Ask questions to facilitate discussion and review: (a) Are there other ways besides taking tests to find out how strong and fit you are? (b) What are some ways you can test yourself at home to find out how fit your body is?* Explain to students that riding your bike to your friend's house, how long you can play tag without getting tired, and so on are all ways to see how fit you are.

GRADES 3 TO 4

NASPE Performance Indicators

- Chooses to participate in structured and purposeful activity. (3–5, #3, 22)
- Participates in selected activities that develop and maintain each component of physical fitness. (3–5, #4, 25)
- Identifies his or her strengths and weaknesses based upon the results of FITNESSGRAM testing. (3–5, #4, 33)
- Chooses to participate in group physical activities. (3–5, #6, 45)
- Defends the benefits of physical activity. (3–5, #6, 50)

Sample Portfolio Task

Ask students to write about someone they consider physically fit. What makes that person seem physically fit? What does that person do to stay physically fit? Would they like to be like that person?

RUBRIC CLUES

To what extent do students

- use correct terms and explanations to describe physical fitness?
- give examples of behaviors that can lead to physical fitness?

Emphasize

Being active is important for you and your body. There are many important benefits to being active.

Ideas for Lesson Development

- Discuss with students why it is important to be active in life. Why is it not good to be a "couch potato?" Relate being active to the body's becoming strong and healthy. Talk about how, just as you need to study to learn, you need to be active to be fit.

- Talk about benefits of being active that students can relate to: builds strong muscles and bones, makes you feel good, produces a healthy heart, helps make friends, helps your brain develop!

- Ask questions to facilitate discussion and review: (a) Why do you think it is good for you to play and be active? (b) What happens if you aren't very active or if you don't move or play very much?

PEC:	Eggs for Fitness	Fitness Pursuit
	Bone Relay	The Skeleton Jig Saw
	Bone Memory	The Bone-a-fyed Rap
	'Dem Bones	Word Association Muscles

You can be active in many different ways.
Moving, playing, working, and exercising are ways you can be active.
There are many fun ways to become active and fit.

- Discuss how moving, playing, and exercising are ways to be active. Ask students to describe specific ways they are active in everyday life.

- Ask students to name the different things they do to be active and fit, such as jumping rope, jogging, dancing, swimming, doing push-ups, playing tag, and throwing footballs. Categorize these according to where they can be done: at home, in the community, or at school.

- Ask students what makes exercising or being active fun for them (some examples might include exercising with a friend, parents or siblings, or a pet dog; and putting on music).

- Ask students for fun suggestions of what they can do to be active with their family.

- Give students an assignment to exercise or do something active with a parent, brother, or sister one time during the week. What they do and for how long is up to them. Have them write a note to their portfolio describing what they did.

Ratliffe: *Shape Up*
PEC: *Fitness Obstacle Course*
        Partner Fitness Fun

It is important to be physically fit.
Being physically fit means you look good, feel good, and have lots of energy to play and work at home and in school.

- Discuss what it means to be physically fit. Ask questions to facilitate discussion: (a) Who do you know who is physically fit? Why? (b) What do you think it means to be physically fit? Why? (c) Are you fit only if you're skinny? Why or why not?

- Have students glue pictures (from home, magazines, and so on) of people they think look physically fit onto a piece of paper, and label who they are. Put these up on a bulletin board. Use a title, such as "Look Whoo's Physically Fit." (Show an owl pointing to the slogan.)

Ratliffe: *Health-Related Circuit*

Physical fitness tests assess your body's fitness levels.
Fitness tests help you find out how fit your body is and whether you need to improve your activity level.
There are other ways to find out how fit you are.

- Explain to students that, just as they take math or spelling tests, they can take physical fitness tests to see how fit their bodies are. Talk about how the results will let them see if they need to be more active.

- Have students describe different things they do at home that let them know their fitness levels.

GRADES 1 TO 2

NASPE Performance Indicators

- States the short-term effects of physical activity on the heart and lungs. (K–2, #2, 17)
- Engages in moderate to vigorous physical activity on an intermittent basis. (K–2, #3, 19)
- Engages in a variety of locomotor activities (e.g., hopping, walking, jumping, galloping, and running) during leisure time. (K–2, #3, 20)
- Recognizes that health-related physical fitness consists of several different components. (K–2, #4, 30)
- Identifies several activities that are enjoyable. (K–2, #6, 48)

Sample Portfolio Task

Have students draw their own pictures on large blank paper of themselves participating in a favorite activity that helps them become physically fit. On a separate piece of ruled paper, the child should explain what he or she is doing in the drawing and why it is fun.

RUBRIC CLUES

To what extent do students

- draw an activity that involves being active?

Emphasize	*Ideas for Lesson Development*
Being active is important for you and your body. Being active is a healthy habit.	• Discuss how being active is a healthy habit, like brushing your teeth, combing your hair, resting, and eating. Being active is something that should happen every day. **Ratliffe:** *Activity Benefits*
You can be active in many different ways. Moving, playing, working, and exercising are ways you can be active.	• Ask students to describe things they do at home and school to be active. What do they think helps the heart, muscles, and bones grow strong? Talk about how fun these activities are. • Have students draw their own pictures doing something that helps them to be active and fit (see Portfolio Task, previously). Post these in the hallway for students and parents to see. **Ratliffe:** *Be Active!* *Human Obstacle Course*
It is important to be physically fit. Being physically fit means your heart, bones, and muscles are strong and healthy.	• Ask students to tell you about someone they think is physically fit. Discuss how these people got to be fit. Are they active and do they exercise? Do they think a person becomes fit by being active infrequently or often? How often? Almost every day? Ask students if they think the people they named were active and exercised when they were in first or second grade. What kinds of things do they think these fit people did? • Discuss with students how their hearts, muscles, and bones grow bigger and stronger every time they play and exercise. **PEC:** *Bone Memory* *Word Association Muscles* *The Skeleton Jigsaw*

KINDERGARTEN

NASPE Performance Indicators

- Identifies several activities that are enjoyable. (K–2, #6, 48)

Sample Portfolio Task

Ask students to draw their own pictures participating in their favorite play or exercise activities. (These drawings are not to be assessed.)

Emphasize	Ideas for Lesson Development
Being active is important for you and your body. Being active is good for your body.	• Conduct a fun activity with students (such as parachute play or jumping rope), then discuss that some fun activities also help their bones and muscles become stronger. • Ask students who they think has big muscles or is very fit; discuss how this person got to be so strong by being active.
You can be active in many different ways. Playing is a fun way to be active.	• Ask students for activities that are fun to do and help their muscles get stronger. Mention an activity and have them raise their hands if they think it helps them become strong (e.g., jumping rope, playing tag, swimming, dancing, playing on the playground). • Play Disney's *Mousercise* (or another activity-related) CD. *Mousercise* has a collection of fun, active aerobic routines introduced by various Disney characters. The medley song is a wonderful activity to do with preschoolers and kindergartners.

Sample Course Standard

By the end of elementary school, students should be able to

- apply the basic concepts of cardiorespiratory fitness to situations in their daily lives.

Cardiorespiratory Fitness

Concepts and Skills	Learnable Pieces
Your heart is an important muscle.	Your heart is special because it is always beating. (K)
	Your heart is in your chest. (K, 1–2)
	Your heart is the size of your fist covered by your other hand. (K, 1–2)
	Your heart is a strong, special muscle that is a pump. (1–2)
	Your heart pumps blood to your muscles and through your body. (1–2)
	Your heart grows bigger as you grow bigger. (1–2)
Your heart acts differently when you exercise.	When you exercise, your muscles need more oxygen and energy to keep moving. (3–4)
	Your heart beats faster when you exercise so it can carry the oxygen from your lungs and the food energy from your blood to your muscles. (5–6)
You can listen to your heart beat.	You can feel your heart beat by putting your hand on your chest. (K)
	You can feel your heart beat at your wrist, your neck, or your chest. (1–2)
	Your heart beats slowly when you sit, sleep, and rest. (K, 1–2)
	Your heart beats fast when you move, play, and exercise. (K, 1–2)
	Your heart rate tells you how hard your heart is working. (3–4)
	Your heart rate, or pulse, is how many times your heart beats in one minute. (3–4, 5–6)
	You can calculate your heart rate by counting your heart beats in six seconds and then multiplying this number by 10. (3–4, 5–6)
	Take your heart rate about five minutes after you have exercised hard. By then it should almost be back to your normal heart rate. (5–6)
It is important to have good aerobic endurance.	Your heart gets stronger when you play and exercise. (1–2)
	Endurance means your heart and muscles can move and exercise for a long period of time—like during physical education class. (3–4)
	Just like your other muscles, your heart gets stronger and has more endurance when you exercise, and it gets weaker when you don't exercise. (3–4, 5–6)

Concepts and Skills	**Learnable Pieces**
It is important to have good aerobic endurance.	Aerobic endurance helps keep your body strong and fit, and it keeps up your energy. (3–4, 5–6)
	Aerobic endurance refers to the fitness level of your heart, lungs, and muscles. (5–6)
	If your heart, lungs, and muscles can be active for a long period of time—about 20 minutes—before you get tired, you probably have good aerobic endurance. (5–6)
	Without good endurance, you cannot be physically fit. (3–4, 5–6)
There are many ways to exercise your heart.	Running, playing tag, and jumping rope are things your heart likes you to do. (K, 1–2)
	Watching too much TV and playing too many indoor games can keep you from having a strong heart (1–2) and good endurance. (3–4)
	You improve your endurance by doing things that keep you moving for at least 10 minutes at a time, three times a day. (3–4, 5–6)
	You increase your aerobic endurance by playing and exercising in activities that make your heart, lungs, and muscles work harder and faster for at least 30 minutes a day. (5–6)
	Biking, swimming, jumping rope, and playing tag are examples of aerobic activities. (5–6)
	If you don't stay active, your aerobic endurance will decrease. (3–4, 5–6)
You should be smart and safe when you exercise aerobically.	You should warm up before you exercise aerobically and cool down afterward. (5–6)
	If you haven't been exercising much, you should gradually work up to being active. (5–6)
There are different ways you can test your aerobic endurance.	The mile-run (1.6 km) test can tell you if you need to be more active. (3–4)
	The mile-run (1.6 km) test is a way to gauge the aerobic endurance of your heart, lungs, and muscles. (3–4, 5–6)
	Seeing how far you can run, walk fast, or ride your bike and how many times you can jump rope are ways to test your aerobic endurance. (3–4, 5–6)

GRADES 5 TO 6

NASPE Performance Indicators

- Maintains a physical activity log (e.g., ACTIVITY-GRAM) for a two- or three-day period documenting activity data (e.g., step count, time). (3–5, #3, 24)
- Engages in appropriate physical activity that results in the development of cardiorespiratory endurance. (3–5, #4, 26)
- Maintains heart rate within the target heart rate zone for a specified length of time during an aerobic activity. (3–5, #4, 31)

Sample Portfolio Task

Ask students to explain in their own words what the term *aerobic* exercise means and to describe why it is important. They should then relate it to their lives by giving examples or keeping a log of their aerobic activities.

RUBRIC CLUES

To what extent do students

- show a correct understanding of the word *aerobic*?
- use appropriate, accurate examples to enhance their explanations?

Emphasize	*Ideas for Lesson Development*
Your heart acts differently when you exercise. Your heart beats faster when you exercise so it can carry oxygen from your lungs and the food energy from your blood to your muscles.	• Discuss the heart pathway with students—how oxygen is taken in by the lungs from the air and passed into the blood, which is pumped through the body. The blood then passes along oxygen and the energy from food they eat. Explain how once the muscles use the oxygen, only carbon dioxide is left over, which enters the blood and is exhaled through the lungs. • Talk with the classroom teachers to see when they teach the "body" units in health or science. You may be able to coordinate teaching much about the heart and lungs between physical education and other classes. • Read the American Heart Association's *Heart Treasure Chest* for a variety of ideas for teaching about the heart. • Borrow a model of the heart and lungs from a local community college or high school biology department to show your students how they look inside the body.

> **Ratliffe:** *Heart Pump Circuit*
> **PEC:** *Cardiac Maze*   *Fitness Monopoly*
>   *Edible Health*

You can listen to your heart beat. Your heart rate, or pulse, is how many times your heart beats in one minute. You can calculate your heart rate by counting your heart	• Have students take their heart rates before and during a vigorous activity. Use a large conversion chart that shows the number of beats in six seconds, and what these numbers mean in terms of a minute. After a few minutes' rest, have students again take their pulses to see how much they have slowed. • Have students guess their heart rates when they are resting and when they have been exercising hard. Then have them take their pulses to see how close they guessed.

beats in six seconds and then multiplying this number by 10. Take your heart rate about five minutes after you have exercised hard. By then it should almost be back to your normal heart rate.

- With the popularity of pedometers, there are many good resources as well as pedometers or pulsemeters themselves to help students find out about their heart rate and how their heart responds to activity. See PE Central's Web site for links to resources and companies that specialize in pedometer use with younger students.

> **PEC:** *How Hard Does Your Heart Beat?*
> *Jump Rope Around the World*
> *Pedometer Partner Fitness Fun*

It is important to have good aerobic endurance.
Aerobic endurance refers to the fitness level of your heart, lungs, and muscles.

- Explain how aerobic endurance involves the heart, lungs, and muscles working together, then ask students if they think a marathoner has good aerobic endurance. How do they know that? What about someone who plays a whole soccer game every Saturday morning? Ask them to give other examples of people with endurance (not necessarily athletes).

Aerobic endurance helps keep your body strong and fit, and it keeps up your energy. If your heart, lungs, and muscles can be active for a long period of time—about 20 minutes—before you get tired, you probably have good aerobic endurance.

- Discuss the benefits of good aerobic endurance and whether it is likely to come with being a couch potato. With aerobic endurance do you have lots of energy, or a little? Do you get sick frequently?

- Encourage students to "keep on moving" for as long as they can. They should see if they can increase the length of time they can stay active and moving. Relate the increased amounts of time with increased aerobic endurance.

> **Ratliffe:** *Keeping the Pipes Clean*
> **PEC:** *Artery Demonstration*
> *Fitness Scavenger Hunt*

Just like your other muscles, your heart gets stronger and has more endurance when you exercise, and it gets weaker when you don't exercise. Without good endurance, you cannot be physically fit.

- Discuss how aerobic endurance is only one aspect of being physically fit, but perhaps the most important aspect. Ask for reasons why this might be so.

- Relate how the heart must be exercised to stay in shape, just like other muscles.

There are many ways to exercise your heart.
You increase your aerobic endurance by playing and exercising in activities that make your heart, lungs, and muscles work harder and faster for at least 30 minutes a day.
You improve your endurance

- Discuss the word *aerobics*. What does it mean? Why is aerobic exercise (in fitness centers) so named? Relate the word *aerobics* to the increased work of the heart and lungs.

- Ask for examples of exercises or activities that can help increase aerobic endurance. Can each of the examples be done for at least 10 minutes without you having to stop?

- Write a list of activities on the board. Ask the class to group or classify them according to whether each helps increase aerobic endurance.

by doing things that keep you moving for at least 10 minutes at a time, three times a day. Biking, swimming, jumping rope, and playing tag are examples of aerobic activities. If you don't stay active, your aerobic endurance will decrease.

- Start a Heart Smart Club. Students who exercise aerobically each day write down the activity and time; every Monday post these heart-smart descriptions on a bulletin board. Post the students' photos with their activity sheets (take pictures or have students bring them from home).

- Ask questions to facilitate discussion and review: (a) What does it mean if an activity is aerobic? What body parts does this involve? (b) How long should you work, play, and be active to get aerobic, or cardiorespiratory, fitness benefits? (c) Can you "save up" aerobic endurance if you do a lot of activity, then stop, and still derive benefits? (d) What are some aerobic activities that you like to do?

Ratliffe: *Run to the Front*
PEC: *Corner Tag*   *Steps to Fitness*
     Follow the Leader Fitness Jog/Walk   *'UNO" Fitness*
     Mission 'Possible" Fitness

You should be smart and safe when you exercise aerobically. If you haven't been exercising much, you should gradually work up to being active. You should warm up before you exercise aerobically and cool down afterward.

- Discuss how, before doing heavy aerobic exercising, you should warm up the heart and other muscles by walking, circling the arms and legs, and then stretching the arms and legs. Then, after finishing, you should cool down by walking, circling the arms, and stretching again.

There are different ways you can test your aerobic endurance.
The mile-run test is a way to gauge the aerobic endurance of your heart, lungs, and muscles. Seeing how far you can run, walk fast, or ride your bike and how many times you can jump rope are ways to test your aerobic endurance.

- Discuss how the mile-run test lets them see how much aerobic endurance they have—it is not given just for the teachers to be mean!

- Set up "heart-smart" stations: jumping rope; walking or jogging on a fitness trail; dancing; hula hooping; playing tag, Frisbee, football, and so forth. On a "heart day," challenge students to choose their stations and to keep moving and being active for as long as they can. They should try to work up to the entire class period. This is a good change of pace and a day when you can talk to individual students about their portfolios and fitness scores.

GRADES 3 TO 4

NASPE Performance Indicators

- Describes how heart rate is used to monitor exercise intensity. (3–5, #2, 11)
- Monitors his or her physical activity by using a pedometer to count the number of steps taken or the distance traveled. (3–5, #3, 23)
- Engages in appropriate physical activity that results

in the development of cardiorespiratory endurance. (3–5, #4, 26)

- Runs the equivalent of two laps around a regulation track without stopping. (3–5, #4, 28)

- Maintains heart rate within the target heart rate zone for a specified length of time during an aerobic activity. (3–5, #4, 31)

Sample Portfolio Task

Students list four activities that can help them improve their cardiorespiratory endurance and four activities that cannot. They should circle the items on either of their lists that they participated in within the past week, either in or out of school.

To what extent do students
- list appropriate examples of activities that are, or are not, good for improving endurance?
- name four examples for each category?

Emphasize	*Ideas for Lesson Development*
Your heart acts differently when you exercise. When you exercise, your muscles need more oxygen and energy to keep moving.	• Discuss how the muscles need oxygen and energy to move, and how during exercise they need even more—which is why the heart beats faster during exercise. • Explain how oxygen from the air goes into the lungs and then into the blood. So, when we move a lot, our lungs breathe faster because the muscles need more oxygen. **Ratliffe:** *Heart Pump Circuit*
You can listen to your heart beat. Your heart rate tells you how hard your heart is working. Your heart rate, or pulse, is how many times your heart beats in one minute. You can calculate your heart rate by counting your heart beats in six seconds and then multiplying this number by 10.	• Discuss how the heart rate tells how fast or slow the heart is beating, or working. A fun fact is that at rest the heart should beat less than 100 times in a minute. During exercise, the heart beats very fast—more than 100 times a minute. • Have students practice taking their heart rates right before, during, and after exercising. Discuss why it was higher during exercise, and why it slowed down afterward.
It is important to have good aerobic endurance. Endurance means your heart and muscles can move and exercise for a long period of time—like during physical education class. Just like your other muscles, your heart gets stronger and has more endurance when you exercise, and it gets weaker when you don't exercise. Aerobic endurance helps keep your body strong and fit and it keeps up your energy. Without good endurance, you cannot be physically fit.	• Compare endurance to the Energizer Bunny—it lets you keep going and going! • Ask students who they sense has good endurance. Why? Give examples for them to reflect on, such as Lance Armstrong, Mia Hamm, Serena Williams, Shaquille O'Neal, and others. • Set up heart-smart stations as described previously. Relate the students' participation in the activities to their endurance. • Discuss how endurance might be the most important part of fitness. • Ask questions to facilitate discussion and review: (a) If your heart works harder when you play for a few minutes, but then you get so tired you can't play anymore, do you think you have good endurance? (b) If you can keep moving for 20 minutes or more during your physical education class time, do you think your heart has good endurance? **Ratliffe:** *Keeping the Pipes Clean* **PEC:** *Mission "Possible" Fitness*

There are many ways to exercise your heart.
You improve your endurance by doing things that keep you moving for at least 10 minutes at a time, three times a day.

- Ask students to tell you some activities that they can do for 10 minutes or more at a time (e.g., walking, running, bicycling, swimming, playing tag). Discuss how these develop endurance because they keep you moving for at least 10 minutes.

- Discuss the kinds of activities that aren't very active and that don't help develop good endurance (watching TV and playing indoor games). Acknowledge that doing this is okay some of the time but that, just like many other things, too much is not good.

Watching too much TV and playing too many indoor games can keep you from developing good endurance. If you don't stay active, your aerobic endurance will decrease.

- Challenge students to keep logs for one week of the activities they do to help their endurance. At the end of the week they should think about their habits: Do they need to be more active? Discuss ways they can start to be more active.

- Ask students to bring in pictures from magazines or photos from home showing people participating in helpful or unhelpful activities for the heart. Post the pictures on a bulletin board.

> **Ratliffe:** *Fitness Club*
> *Run to the Front*
> **PEC:** *Artery Demonstration*   *Uninterrupted*
> *Fire and Ice*

There are different ways you can test your aerobic endurance.
The mile-run test is a way to gauge the aerobic endurance of your heart, lungs, and muscles. The mile-run test can tell you if you need to be more active. Seeing how far you can run, walk fast, or ride your bike and how many times you can jump rope are ways to test your aerobic endurance.

- Discuss how the mile-run test is used to see if the heart has good endurance. What if it doesn't? What can the results tell?

- Encourage students to "keep on moving" at home and test themselves periodically. Challenge them to do this, not because they will be tested in class, but because they are helping themselves by getting in shape.

GRADES 1 TO 2

NASPE Performance Indicators

- Engages in a series of locomotor activities (e.g., timed segments of hopping, walking, jumping, galloping, and running) without tiring easily. (K–2, #4, 25)

- Participates in a variety of games that increase breathing and heart rate. (K–2, #4, 26)

- Sustains activity for increasingly longer periods of time while participating in various activities in physical education. (K–2, #4, 28)

Sample Portfolio Task

Ask students to draw their own pictures doing their favorite heart-smart activities (which help get their hearts in shape). If you wish, have them also explain briefly what they are doing in the drawings.

To what extent do students

- give examples of an activity that can make the heart stronger?

Emphasize	*Ideas for Lesson Development*

Your heart is an important muscle.
Your heart is in your chest.
Your heart is the size of your fist covered by your other hand.
Your heart grows bigger as you grow bigger.

- If possible, bring in a model of the heart (or show a picture of it) to help students understand that the heart is what makes the beating noise in their chests!

Ratliffe: Listening to Your Heart

Your heart is a strong, special muscle that is a pump.
Your heart pumps blood to your muscles and through your body.

- Discuss how the heart pumps blood all over the body—to the muscles, stomach, eyes, and every other part.
- Relate to students that the heart is special because it always pumps blood—even while we sleep.

You can listen to your heart beat.
You can feel your heart beat at your wrist, your neck, or your chest.
Your heart beats slowly when you sit, sleep, and rest.
Your heart beats fast when you move, play, and exercise.

- Have students each feel their own, and a partner's, heart after a vigorous activity. Discuss why the heart was beating faster.
- Have students make fists and squeeze them at the pace they think their hearts pump at rest, and then during exercise.
- Borrow stethoscopes from a doctor's office, health office, or nursing program at a college. Allow students to listen to their hearts through the stethoscopes.

Ratliffe: Listening to Your Heart

It is important to have good aerobic endurance.
Your heart gets stronger when you play and exercise.

- Discuss how the heart, like other muscles, gets stronger when we do things to help it out, like playing and exercising.

There are many ways to exercise your heart.
Running, playing tag, and jumping rope are things your heart likes you to do.
Watching too much TV and playing too many indoor games can keep you from having a strong heart.

- Ask students for activities they can do to help develop a strong heart. Give examples that are inactive or active, to see if they can tell the difference (e.g., playing video games, watching TV, playing tag, jumping rope).
- Make a bulletin board titled "Look Whoo's ... Heart Smart" (borrow a picture of an owl from a classroom teacher if you can). Use pictures that students have drawn of themselves participating in heart-smart activities.
- Set up a Superstars jogging/walking club to help students prepare for the mile-run test. Students can earn their way into the Batman, Spider-Man,

Superman, or Wonder Woman Club, depending on the number of laps they walk or jog. Stickers and certificates are good awards. You also may decide to give decorated pencils as awards for joining the "higher" clubs. (And yes, even boys belong to the Wonder Woman Club!)

Ratliffe: *Endurance Challenge*
Fitness Club
PEC: *Card Suit Aerobics*   *Walking Willie*

KINDERGARTEN

Emphasize	*Ideas for Lesson Development*
Your heart is an important muscle. Your heart is special because it is always beating. Your heart is in your chest. Your heart is the size of your fist covered by your other hand.	• Have students feel their hearts while they are still and then after they exercise. Talk about how the heart is a special muscle.
You can listen to your heart beat. You can feel your heart beat by putting your hand on your chest. Your heart beats slowly when you sit, sleep, and rest. Your heart beats fast when you move, play, and exercise.	• Have students make fists and squeeze them at the pace they think their hearts pump when they are sleeping, running fast, writing at their desks in the classroom, watching TV, playing on the playground, dancing to music, and so forth. • Have students put a hand on a partner's chest and try to feel the heart beat. Do this before and after a vigorous activity. **Ratliffe:** *Listening to Your Heart*
There are many ways to exercise your heart. Running, playing tag, and jumping rope are things your heart likes you to do.	• Use Disney's *Mousercise* as a fun activity that can help the heart.

Muscular Strength and Endurance

Sample Course Standard

By the end of elementary school, students should be able to

- apply the basic concepts relating to the components of muscular strength and endurance to situations in their daily lives.

Concepts and Skills	Learnable Pieces
Muscles are an important part of the body.	You have hundreds of muscles in your body. (K, 1–2) Muscles help you move, stand up straight, and have good posture. (1–2) Muscles help you lift things. When you lift objects, you should bend your knees. (3–4) Muscles help you move, hold you up, and protect the bones and organs inside your body. (3–4, 5–6)
It is important to have good muscle strength.	Firm muscles are strong, healthy muscles. (3–4) Muscle strength relates to how strong your muscles are. (5–6) Good muscle strength helps your body look good and feel good. (5–6) You need strong muscles to become physically fit. (5–6)
It is important to have good muscle endurance.	Muscle endurance relates to how long your muscles can work and play without getting too tired. (3–4, 5–6) Having good muscle endurance is a part of being physically fit. (5–6)
You can achieve muscle strength and endurance in many different ways.	Playing, exercising, and using your muscles can help make them big and strong! (K) You help your muscles become strong and healthy by playing, moving, exercising, and being active. (1–2, 3–4) Certain activities will help certain muscles become stronger and have more endurance. (5–6) Swimming, bicycling, walking, and playing soccer can help increase the strength and endurance of your leg muscles. (5–6) Swimming, climbing, performing push-ups and pull-ups, and jumping rope can help increase the strength and endurance of your arm and shoulder muscles. (5–6)
Exercise is good for your muscles.	When you exercise, you don't get more muscles, but the muscles you have become stronger and bigger. (5–6) The more you exercise and are active, the stronger your muscles become and the more endurance you have. (5–6)

Concepts and Skills

There are different ways you can test your muscle strength and endurance.

Learnable Pieces

You take the pull-ups test to see how strong your arms and shoulders are. (3–4, 5–6)

You take the sit-ups test to see how strong your abdominal muscles are. (3–4, 5–6)

You can test your arm muscle strength at home in many different ways. (3–4, 5–6)

GRADES 5 TO 6

NASPE Performance Indicators

- Chooses to participate in sport activities that require high levels of muscular strength. (3–5, #4, 29)

Sample Portfolio Task

Ask students to complete figure 12.1, rating activities according to how well they can help one improve muscle strength or endurance.

RUBRIC CLUES

To what extent do students

- correctly rate each activity?
- give a logical explanation for their ratings, even if they aren't rated correctly?

Emphasize

Muscles are an important part of the body.
Muscles help you move, hold you up, and protect the bones and organs inside your body.

Ideas for Lesson Development

- Get a life-size chart of the human body showing the muscles.
- Discuss how muscles cover the bones; without them, we would get injured much more easily.

Ratliffe: *The Muscle Circuit*
PEC: *Word Association Muscles*

It is important to have good muscle strength.
Muscle strength relates to how strong your muscles are. Good muscle strength helps your body look good and feel good.
You need strong muscles to become physically fit.

- Ask students for examples of people with good muscle strength. Most likely, they will name athletes; lead them to think about others in their communities who have muscle strength (e.g., nurses, construction workers, firefighters, police officers, and lifeguards).
- Discuss how everyone needs good muscle strength, even nonathletes and those whose work is not physical. Ask students to think of why muscle strength is important for office workers who sit at desks all day (for posture), for homemakers (to clean, lift), and so forth.
- Ask students why they think muscle strength is important in their everyday lives. What does it help them do? What couldn't they do as well if they had poor muscle strength? Try to get them to think beyond activities in physical education.

Name _____ Class _____

Rate the following activities according to how well they can help you improve your muscle strength or endurance.

Activity		Rating	
Playing tag	Great	Good	Not so good
Jumping rope	Great	Good	Not so good
Swimming	Great	Good	Not so good
Playing on the computer	Great	Good	Not so good
Playing in the outfield in baseball/softball	Great	Good	Not so good
Walking to school	Great	Good	Not so good

Which of the above do you like to do the most? _____

least? _____

Figure 12.1   Portfolio task assessment sheet for muscular strength and endurance, grades 5 to 6.

From *Elementary Physical Education Teaching & Assessment: A Practical Guide,* by Christine J. Hopple, 2005 Champaign, IL: Human Kinetics.

It is important to have good muscle endurance.
Muscle endurance relates to how long your muscles can work and play without getting too tired.
Having good muscle endurance is a part of being physically fit.

- Discuss how muscle endurance is similar to aerobic endurance in relating to the muscles working for long periods of time.
- Discuss why muscle endurance is necessary to remain active without tiring.
- Ask students to list at least two things they do in their everyday lives that require muscle endurance. Challenge them to add another activity to their lists over the next month.

You can achieve muscle strength and endurance in many different ways.
Certain activities will help certain muscles become stronger and have more endurance.
Swimming, bicycling, walking, and playing soccer can help increase the strength and endurance of your leg muscles. Swimming, climbing, performing push-ups and pull-ups, and jumping rope can help increase the strength and endurance of your arm and shoulder muscles.

- Discuss how certain activities make specific muscles—not all muscles—stronger. Name an activity, and see if students can figure out the muscle groups that it helps most.
- Ask students to list other activities that help develop muscle strength and endurance, such as walking fast, playing basketball, in-line skating, and weight lifting.

Ratliffe: *Muscle of the Month*
PEC: *Fun Push-Ups*   *Push-Up Routine*
        Macarena Push-Ups

Exercise is good for your muscles.
When you exercise, you don't get more muscles, but the muscles you have become stronger and bigger.
The more you exercise and are active, the stronger your muscles become and the more endurance you have.

- Students, especially girls, often become very conscious of their bodies at this age. Discuss how exercising won't make you get more and more muscles, just firmer ones.

There are different ways you can test your muscle strength and endurance.
You take the pull-ups test to see how strong your arms and shoulders are.
You take the sit-ups test to see how strong your abdominal muscles are.
You can test your arm muscle strength at home in many different ways.

- Discuss why students are given the abdominal and the arm and shoulder muscle strength tests. Have them problem solve other activities they can do at home to determine how strong their arms or abdominals are (e.g., hula hooping, doing push-ups, hanging and swinging, throwing a ball, and performing cartwheels and handstands).
- Partner pull-ups: Students lie on their backs on the floor, and partners (of similar size and weight) stand above the students, extend the arms, grasp the students' hands, and pull them up.
- Secure a bat between two heavy chairs. Students lie on their backs under the bat and practice pull-ups without a pull-up bar. If possible, have family members or friends sit on the chairs to keep them anchored.

GRADES 3 TO 4

NASPE Performance Indicators.

- Chooses to participate in sport activities that require high levels of muscular strength. (3–5, #4, 29)

Sample Portfolio Task

Ask students to describe two things they do at home, either around the house or yard or in sports, that use their muscles and help them develop or maintain strong muscle strength. Ask them to also describe two things that their moms or dads do at home or work to use and develop the muscles.

RUBRIC CLUES

To what extent do students
- accurately give examples of developing muscle strength?

Emphasize	*Ideas for Lesson Development*
Muscles are an important part of the body. Muscles help you move, hold you up, and protect the bones and organs inside your body. Muscles help you lift things. When you lift objects, you should bend your knees.	• Discuss the role of muscles in posture. Have students put their hands on their abdomens, then "slouch" while sitting to feel how the abdominal muscles help hold them up. • Discuss how bending the knees when lifting items helps keep the back muscles from being hurt. • Set up some heavy items that students can practice lifting and, at the same time, challenge them to see how strong their muscles are! Examples can include jumping boxes made from tin cans (see "Jumping and Landing" in chapter 9) or crates filled with objects. **PEC:** *Shopping at the Lift and Carry Store*
It is important to have good muscle strength. Firm muscles are strong, healthy muscles.	• Ask students to name people they know who have strong, firm muscles. • Discuss how the healthiest muscles are firm, not weak and flabby. • Relate good muscle strength to high levels of fitness. • Have students cut out pictures of people with good muscle strength; tack these on a bulletin board. **Ratliffe:** *The Muscle Circuit*
It is important to have good muscle endurance. Muscle endurance relates to how long your muscles can work and play without getting too tired.	• Discuss how strong, healthy muscles can continuously move for a long time—at least 20 minutes (about the length of physical education class). • Ask students to suggest activities that keep them moving and can contribute to muscle endurance (e.g., biking, fast walking, running). **PEC:** *Fun Push-Ups* *Scooter Boats* *Macarena Push-Ups*

You can achieve muscle strength and endurance in many different ways.
You help your muscles become strong and healthy by playing, moving, exercising, and being active.

- Discuss the types of things that students can do to develop muscle strength and endurance.

- List activities on the board and have students name ones beneficial for achieving muscle strength and endurance.

There are different ways you can test your muscle strength and endurance.
You take the pull-ups test to see how strong your arms and shoulders are.
You take the sit-ups test to see how strong your abdominal muscles are.
You can test your arm muscle strength at home in many different ways.

- Discuss why students are given the abdominal and the arm and shoulder muscle strength tests. Have them problem solve other activities they can do at home to determine how strong their arms or abdominals are (e.g., hula hooping, doing push-ups, hanging and swinging, throwing a ball, performing cartwheels and handstands, and so on).

- Have students practice sit-ups or push-ups as a fitness warm-up one time a week, and count how many they do. Have them write the number down, then graph how many they have done over a period of time.

GRADES 1 TO 2

NASPE Performance Indicators

- Demonstrates sufficient muscular strength to be able to bear body weight for climbing, hanging, and momentary body support on the hands. (K–2, #4, 24)

- Increases arm and shoulder strength by traveling hand-over-hand along a horizontal ladder (i.e., monkey bars). (K–2, #4, 27)

- Moves transversely along a rock wall with little teacher assistance. (K–2, #4, 29)

Sample Portfolio Task

Ask students to cut out photos or pictures from newspapers and magazines (from home or school) showing examples of people using their muscles. Have them glue the pictures on paper and label the general muscles of the body that are working (e.g., arm muscles, leg muscles). If pictures are unavailable, students can draw examples.

RUBRIC CLUES

To what extent do students

- give examples that show the muscles in use?
- accurately label each picture?

Emphasize

Ideas for Lesson Development

Muscles are an important part of the body.
Muscles help you move, stand up straight, and have good posture.
You have hundreds of muscles in your body.

- Have students put their hands on their backs and abdomens as they slouch and then straighten up to feel how their muscles help them pull up and sit up straight.

You can achieve muscle strength and endurance in many different ways.
You help your muscles become strong and healthy by playing, moving, exercising, and being active.

- Discuss how, like the heart, other muscles get strong when we move, play, and exercise them.
- Ask students for activities they can do to promote their muscle strength.

Ratliffe: *Muscle Time*
PEC: *Frosty's Meltdown*

KINDERGARTEN

Emphasize

Muscles are an important part of the body.
You have hundreds of muscles in your body.

You can achieve muscle strength and endurance in many different ways.
Playing, exercising, and using your muscles can help make them big and strong!

Ideas for Lesson Development

- Name a muscle area (e.g., arm, leg) and have students quickly point to it.
- Play Simon Says with muscles: Show me your leg muscle ... arm muscle ... abdominal muscles ....

- Discuss activities students can do to make their muscles strong, such as playing outdoors, jumping rope, and skipping.

Sample Course Standard

By the end of elementary school, students should be able to

- apply the basic concepts related to the component of flexibility to situations in their daily lives, as much as possible.

Flexibility

Concepts and Skills	Learnable Pieces
It is important to have good flexibility.	Your muscles like to be stretched every day. This keeps them from getting hurt and makes them feel good. (K, 1–2)
	Flexibility means you can easily move your muscles and joints. (3–4, 5–6)
	Flexibility allows you to move your body easily and protects your muscles from getting stretched too far and hurt. (5–6)
	Flexibility is part of being physically fit. (5–6)
It is important to stretch correctly.	Stretch until you feel a pull; don't stretch farther; you don't want it to hurt. (1–2, 3–4)
	When you stretch, remember to hold the stretch—don't bounce! (1–2, 3–4)
	You should hold a stretch for at least a count of 10. (1–2, 3–4)
	If you stretch with your legs together, keep your knees bent a little so you don't hurt your back. (1–2, 3–4)
	You should stretch your muscles before you do much exercise, to get them warmed up and ready to move. (3–4, 5–6)
	You should especially stretch the muscles you will be using most. (5–6)
	After you exercise, you should again gently stretch your muscles. (5–6)
You can improve your flexibility in many different ways.	You should stretch a little every day to help your flexibility the most. (3–4, 5–6)
	Certain stretches will help certain muscles become more flexible. (5–6)
There are different ways to test your flexibility.	You take the sit-and-reach test to determine the flexibility of your lower back and leg muscles. (3–4, 5–6)

GRADES 5 TO 6

NASPE Performance Indicators

- Explains the personal consequences of poor flexibility on ability to perform various activities. (3–5, #4, 30)

Sample Portfolio Task

Ask students to give two examples of how flexibility is needed in sports and to explain why it is important in these situations. Then ask them to give two examples of how flexibility is needed in everyday life and why it is important.

To what extent do students
- show they understand what flexibility is and how it is important?

Emphasize	*Ideas for Lesson Development*
It is important to have good flexibility. Flexibility means you can easily move your muscles and joints. Flexibility allows you to move your body easily and protects your muscles from getting stretched too far and hurt. Being flexible is part of being physically fit.	• Discuss how flexibility allows us to move our joints and muscles easily. "Just think what would happen if we couldn't stretch!" Give the example of falling off a bike: If you landed on your arm and it bent in a strange way, flexibility would allow it to stretch. • Ask students for examples in sports and everyday life where flexibility is important. • Discuss how flexibility is part of being fit; everyone should have *at least* minimal flexibility. This doesn't mean that everyone needs the flexibility of a gymnast, but some flexibility will help to keep the body feeling good. **Ratliffe:** *Stay Flexed!*
It is important to stretch correctly. You should stretch your muscles before you do much exercise, to get them warmed up and ready to move. You should especially stretch the muscles you will be using most. After you exercise, you should again gently stretch your muscles.	• Discuss why it is important to stretch, even a little, before undertaking a lot of exercise. Use a piece of clay to demonstrate how it breaks apart when cold and how it stretches when it is worked and warmed up. • Discuss how stretching is specific to certain muscles; we should stretch the ones we will be using the most. Cite a few examples of activities, and ask students which muscles are used most in each activity. • Discuss how the best way to increase flexibility is to stretch after exercise, because the muscles are warmed up and ready to stretch. Stretching after exercise can also help cool down the muscles.
You can improve your flexibility in many different ways. Certain stretches will help certain muscles become more flexible. You should stretch a little every day to help your flexibility the most.	• Practice specific stretches that help particular muscle groups. • Discuss how flexibility decreases if it isn't worked on, and it is best to practice stretching as often as possible—even every day. **Ratliffe:** *Stretch It!*
There are different ways to test your flexibility. You take the sit-and-reach test to determine the flexibility of your lower back and leg muscles.	• Discuss how everyone needs a minimal level of flexibility in the lower back to stay healthy; the sit-and-reach test helps to tell if the lower back has that minimum flexibility. • Put out the sit-and-reach boxes so students can test each other, if they wish. They'll enjoy being "the teacher" and helping one another. • Discuss stretches students can do at home if they wish to improve flexibility.

GRADES 3 TO 4

NASPE Performance Indicators

- Explains the personal consequences of poor flexibility on ability to perform various activities. (3–5, #4, 30)

Sample Portfolio Task

Ask students to show their knowledge of what flexibility means by completing figure 12.2.

RUBRIC CLUES

To what extent do students

- show an accurate understanding of what flexibility means and how to stretch correctly?

Emphasize	*Ideas for Lesson Development*
It is important to have good flexibility. Flexibility means you can easily move your muscles and joints.	• Discuss what flexibility means and how it allows people to easily move their muscles and joints. • Ask students for examples of people who have good flexibility. • Have students cut out pictures of athletes from newspapers and magazines that show good flexibility. Post them on a bulletin board. • Questions to facilitate discussion and review include the following: (a) What does it mean if you're very flexible? (b) What kinds of athletes do you think have especially good flexibility? Why? (c) Can you think of occupations that require good flexibility? Why?
It is important to stretch correctly. Stretch until you feel a pull; don't stretch farther; you don't want it to hurt. When you stretch, remember to hold the stretch—don't bounce! You should hold a stretch for at least a count of 10. If you stretch with your legs together, keep your knees bent a little so you don't hurt your back. You should stretch your muscles before you do much exercise, to get them warmed up and ready to move.	• Show students how to practice stretching different muscles correctly; discuss why this is important and have them practice the stretches. **Ratliffe:** *Stay Flexed! Stretch It!*
You can improve your flexibility in many different ways. You should stretch a little every day to help your flexibility the most.	• Discuss how students can make stretching a habit—stretching when they wake up, before they go to bed, or at other regular times.

Name _____ **Class** _____

Stretch Your Thinking!

What are three important things to remember when you stretch?

1.

2.

3.

Describe something that flexibility helps you do better.

Figure 12.2 Portfolio task assessment sheet for flexibility, grades 3 to 4.

From *Elementary Physical Education Teaching & Assessment: A Practical Guide*, by Christine J. Hopple, 2005 Champaign, IL: Human Kinetics.

There are different ways to test your flexibility.
You take the sit-and-reach test to determine the flexibility of your lower back and leg muscles.

• Discuss why students take the sit-and-reach test. After the first test, allow them to practice and test themselves. Give them an "official" test at any time during the year when they are trying to improve their scores. Set aside one day a week or month to test students "officially;" let them know you will test them at least once before a date set toward the end of the year.

GRADES 1 TO 2

Emphasize

Ideas for Lesson Development

It is important to have good flexibility.
Your muscles like to be stretched every day. This keeps them from getting hurt and makes them feel good.

• Try a ball gymnastics routine with students to work on flexibility. Use a large or small playground ball and slow music. While standing, students match your movements as you move the ball slowly around your neck, down and back up your arms, and around your waist. Stretch to move the ball out to both sides, rolling the ball down and up your legs (don't lock the knees), down and up one leg (straddle your legs), and down the other. Then touch the ball to the ground and raise it above the head, sit on the ground and touch the ball to your toes (feet straddled, then together), and roll the ball to the toes and back to the waist. Students also can sit with partners, their straddled feet touching, and roll the ball to each other, leaning forward to reach it. They can roll the ball to their feet while the partners reach to roll it down one leg and then over to the other.

It is important to stretch correctly.
Stretch until you feel a pull; don't stretch farther; you don't want it to hurt.
When you stretch, remember to hold the stretch—don't bounce! You should hold a stretch for at least a count of 10.
If you stretch with your legs together, keep your knees bent a little so you don't hurt your back.

• Demonstrate various safe stretches with students, showing them the correct techniques as noted above; have students stretch with you. It is best to have students stretch at the *end* of their physical education time (this makes a good "relaxation" exercise), after they have been active for a period of time and their muscles are most warm. (At the beginning of the lesson, it is best to start students off with an "Instant Activity"; they don't want to sit and stretch first thing!) Or, have students stretch after the Instant Activity, while they are sitting and you are explaining what they will be doing that day.

Ratliffe: *Stretching Yourself*

KINDERGARTEN

Emphasize

Ideas for Lesson Development

It is important to have good flexibility.
Your muscles like to be stretched every day. This keeps them from getting hurt and makes them feel good.

• Use Disney's *Mousercise* CD (especially the medley); after completing the routine, discuss how stretching is good for the body.

Sample Course Standard

Training and Conditioning

By the end of elementary school, students should be able to

- apply the basic concepts of training and conditioning to their daily lives, as much as possible.

Concepts and Skills	Learnable Pieces
It is important to exercise frequently.	Your body and your muscles feel best if you play and exercise some every day. (K, 1–2)
	To be fit you should try to exercise and be active every day. (3–4, 5–6)
	If you stop exercising or being active for a long time period, your body can become unfit or out of shape. (5–6)
It is important to exercise long enough.	You should try to exercise or be active for at least 10 minutes at a time, three times a day. (5–6)
You can improve your fitness levels.	To improve your fitness, you should exercise a little harder or a little longer. (3–4, 5–6)

GRADES 5 TO 6

NASPE Performance Indicators

- Identifies physical and psychological benefits that result from long-term participation in physical activity. (3–5, #2, 18)
- Recognizes that physiological responses to exercise are associated with their own levels of fitness. (3–5, #4, 27)

Sample Portfolio Task

Ask students to keep a log of their activities for two weeks. What do they do each day to be active? How long? After two weeks they should reflect on their activity levels. Were they active enough? What can they do to be more active?

RUBRIC CLUES

To what extent do students

- show they understand how frequent activity should be?

Emphasize

It is important to exercise frequently.
To be fit you should try to exercise and be active every day.
If you stop exercising or being active for a long time period, your body can become unfit or out of shape.

Ideas for Lesson Development

- Discuss the kinds of things that can keep students from being active: bad weather, homework, not being supervised, and so forth. Talk about possible solutions to these obstacles.

It is important to exercise long enough.
You should try to exercise or be active for at least 10 minutes at a time, three times a day.

You can improve your fitness levels.
To improve your fitness, you should exercise a little harder or a little longer.

- Discuss how exercising for at least 20 to 30 minutes a day benefits the heart and muscles the most and builds endurance.
- Ask students for ideas on fun things they can do to be active for 10 minutes.
- Have students note on a calendar for two weeks the activities that keep them moving for more than 10 minutes at a time.
- Discuss how to improve fitness by exercising a little harder or a little longer each week that you exercise. Give examples, such as walking for three more minutes or running a little faster.

Ratliffe: *Making Stronger Muscles*

GRADES 3 TO 4

NASPE Performance Indicators

- Identifies physical and psychological benefits that result from long-term participation in physical activity. (3–5, #2, 18)
- Recognizes that physiological responses to exercise are associated with their own levels of fitness. (3–5, #4, 27)

Sample Portfolio Task

Ask students to participate in one activity during the next week that lasts at least 20 minutes. They should describe in writing what they did, for how long, and how they felt about doing it. Was it hard? Was it easy? Fun? Would they try it again the next week?

RUBRIC CLUES

To what extent do students

- explain the benefits of the activity in terms of fitness?
- show they understand what kinds of activities can help their physical health?

Emphasize	*Ideas for Lesson Development*
It is important to exercise frequently. To be fit you should try to exercise and be active every day.	• Discuss fun things students can do every day to be physically active. Encourage them to be active with family members, pets, and friends.
You can improve your fitness levels. To improve your fitness, you should exercise a little harder or a little longer.	• Discuss how students may start out being active for only a few minutes, and then increase how long they are active and how hard they exercise to become more fit.

GRADES 1 TO 2

NASPE Performance Indicators

- Participates in chasing and fleeing activities outside of school. (K–2, #3, 21)
- Participates in a variety of activities that involve manipulation of objects in and outside of physical education class (e.g., tossing ball, juggling). (K–2, #3, 22)

Sample Portfolio Task

Ask students to cut out pictures from a newspaper or magazine or draw their own pictures of equipment they can be active and play with (e.g., bike, hula hoop, ball) to help stay in shape.

RUBRIC CLUES

To what extent do students

- show they understand the kinds of activity they can participate in for healthful benefits?

Emphasize	*Ideas for Lesson Development*
It is important to exercise frequently. Your body and your muscles feel best if you play and exercise some every day.	• Discuss how everyone should try to be active and play outside for a little bit every day. Talk about activities that are fun for students to do. • Show students how to make equipment, such as newspaper balls (covered with masking tape) or scoops from gallon milk jugs, to play with at home.

KINDERGARTEN

Emphasize	*Ideas for Lesson Development*
It is important to exercise frequently. Your body and your muscles feel best if you play and exercise some every day.	• Discuss with students ways they can be active and play at home, such as biking, hula hooping, and jumping rope.

Sample Course Standard

By the end of elementary school, students should be able to

- apply basic concepts relative to nutrition and other healthy habits to their daily lives, as much as possible.

Healthy Habits

Concepts and Skills	Learnable Pieces
Good habits are important for good health.	Healthy habits include exercising, eating properly, brushing your teeth, getting enough sleep, washing well, and saying no to drugs, alcohol, and cigarettes. (K, 1–2, 3–4)
Eating right is part of being healthy.	Food is the source of energy for your body. (1–2) Good foods to eat each day are milk and dairy foods, bread and cereal, fruits and vegetables, and meat and fish. (1–2, 3–4) Junk foods that aren't good for you to eat every day include potato chips, candy, and other sweet snacks. (1–2, 3–4)
Everybody is responsible for their healthy habits.	You can make and change your habits, even if it is not always easy. (3–4, 5–6) "Just say no" to drugs, alcohol, and cigarettes. (5–6)
It is important to have good posture.	Good posture helps your bones and body to grow tall and strong. (3–4, 5–6)
Body composition is an important part of fitness.	You can get fat by not exercising, not being active, eating too much, or eating incorrectly. (3–4) Body fat relates to the amount of fat your body has compared with muscles, bones, and organs. (5–6) It isn't good to have too much—or too little—body fat. (5–6) The amount of body fat you have will likely change as you grow older. (5–6) You can control the amount of body fat you have by eating right and exercising. (5–6) If you're concerned about how much body fat you have, you should talk to your parents, doctor, or physical education teacher. (5–6)
Wellness and fitness go together.	Overall wellness means you do healthy things for your body and your mind. (5–6) Fitness is just one part of wellness. (5–6)
Activity and exercise can help in coping with stress.	Stress happens when you worry a lot and feel pressure to do things. (5–6) Exercise, or being active, can help prevent feeling "stressed out" and worried. (5–6)

GRADES 5 TO 6

NASPE Performance Indicators

- Demonstrates good posture while lifting and carrying an object. (3–5, #1, 1)
- Identifies positive feelings associated with participation in physical activities. (3–5, #6, 44)
- Explains that skill competency leads to enjoyment of movement and physical activity. (3–5, #6, 46)

Sample Portfolio Task

Ask students to complete figure 12.3. Meet privately with students to discuss issues of concern.

RUBRIC CLUES

To what extent do students

- have an understanding of what is helpful or not helpful to them as individuals?

Emphasize	*Ideas for Lesson Development*
Everybody is responsible for their healthy habits. You can make and change your habits, even if it is not always easy. "Just say no" to drugs, alcohol, and cigarettes.	• Discuss how each person has the capability to change or make a habit. • Ask students to think of habits they might like to change. Discuss ways that parents, family, and friends can help them change. • Most schools have DARE officers who deliver the DARE Curriculum to students. Find out what topics the students are addressing at various times during the program, and engage them in conversation about the topic, as appropriate. **Ratliffe:** *Goal Setting* **PEC:** *Drugs Abstinence Skills*
It is important to have good posture. Good posture helps your bones and body to grow tall and strong.	• Discuss why good posture is important for the body as well as for looks. • Have students sit slumped over, then ask them to straighten up. Can they feel their muscles work to pull them up? Have them put their hands on their abdominal muscles as they slouch and then straighten to feel how they work.
Body composition is an important part of fitness. Body fat relates to the amount of fat your body has compared with muscles, bones, and organs. It isn't good to have too much—or too little—body fat. The amount of body fat you have will likely change as you grow older.	• Discuss how celebrities on TV and in magazines make us think that having no fat is good. Emphasize that everyone needs body fat to supply energy and keep you from getting sick. • Talk about how body fat can change naturally as people age, but it also depends on how much they eat, what kinds of foods, and how much they exercise. • Discuss how eating correctly and getting exercise can help control how much body fat you have.

Name _____ Class _____

I Feel Good When . . .

Write down five different things that can make you feel good as a person.

1.

2.

3.

4.

5.

Write down three things that can make you feel not so good as a person.

1.

2.

3.

What are three things you do well?

1.

2.

3.

Figure 12.3 Portfolio task assessment sheet for healthy habits, grades 5 to 6.

From *Elementary Physical Education Teaching & Assessment: A Practical Guide,* by Christine J. Hopple, 2005 Champaign, IL: Human Kinetics.

You can control the amount of body fat you have by eating right and exercising.
If you're concerned about how much body fat you have, you should talk to your parents, doctor, or physical education teacher.

- Encourage students to talk to their doctors, parents, or teachers if they are concerned about body fat.

Ratliffe: *Cookie Lesson*
            The Balancing Act
PEC: *Want Ad: Healthy Eater*

Wellness and fitness go together.
Overall wellness means you do healthy things for your body and your mind.
Fitness is just one part of wellness.

- Discuss how fitness is just one part of overall wellness, and how being fit helps people feel better about themselves and, consequently, their overall wellness.
- Ask students to brainstorm and list on the board different things that help them to be "well," not just fit.
- Ask students if they think someone can be well but not fit. Is this possible?
- Use the fitness calendar (figure 12.4) as a supplement to instruction.

Activity and exercise can help in coping with stress.
Stress happens when you worry a lot and feel pressure to do things.
Exercise, or being active, can help prevent feeling "stressed out" and worried.

- Discuss the types of things that might stress students: school, grades, homework, parents. Talk about how jogging, bicycling, or taking a walk can help get the mind off things and can make them feel better.
- List and discuss positive ways of dealing with stress; then list negative ways of dealing with stress.

GRADES 3 TO 4

Sample Portfolio Task

Ask students to keep track of all their daily healthy habits for a week. At the end of the week, ask them to reflect on their habits. Can they improve them? What can help them to improve their habits? What habits do they need to improve?

RUBRIC CLUES

To what extent do students
- show an understanding of healthy habits?

Emphasize

Good habits are important for good health.
Healthy habits include exercising, eating properly, brushing your teeth, getting enough sleep, washing well, and saying no to drugs, alcohol, and cigarettes.

Ideas for Lesson Development

- Discuss the healthy habits and why they are important.

PEC: *Drugs Abstinence Skills*

FEBRUARY

Sunday	Monday	Tuesday	Wednesday	Thursday	Friday	Saturday
Your Name: **Your Teacher:**				**1** February is heart-healthy month! Help your heart today by riding your bike, walking fast, or playing!	**2** A heart pumps about 7 quarts of blood per minute. Plug the sink: dump in 7 x 4 cups of water to see what 7 quarts is.	**3** If there's snow, get outside and play in it! If not, play outside for at least 20 minutes anyway!
4 Children need 10 to 12 hours of sleep to remain healthy. That's each day! Get 10 hours of sleep tonight!	**5** What's your favorite fruit? (Write it below.) Eat it sometime this week.	**6** Do February's "Exercise of the Month." How many can you do? Write it here:	**7** How many jumping jacks can you do in a row? Write the number here:	**8** How many bones are in your body? (See Feb. 29.) Drink extra milk today to help your bones grow strong.	**9** Good posture is good for you! Do some sit-ups today to help your abdominal muscles keep strong.	**10** If you go to the store with your parents today, have them park far away from the store and walk together.
11 While watching cartoons today, stretch your hands to your toes and count to 10!	**12** How many times can you jump rope in a row? Write your answer here:	**13** Use your hands to show your parents how big your heart is. Show them how fast it pumps during exercise.	**14** Today is St. Valentine's Day. Do something for your heart. What did you do? Write it here:	**15** Instead of ice cream for dessert at lunch today, have a piece of fruit!	**16** This weekend, walk up and down some stairs for at least 4 minutes–don't stop. Keep a slow, steady pace!	**17** Lifting heavy objects helps your muscles get stronger. Lift something heavy today (such as groceries).
18 Exercise with a parent today. If it's too cold outside, put music on and move to the music!	**19** Have a healthy snack this week. Try "Ants on a Log": Celery with peanut butter in the groove and raisins on top.	**20** Instead of watching television when you come home, do something active like play inside or do chores.	**21** Draw your teacher a picture of your favorite heart-healthy activity inside a big white heart.	**22** Give your teacher your heart today. Well, the one you drew! Exercise your heart in physical education today.	**23** Pretend you're a skier. Squat down in a tuck, curved shape. How many seconds can you stay like that? Write it here:	**24** The best time to drink liquids is before you get thirsty! Sip some water before you exercise today!
25 Instead of drinking any kind of soda pop today, drink some milk or water. They're best for you!	**26** Push-ups help your arms get stronger. How many can you do? Keep your body straight like a board!	**27** Try to eat at least three servings of vegetables each day; they're full of vitamins! Did you today? Yes No	**28** When you wake up or before bed, stretch your arms up...out...your legs....your body. Stretch tall!	**29** If you guessed 207 bones in your body, you were right! It takes strong muscles to move that many bones!		

Figure 12.4   An example of a fitness calendar, grades 5 to 6.

Eating right is part of being healthy.
Good foods to eat each day are milk and dairy foods, bread and cereal, fruits and vegetables, and meat and fish. Junk foods that aren't good for you to eat every day include potato chips, candy, and other sweet snacks.

• On a "rainy day" or other day when your teaching space is taken, use the classroom to work on a nutrition lesson with the students. Many classroom teachers have a number of nutrition kits (such as from the USDA) that have lessons developed around healthy eating habits that you would be able to easily implement with students.

• Have students cut out pictures of foods from magazines. Working in small groups, have students paste the pictures on large pieces of paper according to food groups. You can also precut pictures for this use.

PEC: *Food Groups and the Food Pyramid*
        Healthy Island

Everybody is responsible for their healthy habits.
You can make and change your habits, even if it is not always easy.

• Ask students to think of their good and bad habits. What are some ways they can change bad habits? Can parents, family, and friends help to change these habits?

Ratliffe: *Goal Setting*

It is important to have good posture.
Good posture helps your bones and body to grow tall and strong.

• Discuss good posture and how it helps people look and feel good.

PEC: *Spinal Cord Cereal*

Body composition is an important part of fitness.
You can get fat by not exercising, not being active, eating too much, or eating incorrectly.

• Body composition is a difficult topic to discuss with children. As children become more aware of their bodies and compare them with others, especially in grade 4, they begin to classify themselves as "fat" and feel pressure to diet, not eat to stay thin, and so on. (Today, we know this issue is not limited to girls.) Discuss with students, especially when the subject comes up, how their bodies will continue to undergo many changes in the next few years. Explain that they should be less concerned about "fat" (as most still have "baby fat"), and more concerned about maintaining an active lifestyle.

Ratliffe: *Cookie Lesson*
        The Balancing Act

GRADES 1 TO 2

Sample Portfolio Task

Have students cut out and glue pictures from magazines or newspapers onto pages called either Good Foods or Junk Foods.

RUBRIC CLUES

To what extent do students
  • correctly identify the food as being in the good-food or junk-food group?

Emphasize	*Ideas for Lesson Development*
Good habits are important for good health. Healthy habits include exercising, eating properly, brushing your teeth, getting enough sleep, washing well, and saying no to drugs, alcohol, and cigarettes.	• Discuss why these healthy habits are important and what can happen if they aren't always followed.

PEC: *Cleanliness*   *Personal Hygiene*
          Outerspace: Frontier for Personal Health and Hygiene   *Rush to Brush*

Eating right is part of being healthy. Food is the source of energy for your body. Good foods to eat each day are milk and dairy foods, bread and cereal, fruits and vegetables, and meat and fish. Junk foods that aren't good for you to eat every day include potato chips, candy, and other sweet snacks.	• Cut out or draw pictures of foods and laminate them. Draw two boxes on the board: good foods and junk foods. After discussing the two types of foods, ask students to stick (using tape) a picture of a food into the correct box. • Play food tag: Pick two to four students to be "it." *It* is a *junk food* (the students decide what kind). The junk food tries to catch the *good food* (everyone else); when tagged, students put their hands up and have to name a good food before they can become "untagged."

PEC: *Fishing for Good Nutrition*

KINDERGARTEN

Good habits are important for good health. Healthy habits include exercising, eating properly, brushing your teeth, getting enough sleep, washing well, and saying no to drugs, alcohol, and cigarettes.	• Ask students to tell you things that are good for the body and things that people do that aren't good for the body. Discuss how exercise and playing are good habits.

PEC: *Bathtime Fun*
          Rush to Brush

Sample Performance Indicators for Selected Themes

Body Awareness

By the end of grade 6, students should be able to

- design, refine, and perform dance or gymnastics sequences in a small group that focus on using different body shapes and body movements.

By the end of grade 4, students should be able to

- move the body in the air using various body movements and shapes after jumping off low- or medium-level equipment;
- use different body shapes and body movements to creatively express the various qualities of effort (i.e., force, flow, speed); and
- design, refine, and perform group dance and gymnastics sequences that focus on using symmetrical or asymmetrical body shapes.

By the end of grade 2, students should be able to

- use different body parts required by different challenges, alone and with a partner;
- mirror the symmetrical or asymmetrical shape of a partner;
- use a variety of bases of support (body parts) to balance on;

- make the different body shapes with and without a partner;
- perform different body movements to a series of beats of varying tempos (i.e., fast or slow);
- make the different body shapes in the air when jumping off the ground or low-level equipment; and
- design and perform simple sequences that focus on body shapes or body movements.

By the end of kindergarten, students should be able to

- make the different body shapes;
- travel while moving in a variety of body shapes;
- use different combinations of body parts to balance on and travel with; and
- move using various body movements.

Space Awareness

By the end of grade 6, students should be able to

- purposefully use pathways, levels, directions, and extensions to change the continuity or flow and add variety to a gymnastics or dance sequence; and
- purposefully use general space to create or deny space when developing or using game strategies in a small-group situation.

By the end of grade 4, students should be able to

- change directions and pathways as they move through general space, in order to not collide with others; and
- define, refine, and perform dance and gymnastics sequences that focus on changes in direction, levels, pathways, and extensions (using one or a combination of two at a time).

By the end of grade 2, students should be able to

- find a self-space in a marked-off area without any prompting;
- purposefully keep out of others' self-space as they travel with or without an object;
- stop and start traveling at a given signal, showing the ability to safely stop in their own self-space;
- travel and change from one direction to another at the signal;
- move a variety of body parts and objects into different levels;
- manipulate different objects through different levels;
- travel and change from one pathway to another at the signal;
- design and perform simple sequences that focus on changes in direction, levels, pathways, and shapes (using one at a time); and
- travel in different ways while using large and small extensions.

By the end of kindergarten, students should be able to

- show the boundaries or limits to their self-space, when alone and when using equipment;
- find a self-space on their own in a large marked-off area with little or no prompting;
- move away from others when traveling in general space;
- travel in general space, starting and stopping in response to a signal;
- move a variety of ways in different directions;
- put a variety of body parts and objects into different levels; and
- move on straight, curved, and zigzag pathways.

Effort

By the end of grade 6, students should be able to

- use the qualities of force, flow, and speed to creatively express feelings, ideas, and actions of the self, others, or groups of others;

- design, refine, and perform gymnastics or dance sequences that show smooth transitions between movements that vary in elements of force, flow, and speed (rhythm); and
- manipulate objects (e.g., kick, throw) using varied amounts of force, flow, and speed appropriate to the given situation.

By the end of grade 4, students should be able to

- move in a variety of ways that focus on accelerating and decelerating their speed;
- move in various ways using definite contrasts of bound- and free-flowing movements;
- use the specific qualities of force, flow, or speed to creatively express feelings, ideas, and actions through dance and other expressive movement sequences;
- design, refine, and perform dance and gymnastics sequences that focus on changes in force, flow, and speed (rhythm); and
- manipulate objects (e.g., kick, throw) using varied amounts of force and speed.

By the end of grade 2, students should be able to

- perform different body movements in time to a signal or music of varying tempos, or speeds;
- manipulate an object in time to a signal or music of varying tempos, or speeds;
- safely change from one speed to another when traveling to a signal or music of varying tempos;
- move in various ways showing definite contrasts of light and strong force;
- express the qualities of light and strong force through a variety of creative dance or gymnastics sequences; and
- express the qualities of fast and slow speed through a variety of creative dance or gymnastics sequences.

By the end of kindergarten, students should be able to

- make fast and slow movements with various body parts;
- travel in various ways at fast and slow speeds; and
- travel and change from one speed to another at a signal.

Relationships

By the end of grade 6, students should be able to

- use a variety of relationships with a partner or small group when designing, refining, and performing repeatable dance, gymnastics, or rope-jumping sequences (e.g., behind, beside, mirroring, matching); and

- use a variety of relationships with others in order to play or design a small-group game.

By the end of grade 4, students should be able to

- move in a variety of ways in relation to a partner, either with or without a piece of equipment;
- mirror and match the movements of a traveling partner;
- use matching or mirroring and meeting or parting to design and perform dance or gymnastics sequences with a partner or small group; and
- design, refine, and perform a repeated on p. 138 sequence with a partner in which the movements of an object (e.g., scarf, ball) are matched as clearly as possible.

By the end of grade 2, students should be able to

- move in a variety of ways in relation to a stationary partner or object;
- mirror the shape and movements of a stationary partner; and
- change from a leading to a following position in relation to a partner.

By the end of kindergarten, students should be able to

- demonstrate a variety of relationships with a stationary partner or object;
- travel while demonstrating a variety of relationships to stationary objects;
- move different objects in a variety of relationships to the self; and
- lead or follow a partner using a variety of locomotor movements.

Locomotor Movements

By the end of grade 6, students should be able to

- run and leap as far and as high as possible;
- run and leap a succession of medium-level obstacles without stopping between;
- design, refine, and perform small-group sequences comprised of even and uneven rhythmic patterns of locomotor movements, body movements, and the use of an object to groups of three or four beats (3/4 or 4/4 time); and
- follow (solo, with a partner, or with a group) given simple

patterns of locomotor skills to 3/4 and 4/4 music from various cultures.

By the end of grade 4, students should be able to

- leap a variety of distances, leading with either the right or left leg;
- run and hurdle a succession of low- to medium-level obstacles, using either leg to lead;
- travel and smoothly change directions or movements to music with sets (measures) of three or four beats;
- combine two or more even locomotor movements into a pattern that can be repeated to music with three- or four-beat groupings, such as one, two, three, (four); one, two, three, (four); and so on;
- combine two or more even and uneven locomotor movements into a pattern that can be performed to music with three- or four-beat groupings, such as one and two, three (four); one and two, three (four); and so on; and
- combine two or more movement patterns based on sets of either three or four beats into repeatable sequences of traveling, manipulating an object, and space awareness concepts (such as levels or pathways) to a counted-out beat or music.

By the end of grade 2, students should be able to

- travel and change from one locomotor movement to another at the signal;
- travel to a signal or music with an even rhythm (walk, run, hop, jump, march);
- travel to a signal or music with an uneven rhythm (slide, gallop, skip);
- perform given or self-designed simple sequences that combine even and uneven locomotor movements into counted-out groups of three, four, or eight beats;
- jump and hop in place while traveling and in relation to an object;
- run and leap, using the favored leg to lead; and
- design a simple sequence using locomotor and body movements to counted-out beats.

By the end of kindergarten, students should be able to

- march in step to a rhythmical (even) beat;
- jump and hop (using both the right and left foot) in place and while traveling;
- gallop forward using a basic or rhythmical galloping pattern; and
- slide sideways using a basic or rhythmical sliding pattern.

Chasing, Fleeing, and Dodging

By the end of grade 6, students should be able to

- cooperatively devise strategies to keep opponents from reaching a specified area, person, or object; and
- cooperatively play a designed or given small-group game with opponents that involves throwing and catching or other skill themes with dodging, chasing, and fleeing.

By the end of grade 4, students should be able to

- travel and dodge stationary opponents; and
- use dodging skills in a small-group situation to avoid a thrown soft, lightweight object.

By the end of grade 2, students should be able to

- follow a fleeing partner's pathway to catch or overtake him or her;
- flee from a partner as quickly as possible at a signal;
- travel and change pathways as quickly as possible at a signal;
- travel and change directions as quickly as possible at a signal; and
- quickly perform dodging skills at a signal.

By the end of kindergarten, students should be able to

- travel and make straight, curved, and zigzag pathways;
- travel around stationary obstacles without touching them; and
- follow the pathway that their partner makes.

Jumping and Landing

By the end of grade 6, students should be able to

- jump a self-turned rope using as many different types of jumps as possible (e.g., skier, bell);
- perform jumping skills in 3/4 or 4/4 time, using ropes, tinikling sticks, elastic jumping bands, and so forth; and
- design and refine a repeatable routine with a partner or a small group using various jumping skills, other movements, and objects to 3/4 or 4/4 time.

By the end of grade 4, students should be able to

- jump for distance using a mature form;
- jump for height using a mature form;
- jump a self-turned rope using buoyant landings;
- jump a self-turned rope using at least five different types of jumps (e.g., hop, skip, forward jump, backward jump, skier); and

- jump into and out of a turning long rope.

By the end of grade 2, students should be able to

- jump and land using a variety of takeoffs and landings in relation to various equipment (e.g., hoops, low hurdles, rope shapes, carpet squares);
- jump a swinging rope with yielding landings;
- jump a self-turned rope both forward and backward with yielding landings; and
- jump a self-turned rope in at least three different ways (e.g., forward direction, backward direction, skip step, fast [buoyant], running skip step).

By the end of kindergarten, students should be able to

- jump and land while bending knees;
- jump and land using a two-to-two, one-to-two, and two-to-one jumping pattern; and
- jump a slowly swinging long rope using a two-to-two jumping pattern.

Rolling

By the end of grade 6, students should be able to

- roll smoothly in a forward and backward direction;
- use different shapes to begin and end rolls when rolling in different directions;
- balance in a variety of upright or inverted positions, move smoothly into a roll, then balance again;
- travel, jump over low equipment, land, and roll;
- travel, jump, land, and roll over low equipment (starting the roll with or without hands on the floor);
- jump off the ground or low equipment to catch an object thrown directly to them, land safely, and roll in at least one direction;
- roll forward or backward on low equipment (bench, beam, table); and
- design, refine, and perform repeatable sequences (with a partner or in a small group) involving rolling and other skills (such as traveling, balancing, and weight transfers).

By the end of grade 4, students should be able to

- roll, starting and ending in different shapes and using different speeds;
- roll forward over a low hurdle, starting with hands on or off the floor;
- jump off low equipment, land safely, and roll; and
- design, refine, and perform (alone or with a partner) simple sequences involving rolling, weight transfers, balances, and movement concepts (levels, shapes, directions, speed).

By the end of grade 2, students should be able to

- roll smoothly and consecutively in a sideways direction, with an extended body position;
- rock smoothly and repeatedly back and forth on the back;
- roll forward smoothly;
- roll in at least two different directions;
- starting from a squatting position, rock backward, placing hands in the appropriate position behind; and
- jump, land, and roll in at least one direction.

By the end of kindergarten, students should be able to

- roll sideways consecutively; and
- on the back, rock back and forth and side to side.

Balancing

By the end of grade 6, students should be able to

- balance on low equipment (tables, benches) in positions using a variety of bases of support;
- balance with partners using principles of counterbalance (pushing) and counter-tension (pulling);
- incorporate balance into a small-group designed sequence;
- balance in a variety of shapes while hanging from equipment; and
- balance in an inverted position.

By the end of grade 4, students should be able to

- balance in a symmetrical or asymmetrical shape on large gymnastics equipment (e.g., beams, tables, benches);
- move smoothly from one balanced position to another in a variety of ways;
- balance on a variety of moving and other balancing objects (e.g., stilts, balance boards) (dynamic balance);
- balance in inverted positions using the least number of bases of support possible;
- balance in a variety of positions using different bases of support and directions when on large gymnastics equipment; and
- cooperatively balance as part of a small group by connecting with or supporting each other's body weight.

By the end of grade 2, students should be able to

- balance on different numbers of bases of support;
- balance using a variety of symmetrical and asymmetrical body shapes, either with or without a partner;
- balance using a variety of inverted symmetrical or asymmetrical body shapes;

- balance using different bases of support on low equipment;
- balance while traveling and changing directions and levels on low- to medium-level equipment; and
- design and perform simple sequences involving balancing along with other skills (weight transfers, rolling) or concepts (levels, shapes).

By the end of kindergarten, students should be able to

- balance on a variety of combinations of body parts;
- travel and stop in balanced positions; and
- follow different pathways while moving forward and sideways on the ground or on low equipment.

Weight Transfer

By the end of grade 6, students should be able to

- travel and smoothly move into weight transfers from feet to hands;
- travel into a spring takeoff and then transfer weight onto a large apparatus (e.g., bars, beam, vault box);
- transfer weight off low apparatus (beam, bench, table) using a variety of body actions, starting with hands and feet stationary on the apparatus (e.g., stretching, twisting, turning); and
- transfer weight in a variety of ways along low- to medium-level apparatus (beam, benches) in a variety of ways, using changes in directions, levels, speeds, and body shapes.

By the end of grade 4, students should be able to

- transfer weight from one body part to another (hands, knees, feet) in a variety of ways when on a large apparatus (e.g., climbing apparatus, bars);
- use safe methods to recover from unstable feet-to-hand weight transfers;
- use a variety of body actions to move into and out of a number of weight transfers from feet to hands with large extensions (e.g., stretching legs wide, torso twisting, rolling, curving feet over to land on one or two feet);
- step into weight transfers from feet to hands over low equipment or apparatus (e.g., box, crate, beam);
- transfer weight in various ways off low equipment or apparatus (beam, bench, box) onto floor level, starting with hands on the floor;
- use balances to move smoothly into and out of different weight transfers;
- travel into a spring takeoff and then transfer weight from the feet to hands onto low- to medium-level equipment or apparatus (e.g., beam, bench, table, large tire); and

- transfer weight onto low- to medium-level equipment or apparatus by placing the hands on equipment and springing off of two feet (land on hands and feet or knees).

By the end of grade 2, students should be able to

- transfer weight from one set of body parts to another in a variety of ways (e.g., twist, turn);
- transfer weight over low equipment (e.g., hurdles, hoops, mats) in a variety of ways, beginning with hands on the opposite side of the hurdle;
- transfer weight from feet to hands in a variety of ways;
- transfer weight from feet-to-hands, making the legs land in different places around the body;
- transfer weight across a mat in as many ways as possible; and
- transfer weight by traveling into a spring takeoff.

By the end of kindergarten, students should be able to

- transfer weight from one body part to another in a variety of ways, using rocking, rolling, and feet-to-hand actions with small extensions; and
- take weight momentarily onto the hands by transferring weight from feet to hands with large extensions.

Dribbling With the Hands

By the end of grade 6, students should be able to

- dribble while traveling in a group (in a large marked-off area) without touching others or stationary objects;
- dribble and smoothly change from one direction to another without stopping;
- dribble and smoothly change from one speed to another without stopping;
- dribble continuously while stopping and starting traveling at the signal;
- dribble and then throw a leading pass to a moving partner using a chest or bounce pass;
- travel, dribble, and pivot on one foot to begin dribbling in another direction;
- shoot toward an appropriate-height goal from different distances;
- dribble and keep the ball away from an opponent in a one-on-one situation;
- dribble and pass in a small-group keep-away game; and
- cooperate and play a small-group game using passing, receiving, and shooting toward an appropriate-height goal.

By the end of grade 4, students should be able to

- dribble a ball in self-space using one, then the other, hand with proper form;
- dribble while moving to the right of left, using the appropriate hand;
- dribble and change direction at the signal;
- dribble and quickly change the pathway they are moving on at the signal;
- dribble and change from one speed to another at the signal;
- dribble while keeping the ball away from stationary opponents; and
- travel, dribble, and chest- and bounce-pass the ball to a stationary partner.

By the end of grade 2, students should be able to

- dribble a ball in self-space using one, then the other, hand;
- dribble a ball in self-space while switching from one hand to the other;
- dribble a ball in self-space at the different levels;
- dribble while slowly traveling in different directions; and
- dribble while slowly traveling on different pathways.

By the end of kindergarten, students should be able to

- use two hands to bounce and catch a large playground ball; and
- use two hands to bounce and catch a ball while slowly traveling forward.

Kicking and Punting

By the end of grade 6, students should be able to

- dribble and change speeds at the signal;
- dribble with a group in a marked-off area without losing control of the ball and while avoiding contact with others or opponents;
- use the inside of the foot to dribble and kick a leading pass to a moving partner;
- punt a ball using a two- or three-step approach;
- punt a ball to targets at varying distances;
- collect a thrown or kicked ball using the thigh and chest;
- defend a goal by catching or deflecting balls kicked to them with appropriate force;
- dribble and pass in a small-game keep-away situation; and
- cooperate to play a designed or given small-group game involving dribbling, passing, kicking, or punting to keep the ball away from opponents and to reach a goal area.

By the end of grade 4, students should be able to

- run and kick a ball that is moving slowly toward and away from them, using the instep;
- use the insides or outsides of the feet to slowly dribble the ball;
- dribble while changing pathways and directions at the signal;
- dribble in a group in a marked-off area without losing control of the ball or colliding with others;
- dribble around stationary opponents and avoid losing the ball;
- dribble and then kick the ball to a large target area from a distance of choice, using the instep;
- dribble and then kick the ball to a target or stationary partner while using the inside of the foot;
- use the inside of the foot to collect a ball coming toward them; and
- punt a ball as high and as far as possible.

By the end of grade 2, students should be able to

- kick a slowly rolling ball by using the instep;
- run up to and kick a stationary ball as far as possible using the instep;
- kick a stationary ball along the ground toward a stationary partner or target while using the inside of the foot;
- dribble and slowly jog while using the inside of either foot;
- dribble and slowly jog around stationary obstacles while using the inside of each foot;
- trap a slowly moving ball rolling toward and away from them, contacting it with the ball of the foot; and
- punt a ball into the air using the instep.

By the end of kindergarten, students should be able to

- walk and "roll" the ball forward, using the inside of either foot;
- kick a large stationary playground ball, using any part of the foot; and
- move up to and kick a stationary ball, using any part of the foot.

Throwing and Catching

By the end of grade 6, students should be able to

- throw to a partner or at a target, using varying degrees of force and speed;
- throw and catch a Frisbee;
- throw a leading pass overhand to a moving partner using a variety of objects;
- catch objects of different sizes and weights while moving toward a specified area;
- move in order to throw to a (stationary) partner while being guarded in a small-group keep-away situation; and
- throw and catch in a self-designed or given small-group game to keep the ball away from opponents or to reach a goal area.

By the end of grade 4, students should be able to

- throw a variety of objects to target areas using a smooth underhand motion;
- throw as far as possible using a smooth overhand motion;
- throw balls of various sizes and weights to an appropriate target or partner using a smooth overhand motion;
- throw, using an overhand motion, so the ball travels in different pathways in the air and covers different distances;
- catch a ball, tossed by themselves or by others, at different levels;
- move in different directions to catch a ball thrown by a partner; and
- move to catch an object in a small-group (two-on-one) keep-away situation.

By the end of grade 2, students should be able to

- catch a self-tossed yarn or other soft ball;
- catch a softly thrown ball at different levels;
- catch a softly thrown ball at different places around the body;
- throw a variety of objects using an underhand motion;
- throw as far as possible using an overhand motion; and
- throw (underhand) and catch a self-tossed object, using a scoop or other implement.

By the end of kindergarten, students should be able to

- catch a softly rolled large ball;
- catch a self-tossed yarn or other soft ball;
- throw to a variety of large targets using an underhand throwing motion; and
- throw a yarn or other soft ball using an overhand arm motion.

Volleying

By the end of grade 6, students should be able to

- cooperate in a small group to strike a lightweight ball with various body parts while keeping it off the ground;
- underhand-strike a lightweight ball over a medium-level net or rope (from an appropriate distance);
- overhead-volley a lightweight ball back and forth with a partner across a medium-level net or rope;
- move to forearm-pass or overhead-volley a lightweight ball back to a partner;
- forearm-pass a lightweight ball to an area other than the direction it came from;
- forearm-pass a lightly tossed lightweight ball back to a partner across a medium-level rope or net;
- use underhand and overhead volleys and forearm passes to cooperatively keep a ball in play over a medium-level net or rope with a partner or a small group; and
- use underhand and overhead volleys and forearm-passes in a given or self-designed small-group game.

By the end of grade 4, students should be able to

- strike a lightweight ball in succession using at least two different body parts, keeping it in self-space;
- strike a lightly tossed lightweight ball back to a partner using a variety of body parts;
- underhand-strike a lightweight ball back and forth across a line or low net to a partner after one bounce;
- overhead-volley a self-tossed lightweight ball to a wall or partner (to an appropriate height, if desired); and
- forearm-pass a lightly tossed lightweight ball back to a partner.

By the end of grade 2, students should be able to

- strike a lightweight ball with at least three different body parts (e.g., knee, foot, elbow), keeping it in self-space;
- underhand-strike a soft, lightweight ball or balloon upward with the hand, keeping it in self-space; and
- travel slowly and underhand-strike a soft, lightweight ball or balloon upward with the hand or other body parts.

By the end of kindergarten, students should be able to

- using both right and left hands, continuously push a balloon upward with the hands, keeping it off the ground; and
- using the palm, strike a balloon underhand (upward) continuously.

Striking With Short-Handled Implements

By the end of grade 6, students should be able to

- repeatedly strike a rebounding ball from a wall with a paddle or lightweight racket using a forehand stroke;
- strike a gently tossed ball from a partner, using a backhand motion;
- repeatedly strike a rebounding ball from a wall using forehand or backhand strokes, moving back to a ready position in between strokes; and
- strike a self-dropped ball with a racket over a low-level line or net to various designated areas, using a forehand stroke.

By the end of grade 4, students should be able to

- bounce and then strike a small object to a wall or across a low net using an underhand motion with a lightweight paddle or racket;
- bounce and then strike a small object using a forehand motion with a lightweight paddle or racket;
- strike a small object with a forehand motion using both strong and light force; and
- bounce and then strike a small object using a backhand motion with a lightweight paddle or racket.

By the end of grade 2, students should be able to

- strike a small, lightweight ball upward with a hand or lightweight paddle, letting it bounce between strikes (i.e., bounce, strike, bounce);
- continuously strike a small, lightweight ball or balloon upward using a hand or lightweight paddle;
- continuously strike a suspended ball, using a forehand motion, with either a hand or lightweight paddle; and
- bounce then strike a small, lightweight ball using a hand or lightweight paddle.

By the end of kindergarten, students should be able to

- repeatedly strike a balloon upward with a hand or lightweight paddle; and
- repeatedly strike a small suspended ball with a hand or other lightweight paddle.

Striking With Long-Handled Implements

By the end of grade 6, students should be able to

- strike a gently tossed ball using a bat;
- use a hockey stick to control-dribble a ball in a large group and not collide with others or obstacles;

- use a hockey stick to dribble a ball around stationary obstacles without losing control of the ball;
- dribble and then strike a ball to a stationary target or partner, using a hockey stick;
- strike a ball toward large target areas from an appropriate distance using a golf club or hockey stick; and
- design and play small-group keep-away games involving dribbling and shooting with a hockey stick toward a goal area.

By the end of grade 4, students should be able to

- strike a softly pitched ball with a bat as far as possible;
- dribble a Wiffle ball with a hockey stick and change directions and pathways at the signal;

- strike a Wiffle ball along the ground to a stationary partner using a hockey stick; and
- strike a Wiffle ball in the air using a golf club or hockey stick.

By the end of grade 2, students should be able to

- strike a Wiffle ball off a tee with a bat;
- use an underhand swing to strike a Wiffle ball with a hockey stick or golf club; and
- travel slowly in different directions and dribble a Wiffle ball with a hockey stick.

By the end of kindergarten, students should be able to

- strike a small playground ball off a tee or cone using the hand.

NASPE Performance Indicators

Here is a list of the NASPE Performance Indicators, organized by grade level and standard.

Grades K-2

Standard #1

(K-2, #1) 1. Skips (or hops, gallops, slides, etc.) using mature form (e.g., step-hops, swings arm, swings knee, shows smooth and continuous motion, shows rhythmical weight transfer, and use of arms).

(K-2, #1) 2. Performs a simple dance step in keeping with a specific tempo (e.g., slow-slow-fast-fast-fast).

(K-2, #1) 3. Demonstrates clear contrasts between slow and fast movement when skipping (or hopping, galloping, sliding, etc.).

(K-2, #1) 4. Travels forward and sideways, changing directions quickly in response to a signal or obstacle using a variety of locomotor skills.

(K-2, #1) 5. Demonstrates a smooth transition between locomotor skills in time to music.

(K-2, #1) 6. Taps the ball from foot to foot, shifting weight and balancing the body on the non-dribbling foot, while in one location (i.e., not moving).

(K-2, #1) 7. Drops a ball and catches it at the peak of the bounce.

(K-2, #1) 8. Throws a ball underhand using mature form (e.g., places feet together and shoulders square to target, swings throwing arm straight back, shifts weight forward by stepping forward onto opposite foot, rolls ball off fingers, and finishes with throwing arm outstretched toward target).

(K-2, #1) 9. Discovers how to balance on different body parts, at different levels, becoming "like" a statue while making symmetrical and nonsymmetrical shapes.

Standard #2

(K-2, #2) 10. Identifies correctly body planes (i.e., front, back, side).

(K-2, #2) 11. Identifies correctly various body parts (e.g., knee, foot, arm, palm).

(K-2, #2) 12. Explains that warm-up prepares the body for physical activity.

(K-2, #2) 13. Recognizes appropriate safety practices in general space by throwing balls only when others are not in direct line of the throw.

(K-2, #2) 14. States that best effort is shown by trying new or hard tasks.

(K-2, #2) 15. Repeats cue words for jumping

vertically (e.g., crouch, straighten, land on both feet, and bend knees) and demonstrates/explains what is meant by each.

(K–2, #2) 16. Corrects movement errors in response to corrective feedback (e.g., remember to twist your tummy when throwing the ball).

(K–2, #2) 17. States the short-term effects of physical activity on the heart and lungs.

(K–2, #2) 18. Explains that appropriate practice improves performance.

Standard #3

(K–2, #3) 19. Engages in moderate to vigorous physical activity on an intermittent basis.

(K–2, #3) 20. Engages in a variety of locomotor activities (e.g., hopping, walking, jumping, galloping, and running) during leisure time.

(K–2, #3) 21. Participates in chasing and fleeing activities outside of school.

(K–2, #3) 22. Participates in a variety of activities that involve manipulation of objects in and outside of physical education class (e.g., tossing ball, juggling).

(K–2, #3) 23. Participates regularly in a variety of nonstructured and minimally organized physical activities outside of physical education class (e.g., tag, hide-and-seek).

Standard #4

(K–2, #4) 24. Demonstrates sufficient muscular strength to be able to bear body weight for climbing, hanging, and momentary body support on the hands.

(K–2, #4) 25. Engages in a series of locomotor activities (e.g., timed segments of hopping, walking, jumping, galloping, and running) without tiring easily.

(K–2, #4) 26. Participates in a variety of games that increase breathing and heart rate.

(K–2, #4) 27. Increases arm and shoulder strength by traveling hand-over-hand along a horizontal ladder (i.e., monkey bars).

(K–2, #4) 28. Sustains activity for increasingly longer periods of time while participating in various activities in physical education.

(K–2, #4) 29. Moves transversely along a rock wall with little teacher assistance.

(K–2, #4) 30. Recognizes that health-related physical fitness consists of several different components.

Standard #5

(K–2, #5) 31. Practices specific skills as assigned until the teacher signals the end of practice.

(K–2, #5) 32. Follows directions given to the class for an all-class activity.

(K–2, #5) 33. Shows compassion for others by helping them.

(K–2, #5) 34. Handles equipment safely by putting it away when not in use.

(K–2, #5) 35. Uses equipment and space safely and properly.

(K–2, #5) 36. Honestly reports the results of work.

(K–2, #5) 37. Works in a diverse group setting without interfering with others.

(K–2, #5) 38. Invites a peer to take his or her turn at a piece of apparatus before repeating a turn.

(K–2, #5) 39. Assists a partner by sharing observations about skill performance during practice.

(K–2, #5) 40. Enjoys participating alone while exploring movement tasks.

(K–2, #5) 41. Accepts all playmates without regard to personal differences (e.g., ethnicity, gender, disability).

(K–2, #5) 42. During class closure, identifies sharing with a partner as a way to cooperate.

(K–2, #5) 43. Displays consideration of others while participating on the playground.

(K–2, #5) 44. Demonstrates the elements of socially acceptable conflict resolution during class activity.

Standard #6

(K–2, #6) 45. Exhibits both verbal and nonverbal indicators of enjoyment.

(K–2, #6) 46. Willingly tries new movements and skills.

(K–2, #6) 47. Continues to participate when not successful on the first try.

(K–2, #6) 48. Identifies several activities that are enjoyable.

(K–2, #6) 49. Expresses personal feelings on progress made while learning a new skill.

Grades 3-5

Standard #1

(3-5, #1) 1. Demonstrates good posture while lifting and carrying an object.

(3-5, #1) 2. Balances with control on a variety of objects (e.g., balance board, large apparatus, skates).

(3-5, #1) 3. Catches a fly ball using mature form (e.g., has eyes on ball, moves to position, reaches with hands, catches with hands only rather than trapping the ball, and bends elbows to pull ball into chest to absorb force).

(3-5, #1) 4. Performs a basic tinikling step to 3/4 time (close, tap, tap).

(3-5, #1) 5. Jumps vertically to a height of 9 inches and lands using mature form (e.g., stands, crouches with arms back and weight on toes, lifts off with hands high, lands on both feet).

(3-5, #1) 6. Throws a ball overhand and hits a target on the wall (6-foot square centered 4 feet above the ground) from a distance of 40 feet.

(3-5, #1) 7. Develops and refines a gymnastics sequence (or creative dance sequence) demonstrating smooth transitions.

(3-5, #1) 8. Dribbles then passes a basketball to a moving receiver.

(3-5, #1) 9. Throws a ball overhand to a partner 15 yards away using mature form (e.g., turns side to target, uses T-position [ball held close to and behind ear], rotates hips and chest toward target, twists, releases, follows through across body) after fielding a ball.

(3-5, #1) 10. Demonstrates correct pattern for the polka step (hop-step-together-step).

Standard #2

(3-5, #2) 11. Describes how heart rate is used to monitor exercise intensity.

(3-5, #2) 12. Identifies and demonstrates key elements of a proper grip when holding a racket to perform the forehand strike.

(3-5, #2) 13. Explains the necessity of transferring weight from the back leg to the front leg during any action that propels an object forward.

(3-5, #2) 14. Accurately recognizes the critical elements of a catch made by a fellow student and provides feedback to that student.

(3-5, #2) 15. Describes the difference in foot placement when kicking a stationary ball, a ball moving away, and a ball moving toward.

(3-5, #2) 16. Explains how appropriate practice improves performance.

(3-5, #2) 17. Designs a new game incorporating at least two motor skills, rules, and strategies.

(3-5, #2) 18. Identifies physical and psychological benefits that result from long-term participation in physical activity.

Standard #3

(3-5, #3) 19. Consciously chooses to participate in moderate to vigorous physical activity outside of physical education class on a regular basis.

(3-5, #3) 20. Participates in organized sport activities provided through local community programs.

(3-5, #3) 21. Participates in an intramural sports program provided by the school.

(3-5, #3) 22. Chooses to participate in structured and purposeful activity.

(3-5, #3) 23. Monitors his or her physical activity by using a pedometer to count the number of steps taken or the distance traveled.

(3-5, #3) 24. Maintains a physical activity log (e.g., ACTIVITYGRAM) for a two- or three-day period documenting activity data (e.g., step count, time).

Standard #4

(3-5, #4) 25. Participates in selected activities that develop and maintain each component of physical fitness.

(3-5, #4) 26. Engages in appropriate physical activity that results in the development of cardiorespiratory endurance.

(3-5, #4) 27. Recognizes that physiological responses to exercise are associated with their own levels of fitness.

(3-5, #4) 28. Runs the equivalent of two laps around a regulation track without stopping.

(3-5, #4) 29. Chooses to participate in sport activities that require high levels of muscular strength.

(3-5, #4) 30. Explains the personal consequences of poor flexibility on ability to perform various activities.

(3-5, #4) 31. Maintains heart rate within the target heart rate zone for a specified length of time during an aerobic activity.

(3-5, #4) 32. Meets the age- and gender-specific health-related fitness standards defined by FITNESSGRAM.

(3-5, #4) 33. Identifies his or her strengths and weaknesses based upon the results of FITNESSGRAM testing.

Standard #5

(3-5, #5) 34. In preparation for a kicking on goal task, arranges soccer equipment safely in a manner appropriate to practice.

(3-5, #5) 35. Takes seriously the role of teaching an activity or skill to his or her team.

(3-5, #5) 36. Cooperates with all class members by taking turns and sharing equipment.

(3-5, #5) 37. Works productively with a partner to improve performance of a dance sequence by following a detailed diagram of the process.

(3-5, #5) 38. Accepts the teacher's decision regarding a personal rule infraction without displaying negative reactions toward others.

(3-5, #5) 39. Assesses and takes responsibility for his or her own behavior problems without blaming others.

(3-5, #5) 40. Recognizes and appreciates similar and different activity choices of peers.

(3-5, #5) 41. During class discussion of various dance forms, shows respect for the views of a peer from a different cultural background.

(3-5, #5) 42. Demonstrates respect and caring for a wheelchair-bound peer through verbal and nonverbal encouragement and assistance.

(3-5, #5) 43. Regularly encourages others and refrains from put-down statements.

Standard #6

(3-5, #6) 44. Identifies positive feelings associated with participation in physical activities.

(3-5, #6) 45. Chooses to participate in group physical activities.

(3-5, #6) 46. Explains that skill competency leads to enjoyment of movement and physical activity.

(3-5, #6) 47. Interacts with others by helping with their physical activity challenges.

(3-5, #6) 48. Selects and practices a skill on which improvement is needed.

(3-5, #6) 49. Develops a dance sequence (or game) that is personally interesting.

(3-5, #6) 50. Defends the benefits of physical activity.

Glossary

alternative assessment – Assessments that ask students to construct, perform, or demonstrate their learning in a manner that allows for a full understanding of their learning to be measured. Also termed *performance assessment*.

assessment – The combined processes of measurement and evaluation; the gathering of information so that one can make a judgment about the collected data.

authentic assessment – Assessment that takes place in a real-life context, or one that approximates how the skill or knowledge would be used in the "real world."

benchmarks – Statements whose purpose is to give further definition to content standards at various points in the educational process.

checklist – A method of scoring performance-based assessments that delineates a set of separately considered criteria that students perform in order to successfully complete a specific assessment task.

content delineation – The process of defining all the skills and concepts (curricular content) that should be taught in order for students to be able to reach the desired course standards.

content standards – Those standards that describe the information or skills children should learn that are specific to a particular discipline or content area.

course standards – Statements that define what students at a specific school level or in a specific course should achieve by the time they leave that particular level of school.

curriculum frameworks – General guidelines describing what should be taught in schools.

designing-down – The process of purposefully planning a curriculum by beginning with the main goals or outcomes desired for students to achieve by the time they graduate from high school, and then planning one's curriculum *backward* from that point.

evaluation – The process of comparing raw data scores to a standard or norm in order to place a value on the test scores.

exit standards – The academic standards that students should achieve by the time they graduate from high school; these standards set the tone and give focus for what students should learn at the underlying grade levels.

formal assessment – A standardized assessment that takes place in a structured, controlled situation.

formative assessment – Typically informal assessment that takes place on a daily basis and allows teachers to determine whether students are progressing toward the attainment of important objectives and standards.

grading – The process by which assessment data is translated into predetermined marks or letter (e.g., such as "E," "S," or "U") that indicate the quality of students' knowledge, performance, or behavior.

informal assessment – Assessments that take place in a more "open" context through the use of techniques such as observation, alternative assessments, and written records.

learnable pieces – A specific focus for what students can realistically achieve in a lesson.

lesson standards – Statements that define the goals for instruction and students' learning over the course of a lesson.

measurement – The combined processes of testing students to determine how much they have learned and then subsequently scoring the test.

No Child Left Behind Act (Public Law 107-110) – Legislation signed into law by President George W. Bush. It calls for, in part, the mandatory annual testing of students in grades 3 to 8 beginning in the 2005-2006 school year, with consequences for schools that repeatedly do not help students "succeed" in their educational endeavors.

Opportunity to Learn standards – The part of the Goals 2000 Act that specifies the conditions and resources that are necessary in order to give all students an equal chance to meet content and performance standards.

performance – Observable affective or psychomotor behaviors demonstrated by students.

performance indicators – The part of the content standard that defines the skill or performance desired for students to demonstrate.

performance standards – The measure of how well students know and are able to work with (apply) the desired content standards. The standards describe what students must do, and how well they must do this, in order to show they have achieved the content standard.

performance task – Used interchangeably with *alternative assessment task* and *performance assessment task;* those specific assessment tasks that require students to apply or do something with their learning in order to show their progress toward meeting desired standards.

portfolio – A collection of a student's work over time that demonstrates his or her progress toward the attainment of specific learning standards.

products – Tangible, concrete items that a student produces or creates through the written, visual, or auditory media.

program standards – Broad statements that delineate the overall K–12 goals for a specific subject area for students in a particular state or district.

rating scale – A method of scoring performance-based assessments that requires a judgment to be made as to the *degree* to which specific criteria are present.

rubric – A scale of criteria that explains in detail the possible levels of performance for an alternative assessment task.

standards – Statements that delineate what students should know and be able to do by the time they graduate from K–12 education.

strands – Similar areas (e.g., fitness, health, manipulative skills) in a curricular content area (e.g., physical education) by which states or districts group standards.

summative assessment – Assessment that typically occurs at the end of a unit of instruction; used for determining what students have learned over a long period of time.

testing – The process of administering a set of questions or situations designed to gain information about the student, which then permits an inference about what he or she knows or can do. It is typically administered under strict conditions.

unit standards – Statements that define what students should be learning over the course of an instructional unit (series of lessons with a similar theme).

Bibliography

Allen, V. (1997). Assessment: What to do with it after you've done it. *Teaching Elementary Physical Education, 8*(6), 12-15.

American Council on Education. (1999). *Alignment of national and state standards: A report by the GED testing service.* Washington, DC: General Educational Developmental Testing Service.

Anderson, L. (2003). *Classroom assessment: Enhancing the quality of teacher decision making.* Mahwah, NJ: Lawrence Erlbaum Associates.

Andrade, H. (2000). Using rubrics to promote thinking and learning. *Educational Leadership, 57*(5), 13-18.

Ardovino, J., Hollingsworth, J., & Ybarra, S. (2000). *Multiple measures: Accurate ways to assess student achievement.* Thousand Oaks, CA: Corwin Press.

Asp, E. (1998). The relationship between large-scale and classroom assessment: Compatibility or conflict? In R. Brandt (Ed.), *Assessing student learning: New rules, new realities* (pp. 17-46). Arlington, VA: Educational Research Service.

Barlin, A.L. (1979). *Teaching your wings to fly: The nonspecialists' guide to movement activities for young children.* Santa Monica, CA: Goodyear.

Baron, M. & Boschee, F. (1995). *Authentic assessment: The key to unlocking student success.* Lancaster, PA: Technomic.

Birenbaum, M. (1996). Assessment 2000: Towards a pluralistic approach to assessment. In M. Birenbaum & F. Dochy (Eds.), *Alternatives in assessment of achievements, learning processes, and prior knowledge* (pp. 3-30). Norwell, MA: Kluwer Academic.

Brandt, R. (1992a). On outcome-based education: A conversation with Bill Spady. *Educational Leadership, 50*(4), 66-70.

Brandt, R. (1992b). On performance assessment: A conversation with Grant Wiggins. *Educational Leadership, 50*(8), 35-37.

Brandt, R. (1998). Introduction. In R. Brandt (Ed.), *Assessing student learning: New rules, new realities* (pp. 1-16). Arlington, VA: Educational Research Service.

Brualdi, A. (2002a). Traditional and modern concepts of validity. In Rudner, L.M. & Schafer, W.D. (Eds.), *What teachers need to know about assessment* (pp. 13-16). Washington, DC: National Educational Association of the United States.

Brualdi, A. (2002b). Implementing performance assessment in the classroom. In Rudner, L.M. & Schafer, W.D. (Eds.), *What teachers need to know about assessment* (pp. 81-85). Washington, DC: National Educational Association of the United States.

Brualdi, A. (2002c). Teacher comments on report cards. In Rudner, L.M. & Schafer, W.D. (Eds.), *What teachers need to know about assessment* (pp. 111-114). Washington, DC: National Educational Association of the United States.

Calfee, R.C. (1994). Observations on assessment. *Educational Assessment, 2*(1), 1-5.

Calfee, R.C. (2000). A decade of assessment. *Educational Assessment, 6*(4), 217-219.

Carr, J. (2000). Technical issues of grading methods. In Trumbull, E. & Farr, B. (Eds.), *Grading and reporting student progress in an age of standards* (pp. 45-70). Norwood, MA: Christopher-Gordon Publishers, Inc.

Carr, J.F. & Harris, D.E. (2001). *Succeeding with standards: Linking curriculum, assessment, and action planning.* Alexandria, VA: Association for Supervision and Curriculum Development.

Cawyer, C.S. & Caldwell, D.A. (2002). Performance-based assessment of teacher education: Some contextual considerations. *Action in Teacher Education, XXIII*(4), 1-3.

Chappuis, S. & Stiggins, R. (2002). Classroom assessment for learning. *Educational Leadership, 60*(1), 40-43.

Cohen, P. (1995). Designing performance assessment tasks. *Education Update, 37*(6), 1, 4-5, 8.

Florida Department of Education, 1996. Retrieved May 27, 2003 from http://www.firn.edu/doe/curric/preK12/frame2.htm.

Franck, M., Graham, G., Lawson, H., Loughery, T., Ritson, R., Sanborn, M., & Seefeldt, V. (1992). *Outcomes of quality physical education programs.* Reston, VA: National Association for Sport and Physical Education.

Gandal, M. & Vranek, J. (2001). Standards: Here today, here tomorrow. *Educational Leadership, 59*(1), 6-13.

Graham, G. (2001). *Teaching children physical education: Becoming a master teacher* (2nd edition). Champaign, IL: Human Kinetics.

Graham, G., Holt/Hale, S., & Parker, M. (2004). *Children moving: A reflective approach to teaching physical education* (6th ed.). New York: McGraw-Hill.

Hellison, D. (2003). *Teaching responsibility through physical activity* (2nd ed.). Champaign, IL: Human Kinetics.

Hopple, C. (1995). *Teaching for outcomes in elementary physical education: A guide for curriculum and assessment.* Champaign, IL: Human Kinetics.

Janesick, V.J. (2001). *The assessment debate: A reference handbook.* Santa Barbara, CA: ABC-CLIO.

Khattri, N., Reeve, A., & Kane, M. (1998). *Principles and practices of performance assessment.* Mahwah, NJ: Lawrence Erlbaum Associates.

Kuhs, T.M., Johnson, R.L., Agruso, S.A., & Monrad, D.M. (2001). *Put to the test: Tools and techniques for classroom assessment.* Portsmouth, NH: Heinemann.

Lambert, L.T. (2003). In Silverman, S. & Ennis. C. (Eds.) *Student learning in physical education: Applying research to enhance instruction* (2nd ed.), pp. 129-146. Champaign, IL: Human Kinetics.

Lin, Q. (2002). Beyond standardization: Testing and assessment in standards-based reform. *Action in Teacher Education, 23*(4), 43-49.

Mabry, L. (1999). *Portfolios plus: A critical guide to alternative assessment.* Thousand Oaks, CA: Corwin Press.

Madaus, G.F. & Raczek, A.E. (1996). A turning point for assessment: Reform movements in the United States. In Little, A. & Wolf, A. (Eds.) *Assessment in transition: Learning, monitoring and selection in international perspective* (pp. 101-117). Tarrytown, NY: Elsevier Science.

Manross, M. (n.d.). *PE central assessment sheet.* Retrieved August 24, 2001 from www.pecentral.org.

Marzano, R.J. & Kendall, J.S. (1998). *Implementing standards-based education.* Washington, DC: National Educational Association of the United States.

Marzano, R.J., Pickering, D., & McTighe, J. (1993). *Assessing student outcomes: Performance assessment using the dimensions of learning.* Alexandria, VA: Association for Supervision and Curriculum Development.

McMillan, J.H. (1997). *Classroom assessment: Principles and practices for effective instruction* (2nd ed.). Boston: Allyn and Bacon.

McMillan, J.H. (2001). *Classroom assessment: Principles and practices for effective instruction* (2nd ed.). Boston: Allyn and Bacon.

McMillan, J.H. (2002). Fundamental assessment principles for teachers and school administrators. In Rudner, L.M. & Schafer, W.D. (Eds.), *What teachers need to know about assessment* (pp. 6-12). Washington, DC: National Educational Association of the United States.

McTighe, J. & Ferrara, S. (1998). *Assessing learning in the classroom.* Washington, DC: National Educational Association of the United States.

Moskal, B.M. (2002). Scoring rubrics: What, when and how? In Rudner, L.M. & Schafer, W.D. (Eds.), *What teachers need to know about assessment* (pp. 86-94). Washington, DC: National Educational Association of the United States.

Moskal, B.M. & Leydens, J.A. (2002). Scoring rubric development: Validity and reliability. In Rudner, L.M. & Schafer, W.D. (Eds.), *What teachers need to know about assessment* (pp. 95-106). Washington, DC: National Educational Association of the United States.

Mustain, W. (1994). Authentic assessments: More than 'Grist for the grading mill'. *Teaching elementary physical education, 5*(3), 1, 4-5.

National Association for Sport and Physical Education. (2004). *Moving into the future: National standards for physical education* (2nd ed.). Reston, VA: Author.

National Education Goals Panel. (1996). *Profile of 1994-95 state assessment systems and reported results.* Washington, DC: United States Department of Education.

Priestly, M. (1982). *Performance assessment in education and training.* Englewood Cliffs, NJ: Educational Testing Publications.

Puckett, M.B. & Black, J.K. (1994). *Authentic assessment of the young child: Celebrating development and learning.* New York: Macmillan.

Ravitch, D. (1995). *National standards in American education: A citizen's guide.* Washington, DC: The Brookings Institute.

Reeves, D. (2002). *The leader's guide to standards: A blueprint for educational equity and excellence.* San Francisco: Jossey-Bass.

Robinson, G. & Craver, J. (1989). *Assessing and grading student achievement.* Arlington, VA: Educational Research Service.

Rudner, L.M. & Schafer, W.D. (2002). Reliability. In Rudner, L.M. & Schafer, W.D. (Eds.), *What teachers need to know about assessment* (pp. 17-23). Washington, DC: National Educational Association of the United States.

Scherer, M. (2001). How and why standards can improve student achievement: A conversation with Robert J. Marzano. *Educational Leadership, 59*(1), pages 14-18.

Schiemer, S. (2000). *Assessment strategies for elementary physical education.* Champaign, IL: Human Kinetics.

Schulman, J.H., Whittaker, A., & Lew, M. (2002). Introduction. In Schulman, J.H., Whittaker, A., & Lew, M. (Eds.), *Using assessments to teach for understanding: A casebook for educators* (pp. 1-9). New York: Teachers College Press.

Scriven, M. (2000). The logic and methodology of checklists. Address given at Claremont Graduate University, June. (Available at www.wmich.edu/evalctr/checklists).

Segers, M., Dochy, F., & Cascallar, E., Eds. (2003). *Optimizing new modes of assessment: In search of qualities and standards.* Norwell, MA: Kluwer Academic Pub.

Shafer, S. (1997). *Writing effective report card comments.* New York, NY: Scholastic Professional Books.

Shellhase, K. (1998). Grades K-6 Assessment System. Blacksburg, VA: PE Central.

Smith, J.K., Smith, L.F., & DeLisi, R. (2001). *Natural classroom assessment: Designing seamless instruction and assessment.* Thousand Oaks, CA: Corwin Press.

Solomon, P.G. (2002). *The assessment bridge: Positive ways to link tests to learning, standards, and curriculum improvement.* Thousand Oaks, CA: Corwin Press.

Spady, W.G. (1988). Organizing for results: The basis of authentic restructuring and reform. *Educational Leadership, 46*(2), 4-8.

Stiggins, R. (1997). *Student-centered classroom assessment* (2nd ed.). Upper Saddle River, NJ: Prentice-Hall.

Stiggins, R. (1998). *Classroom assessment for student success.* Washington, DC: National Educational Association of the United States.

Tienken, C. & Wilson, M. (2002). Using state standards and assessments to improve instruction. In Rudner, L.M. & Schafer, W.D. (Eds.), *What teachers need to know about assessment* (pp. 45-54). Washington, DC: National Educational Association of the United States.

Trice, A.D. (2000). *A Handbook of classroom assessment.* New York: Longman.

Weikart, P. (1998). *Teaching movement and dance: A sequential approach to rhythmic movement* (4th ed.) Ypsilanti, MI: High-Scope Press.

Werner, P. (2004). *Teaching children gymnastics* (2nd ed.). Champaign, IL: Human Kinetics.

Wiggins, G. & McTighe, J. (1998). *Understanding by design.* Alexandria, VA: Association for Supervision and Curriculum Development.

About the Author

Christine J. Hopple, MS, has taught elementary physical education for eight years in Florida and Virginia. She has also taught physical education teacher preparation courses at Ithaca College for five years. Hopple authored *Teaching for Outcomes in Elementary Physical Education: A Guide for Curriculum and Assessment*, and she coauthored the first edition of NASPE's *Developmentally Appropriate Physical Education Practices for Children*. Hopple, currently at work on her PhD, has presented on assessment and other topics at numerous state and national conferences, and has worked with numerous teachers and school districts across the country on this subject.

Hopple is a member of AAHPERD (American Alliance for Health, Physical Education, Recreation and Dance), a past editor of *TEPE (Teaching Elementary Physical Education)*, and an instructor for the American Master Teacher Program for Children's Physical Education.

You'll find other outstanding
physical education resources at
www.HumanKinetics.com

In the U.S. call 1.800.747.4457
Australia 08 8372 0999
Canada. 1.800.465.7301
Europe . . . . .+44 (0) 113 255 5665
New Zealand 0800 222 062